Latin American Political Economy

Latin American Political Economy publishes new, relevant, and empirically-grounded scholarship that deepens our understanding of contemporary Latin American political economy and contributes to the formulation and evaluation of new theories that are both context-sensitive and subject to broader comparisons. Inspired by the need to provide new analytical perspectives for understanding the massive social, political, and economic transformations underway in Latin America, the series is directed at researchers and practitioners interested in resurrecting political economy as a primary research area in the developing world. In thematic terms, the series seeks to promote vital debate on the interactions between economic, political, and social processes; it is especially concerned with how findings may further our understanding of development models, the socio-political institutions that sustain them, and the practical problems they confront. In methodological terms, the series showcases cross-disciplinary research that is empirically rich and sensitive to context and that leads to new forms of description, concept formation, causal inference, and theoretical innovation. The series editors welcome submissions that address patterns of democratic politics, dependency and development, state formation and the rule of law, inequality and identity, and global linkages. The series editors and advisory board members belong to Red para el Estudio de la Economía Política de América Latina (REPAL) (http://redeconomiapoliticaamlat.com/). Advisory Board Ben Ross Schneider and Andrew Schrank.

More information about this series at
http://www.springer.com/series/14825

María José Álvarez-Rivadulla

Squatters and the Politics of Marginality in Uruguay

palgrave
macmillan

María José Álvarez-Rivadulla
Universidad de los Andes
Bogota, Colombia

Latin American Political Economy
ISBN 978-3-319-85415-1 ISBN 978-3-319-54534-9 (eBook)
DOI 10.1007/978-3-319-54534-9

Softcover reprint of the hardcover 1st edition 2017

Cover design: Jenny Vong

Printed on acid-free paper

This Palgrave Macmillan imprint is published by Springer Nature
The registered company is Springer International Publishing AG
The registered company address is: Gewerbestrasse 11, 6330 Cham, Switzerland

For Martin, who put my whole life in perspective, including this book, and therefore made it possible for me to finish it.

Acknowledgements

This book emphasizes the power of networks. Without mine, my support, academic, and in-field networks, I would never have been able to write it. Time and my maturing process did their work too. When I finished my dissertation at the University of Pittsburgh under the guidance of the most generous and wise man I have ever met, John Markoff, and of my wonderful and very much involved committee including Kathy Blee, Javier Auyero, and Pat Doreian, I wanted to publish right away. Many obstacles impeded this, leading to great frustration despite the joys and challenges of a new job in a new country. Now, 7 years later, having returned to the field numerous times, written several articles about the topic, and having a longer longitudinal perspective, as well as a few more years under my belt, I feel a smoother pen, one that flows more easily, and that is more certain, more me.

The book would have remained on a desk had it not been for the two people that pushed me to get it out from there. Juan Carlos Rodríguez Raga, my partner in crime and love, knew that this was a painful debt I had to pay myself and reminded me of that, every time I wanted to give up. Juan Pablo Luna, a friend and admired colleague with whom I learned most of what I know about clientelism in our country, was the other force pushing me to send this book out. I could not be more grateful for that encouragement. My parents, sister, nephew, and brother-in-law are of course the most basic network, the basic emotional network, which is always the happiest and proudest even if what

I publish is a mere tweet. I owe them everything I have accomplished, including this book.

Writing a book for an English-speaking publisher, trying to engage in a global academic conversation, when one works in the Local South as I like to put it (the Global South seems too grandiloquent or idealistic to me) is neither easy nor a priority. There are satisfactory yet very time-consuming institutional tasks to complete and eager students to be taught in our primarily teaching universities. Trying to escalate in the very unfair competition for global rankings, universities in the Third World push us to publish articles in renowned indexed journals. Books are not a priority any more. Besides, working in the Local South, it is not easy to find a publisher that wants to engage in conversation with what we have to say. I thank the Palgrave Latin American Political Economy Series for undertaking this publication project and for the respectful and substantial comments of two anonymous reviewers who greatly improved the final and very different version of this book.

Two wonderful colleagues and friends undertook the invisible yet fundamental work of commenting on the chapter drafts. Thanks to Thomas Ordóñez and Catalina Vallejo for their sharp comments and for reinforcing my belief in academia as a collective enterprise. I am also deeply grateful to Paul Almeida, Paul Dosh, and Michael Burawoy for reading a previous version of the whole book and suggesting routes for reorganization. Research assistants are often forgotten fundamental blocks in knowledge building. To Denise Gelber, Magdalena Marsiglia, and more recently, to María José Bolaña, thanks for engaging in the fieldwork with the passion, empathy, and rigorousness it deserves.

I thank Universidad de los Andes, my new academic home, for supporting and encouraging this publication (via Felipe Castañeda, Vice-Dean of Research in the School of Social Sciences), and for providing the financial help for the copyediting, fantastically undertaken by Tiziana Laudato.

Finally and fundamentally, to Jacque, Julio, and so many other squatters who shared their stories of resistance and suffering with me, and who patiently answered my rather odd questions, opening their homes, picking me up at the bus stop, showing me around, introducing me to other people, and offering me *mates.* I owe most of what I know to them. I am still puzzled by their generosity and I hope this book honors their bravery in fighting for their right to live in the city and their willingness in opening up their experiences to me.

Contents

List of Figures

List of Tables

CHAPTER 1

Introduction

The last decades of the twentieth century combined two conditions that triggered mobilizations throughout Latin America: neoliberal reforms and democratization (Johnston and Almeida 2006). As such, we have witnessed the flourishing of indigenous rights movements in several countries, from the Zapatistas in Mexico to the Mapuches in Chile, great activity by the MST (Movement of Rural Landless Workers) in Brazil, the mushrooming of NGOs and other civil society organizations, the emergence of the unemployed *piquetero* movement in Argentina and many other similar forms of austerity, and anti-privatization protests especially among the popular classes (Walton and Ragin 1990). Although Montevideo's squatters were not protesting against economic policy, they were clearly part of its consequences and, as we will see, some of them implied collective action in the context of a democratizing society. Housing, labor, and other basic needs were behind the two waves of squatters' mobilization in the Montevideo of the 1980–2000 period. Yet, unless we look at how politics mediated between people in need of housing and land seizures, the picture remains incomplete. As much as it was shaped by economic changes, the squatters' mobilization was also shaped by democratization.

Uruguay was not an exception to this wave of mobilizations. The end of the military dictatorship in 1984 was repelled and subsequently welcomed by such a wave of mobilizations and a revival of civil society (Filgueira 1985). The labor movement, the cooperative housing movement, the human rights movement, and the student movement took the

M.J. Álvarez-Rivadulla, *Squatters and the Politics of Marginality in Uruguay*, Latin American Political Economy, DOI 10.1007/978-3-319-54534-9_1

lead and were quickly followed by a myriad of smaller forms of collective action such as soup kitchens and neighborhood associations (Rodé et al. 1985). In this context of active mobilization, a group of very poor accretion invasions that had slowly grown in the outskirts of the city and the state, mobilized as a reaction to evictions and managed to set up an umbrella movement. This unlikely mobilization of the destitute requires more explanation than the mere need for housing. The brokerage role of NGOs and church networks were crucial allies in this mobilization born at a time when the dictatorship started to crack but when parties were as yet forbidden. Most of the mobilization dissipated during the first 5 years of democracy (1984–1989); once political parties recovered their traditional central role in a very party-centric society (Caetano et al. 1987) channeling and co-opting civil society demands (Canel 1992).

Soon, opposition to state retrenchment triggered a new wave of mobilization including different forms of collective action, especially among the middle and working classes that had enjoyed the benefits of the early and relatively robust Uruguayan welfare state during the twentieth century. A landmark in that fight was the 1992 anti-privatization referendum (Moreira 2011). Another was the successful campaign against water privatization which ended in a constitutional amendment popularly voted for an election day in 2004 (Santos et al. 2006). It was exactly that day that *Frente Amplio*, a coalition of leftist parties, won national office breaking away from 175 years of electoral dominance by the traditional *Colorado* and *Blanco* parties. This victory can also be interpreted as Frente Amplio's consistent opposition to neoliberal reforms, in a context of deep economic crisis, albeit combined with programmatic moderation (Luna 2007).[1]

In the midst of this reaction against neoliberalism, a silent urban revolution was taking place. During the 1990s, Montevideo squatters suffered a quantitative and qualitative change. On the one hand, they peaked in number. Between 1984 and 1994, the number of houses in squatter settlements tripled (INTEC 1995), the population living in squatter settlements grew to almost 145.000 in a city of less than 1.5 million inhabitants (INE-PIAI 2006), and the number of informal settlements rose to about 400. These figures become more puzzling considering the fact that the city's population had stagnated for decades. The informal city grew without the population as a whole growing. On the other hand, land invasions became increasingly planned and organized. Structural conditions, such as persistent deindustrialization; poverty; state retrenchment; low real wages; and perhaps, and even more directly, rising rent prices were undoubtedly behind these changes (Alvarez-Rivadulla 2000; Amarante and Caffera 2003; Kaztman et al. 2005). However, as mentioned earlier, political variables tended to interact with economic needs. In particular, the electoral competition for the urban poor's votes was an incentive for political networks and brokers to develop and facilitate squatters' access to land and state services. This book unveils the political economy of land invasions in Montevideo. Through a multi-method project that involved a year of fieldwork in 2006–2007 and several follow-ups, this book describes and explains the origins and trajectories of squatting in Montevideo as an elusive form of collective action since it began in the late 1940s. Putting together ethnographic and archival data with official records and maps, I was able to reconstruct the yearly time series of squatting events. Through historical press articles and documents, 80 interviews with squatters, politicians, government authorities, bureaucrats, and other key informants, and visits to 25 different neighborhoods in Montevideo, I was able to reconstruct the land invasion histories of different types of neighborhoods that squatted at different points in time. I describe the peaks and changes in squatting, and conduct the statistical analysis that shows how relevant electoral and post-electoral years were for squatting, particularly during the 1984–2004 period, even after controlling for hardship measures such as real wages. Thus, in this book, I illustrate how the relationship to politics varies depending on the type of settlement and the political context. Brokerage emerged as a powerful mechanism explaining how disenfranchised people reached valuable resources such as land security. Yet, the type of brokerage changed depending on the political context; while toward the end of dictatorship some NGOs and local parishes acted as brokers for squatters, this role was later taken over by local leaders or party activists tied to political parties and the state.

On Squatting

For the first time in history, the majority of the world's population lives in cities (54% in 2014). The vast part of this growth, 90% in fact, is taking place in the developing world, and a big portion of it happens in squatter settlements that are residential communities which are mostly or completely inhabited by poor residents who build their own houses on illegally occupied land. One-third of the population of the developing world currently lives in squatter settlements (UN-Habitat 2014).

Different perspectives have attempted to explain this enormous, informal urban growth. On the one hand, Davis' (2006) famous *Planet of Slums* offers a catastrophic yet compelling prospective. He relates the growth of squatters around the world with neoliberalism, including state retrenchment and the making of a more atomized and insecure lower class, very fitting to the case of Uruguay. Yet, his interpretation leaves us paralyzed in the face of an inevitable process of societal polarization between the shrinking haves and the growing have-nots that may not be completely accurate.[2] Moreover, Davis sees the urban as an automatic mirror of the inequalities in the economic arena. And he forgets a very important variable: the trends he describes coincide with another global trend, that of a new wave of democracy (Markoff 2015), and that this may have empowering consequences even for the most destitute of all.

On the other hand, other authors emphasize the constrained yet existing possibilities for agency among the poorest. Holston (2009), for example, highlights the coexistence of urbanization and democratization as a generative combination that leads to "insurgent citizenships" in the peripheries of the world. It is in their daily life struggles, rather than in the civic square that the poor generate new ways of solving their problems and fight for their right to belong to the city. Far from idealizing these insurgent citizenships, the author recognizes their limited and unequal nature. Yet, from his anthropological perspective, he highlights the heterogeneity among those that remain voiceless and faceless in more structural accounts. This book follows this perspective and advances it by showing how the possibilities for insurgent citizenship change with changing political conditions.

I see squatter settlements as sites of both suffering and agency. More often than not, the media, politicians, policy makers, and the public portray squatters as suffering individuals, as citizens that lack what others have. This is indeed objectively true given that they are poor, and they do not have access to a decent life in the city. Moreover, many squatters perceive themselves as suffering individuals, who lack what they need or what they are entitled to, such as land titles. And this is what you see when you enter into deprived households, when you talk to people who do not have jobs, health insurance or hope, when you walk along the streets of neighborhoods that look like lost nonplaces in the middle of nowhere, and see barefoot children playing with rundown toys close to a smelly, polluted river. However, there are many poor people with similar needs and rights who do not squat. I do not know whether "it takes a certain personality" to be a squatter, as I was told by a social worker, referring to how tough one needs to be to survive the ordeal of being cold, hungry, or having no running water, especially at the beginning of a land invasion. What is clear is that squatting takes a lot of individual, family, and collective work. In more academic terms, it takes a lot of agency. As Gay (1994: 1) puts it, "victims they undoubtedly are; innocent however, they are not. Indeed, there's increasing evidence from a variety of contexts that the urban poor have been active, organized, and aggressive participants in the political process and that the popular organizations, in particular, have had a significant impact on the relationship between the urban poor and political elites."

Squatter settlements all over the world share their illegality and their most important demand: land security, their right to the city. Yet they vary from city to city, within cities, and in time. They vary, for instance, in the social composition of their dwellers, from the poorest of the poor or immigrants to the working classes. They vary in their construction materials, depending on climate conditions, available materials, dwellers' assets, eviction expectations, and so on. Their landscapes differ, from crowded slums to neighborhoods with streets and blocks that look just like regular neighborhoods in the formal part of the city, and their location within the city is also heterogeneous. While some of Rio's *favelas* are in the middle of the city alongside other more affluent neighborhoods, in most cities, squatters locate in the periphery, but in others, like Mumbai, for example, they populate the fringes of the railway lines. They vary in their degree and type of organization both initially and through time (e.g., accretion, planned, and fraudulent sale). This variation also relates to their relationship to external agents such as NGOs, religious organizations, other social movements or political parties, and the state.

The prevalence and the mobilization of squatters greatly depend on population pressures, the housing market, and the labor market. But it also depends on the relationship between the popular classes and the state, which involves housing policy and specific actions for the benefit of those who squat. State agencies may encourage, tolerate, forbear, ignore, harass, or crush squatter settlements. More often, however, their acts fall within a gray zone that includes some tolerance, some repression, some cooptation, and some assistance. In addition, and to add one more layer of complexity, the state is not monolithic. Different state agencies may pursue different policies or specific actions and those policies may change. State actions tend to depend, in turn, on squatters' levels of organization and the elite's interest in the political support of squatters. In other words, the argument that guides this book is an interactive one. Harsh economic conditions are a necessary but not sufficient condition for the prevalence and mobilization of squatter settlements in a city or at a point in time in the same city. Economic conditions interact with political factors to make squatting happen, and to shape how it happens.

The relationship between squatter settlements and politics in Latin America has received much more attention than in other parts of the world, in part, because this relationship has been much stronger here than elsewhere. Collier's (1976) seminal work in Lima persuasively unveils how intertwined *squatters* and *oligarchs* are, and how extensively, though often silently, the Peruvian elite has been involved in the creation of the dozens of settlements that make Lima one of the most informal cities of the region. Also for the case of Lima, perhaps the most frequently studied city when it comes to urban informality, Dietz (1998) analyzes formal (vote) and informal (community participation) political participation, in six poor neighborhoods in Lima over a 20 year time span, finding more participation in newer settlements and more radicalism in older ones. More recently, and comparing political contexts, Dosh (2010) finds that Lima's land invasions keep growing because the government is much more permissive than it is in Quito. For the Chilean case, another of the most frequently studied, Schneider (1995) investigates how the Pinochet military regime reduced political opportunities for Santiago's squatters—who had previously been highly mobilized—and repressed them. Hipsher (1998), in turn, looks at how democratization revived great, though not long lasting, mobilization in Chilean *poblaciones*. More recently, and after dozens of removals and massive social housing construction and relocation, there are basically no more *poblaciones* in Chile, and Murphy (2015) questions the important yet limited effects of property on citizenship among the still urban poor (and currently also segregated) of Santiago. Similar research has been carried out for almost every city in Latin America and for different points in time, from which we learn that the relationship between squatters and politics varies through time and space but that, in the region, it is often fluid.[3]

Specialists on different global regions often point out the distinctiveness of Latin American squatters. In their attempt to bring together different traditions in the study of urban informality, Alsayyad (1993) and Alsayyad and Roy (2003) argue that, in contrast to what happens in Latin America, in the Middle East, it is the relative depoliticization and invisibility of squatters that has enabled their survival. Also, in her comparison of squatters in Brazil and South Africa, Huchzermeyer (2002) notes huge differences between the slum upgrading programs of Brazilian cities and the eradication policies as a violent shortcut to meet the Millennium goals of current South Africa.

Yet, even in Latin America, and even within one same city, the relationship of different types of squatter settlements with the state varies depending on the organizational capacity of residents and the availability of allies and brokers, and, moreover, these relationships change over time depending on the available political opportunities and the existing level of hardship. This book tells the story of the relationship of squatters and politics in one particular context throughout history to show its relevance and changes over time: Montevideo, from the mid-twentieth century to present day.

The Case in a Nutshell

The explosion of squatting in Montevideo took place later than in the region's other metropolises. Some land invasions, dubbed *cantegriles*, existed in Montevideo before squatting peaked in the 1990s. Mostly populated by recyclers and other very poor workers that squatted one family at a time, cantegriles had very precarious housing and little urban planning. Yet, the Uruguayan capital developed differently to other Latin American cities. Despite already starting to show signs of urban socioeconomic inequality in the 1980s (Portes 1989), Montevideo was more egalitarian than other cities of the continent, both economically and spatially. Today, about 8.5% of the city's population lives on illegally occupied land (PMB-PIAI 2013).[4] This percentage is low by regional standards even today if we consider cities like Lima where half of its almost 7 million inhabitants lived in one of about 300 settlements in the 90s (Dietz 1998). Yet Montevideo's smaller but a little more than 300 current squatter settlements have expanded the city limits leaving a very concrete and profound trace of urban and social fragmentation. Aerial pictures of Montevideo today look very different from those taken in the 1960s. Areas that in the past were green are now gray.

So far, no one has written about the history of land squatting in Montevideo. This work recovers this history from oblivion and puts it in dialog with the literature on popular politics. From a social movement/contentious politics perspective, in this book, I challenge the assumption that socioeconomic factors such as poverty were the only causes triggering land squatting. I argue that the political scenario also shaped the number and type of land invasions. Although politics were crucial throughout the cycle, in particular the various mechanisms of democratization, it affected different types of land invasions in different ways.

Thus, while accretion invasions, cantegriles, have always been mostly invisible to the state, with the exception of police raids or the occasional visit paid by politicians before elections, they were main characters in the mobilization during the democratization wave in the 1980s. The first signs of political opening, still under the dictatorship, combined with threats of eviction and with nonpartisan allies, and the church and NGOs with international funding both interested in working with grassroots movements among the excluded, created a configuration that led to an unprecedented mobilization of squatters. Hence, squatters from the city's poorest cantegriles, together with young motivated professionals and volunteers inspired by Paulo Freire's ideas and priests from a Catholic Church inspired by Liberation Theology, created an umbrella movement, MOVIDE.

MOVIDE turned reaction into action and shifted from the initial concern and fear about eviction to the members constructing their own houses drawing from the important cooperative housing movement in Uruguay (FUCVAM) and later to the streets, participating in the public arena as never before. They were invited to the negotiation table that led the democratic transition (CONAPRO) where, together with other social organizations, they made the housing deficit and high renting prices a priority among social demands. They appeared in the news for the first time in the early 80s, and they participated in the first and a few of the following Homeless Day (Día de los Sin Techo) marches, which have taken place every October since 1987. However, as I mentioned earlier, the wave of mobilization which MOVIDE was part of started fading, and the parties recovered their traditional central power during the first democratic period.

A second wave of mobilization followed, also triggered by structural economic needs combined with politics, but this time, it was party and electoral politics instead of social mobilization in times of democratization. An unprecedented peak of land invasions occurred in 1989 and 1990 and a lower peak followed in 1994 and 1995 (electoral and post-electoral years respectively). Land invasions became increasingly popular and planned, with streets and blocks and with a clear intention to belong to the city. Their leaders reached the state often through political networks, and politicians helped or forbore (Holland 2017) in a context of pronounced electoral competition for popular votes.

Through the Lens of Social Movements Theory

Through the study of squatter settlements, we learn about urban popular politics in Uruguay. They provide a window through which to understand broader changes in the country and the whole region: from industrialization and its related problems to deindustrialization and state retrenchment ending with the rise of the left in the 2000s. However, this book also contributes to the literature on urban studies, showing the processes behind and the consequences of two of the greatest societal trends of the last century: unstoppable urbanization and growing inequality. It shows the politics and the agency behind the informal urbanization of our cities. In fact, Montevideo is an excellent case for discussions on informality, given that they normally assume either that informality is in Third World cities to stay or that it will disappear in time as it did in the First World. Montevideo is therefore interesting in its outlier condition, as a city that increased its informality after being almost completely formal without immigration or natural disasters. A city which expelled its former dwellers from its core, and, in so doing, challenged many of the assumptions about old and new versions of Modernization theory (informality is just a stage in development) and sides with more structural accounts of informality, which are a product of processes of expulsion in the midst of neoliberalism (Sassen 2014).

The main theoretical contributions of this book, however, because of its questions, regard the literature on social movements or, broadly speaking, contentious politics. First, it expands its scope to less visible and structured forms of collective action more generally, forms that I dub here as *elusive*. Most of the literature on collective action, and concretely that of the political process theory, has been based on empirical research conducted in wealthy Western democracies about more or less clearly structured movements such as the labor or civil rights movements that leave traces in archives or the press. Political opportunities are dimensions of the political system that suggest that effective action is possible and thereby encourage people to engage in contentious politics (Tarrow 1998; McAdam et al. 1996). This book shows that such a concept is useful also in understanding less organized forms of collective action, that often do not even consider themselves social movements. The same happens with concepts such as the protest cycle, political opportunities, repertoires of contention, and threats or influential allies, as I will show here through the case of squatters in Montevideo.

Second, this book illustrates the interactive effect of grievances and political opportunities in spiking squatters' mobilizations. Because they wanted to quarrel with the engrained idea that relative deprivation was the cause of (irrational) mobilization, exponents of resource mobilization theory first, and political opportunities theory later, downplayed the role of hardships or grievances completely. In a beautifully provocative statement in 1974, Tilly wrote:

> Grievances are fundamental to rebellion as oxygen is fundamental to combustion. But just as fluctuations in the oxygen content of the air account for little of the distribution of fire in the workaday world, fluctuations in grievances are not a major cause of the presence or absence of rebellion. For that, the political means of acting on grievances which people have at their disposal matter a good deal more (Tilly 1974: 302)

Here, Tilly assumes grievances as if they were a constant but they are not. For instance, the mobilization that generated MOVIDE started in the midst of democratization (political opportunity) but only among those squatter settlements that had suffered the threat of eviction. It was because of these threats that neighbors from two different very poor settlements went to knock at their local parishes' doors, as the first step in their mobilization. In turn, when looking at the time series of new land invasions in the city from 1947 to 2006 (Appendix B), we see that when hardships are low (real wages) new land invasions are less likely. It was only when hardships were high and political opportunities present that land invasions did spike. Grievances and opportunities tend to interact with each other to make people mobilize.

Finally, by considering the macro and micro dimensions and conducting protest event analysis at the same time as ethnographic analyzes, this work sheds light not only on the when or what but also on the *how*, and in so doing, it both specifies political opportunities and uncovers mechanisms that connect structures or conditions of possibility for mobilization with real people actually mobilizing (Goodwin and Jasper 1999). Democratization is a political opportunity for excellence (Hipsher 1998).

Yet, its effects are neither automatic nor the same at different points through history or for different social actors. This research shows two different effects: in the first wave of mobilization, the effect of democratization is that of political opening and a relaxation of repression. In the second wave of mobilization, the effect of a more institutionalized democracy was created through increased political competition for popular votes. Many have criticized political opportunities for being a sponge concept that explains everything, and therefore runs the risk of explaining nothing (Gamson and Meyer 1996; Goodwin and Jasper 1999; Meyer 2004). This work helps to more precisely specify the different channels through which democratization may become a political opportunity.

Finally, it emphasizes a common mechanism through which democratization can turn into mobilization, especially for those that are otherwise disenfranchised: brokerage (McAdam et al. 2001: 141). Throughout the analyzed period, what appears as a commonality linking needs and political opportunities to action is the presence of a broker; that is, an institution or person that links those in need with other groups and/or different types of resources. It was through the local priest, who acted as a broker connecting one squatter neighborhood in Montevideo to other squatters with the same needs, to members of a much wealthier parish and to international funding that one of the studied accretion invasions managed to resist eviction, buy their land and pay for construction materials to build self-help housing. It was through a variety of political ties that a local leader, a master in political relations, managed to bring the state to his neighborhood in different ways, from roads to public transportation and water. Brokers can be external, for example, a priest or an NGO, or internal, such as a neighborhood leader, but what they share is their capacity to connect squatters with the outside. Therefore, brokers are often crucial for the mobilization of those with little resources for mobilization.

The book is organized into seven chapters. Following this introduction, Chap. 2 introduces us to the Uruguayan case, focusing on its party-centered and state-centered features as well as describing some of the main structural changes which have taken place in the last century such as the passage from import substitution to deindustrialization and their urban consequences for squatters. It also introduces squatting in Montevideo, using secondary data to characterize squatters at different times. While the squatters of the past were on average extremely marginalized in terms of education and labor, squatters of the present tend to be a product of the recent changes in the labor market without the housing policy having undergone many changes. Current squatters have, on average, better education and better labor conditions, even if these are precarious, as well as more previous experiences of participation in unions or cooperative organizations; they used to live in the formal city and want to belong to the formal city, they plan their neighborhoods and want to be regularized/legalized, and to have all the urban services they feel entitled to.

Chapter 3 describes the cycle of land squatting in Montevideo from its beginnings in the late 1940s until the end of the study period in 2011. It shows that until the late 1980s, squatter settlements were rare events in the city. In contrast to most other cities, Montevideo's squatting started after the rural–urban migration process, which was already over by the 1960s. Accretion invasions grew slowly but steadily until the mid-80s. Around 1990, there was a notorious peak in land invasions, but many of them were planned land invasions, with a group organizing to seize a plot, establish blocks and streets and demand that the state provide them with public services. All types of land invasions have declined since the end of the 1990s and they once more became rare in the city. Still, the urban and social consequences of this wave changed the form and nature of the city forever and, although some settlements have been regularized, most of them are still informal.

Chapters 4 and 5 tell the stories of the two waves of squatters' mobilizations in Montevideo. While Chap. 4 tells the story of the unlikely mobilization of the poorest of the poor, those threatened by evictions in accretion invasions toward the end of dictatorship, Chap. 5 is dedicated to the analysis of the peak in planned land invasions around 1990. Chapter 4 is based mainly on historical data such as press articles and various documents, while Chap. 5 is mostly based on ethnographic data reconstructing the history of different neighborhoods. Both attempt to connect the structures that made mobilization possible with the actors and stories that where crucial in that mobilization. As mentioned before, they both emphasize the role of brokerage as an enabling mechanism for squatters' mobilization.

Chapter 6 is deeply ethnographic in the sense that it tries to take the reader to the study setting, by choosing a story of a planned land invasion and scrutinizing the relationship between squatters and the state through political brokerage. It puts the mobilization literature in dialogue with the literature on clientelism, showing that political networks can at times be mobilizing rather than demobilizing, and shows the relational nature of political networks considering the different sides, the politicians or state officials, the broker, and the clients or ordinary residents. Finally, after the concluding chapter, there are two methodological appendixes for interested readers. The first details the methods, showing the different ways in which quantitative and qualitative methods are combined in this work. The second presents a summary of the main results from the quantitative protest event analysis that are crucial for one of this books' main arguments: both political opportunities and grievances are needed for mobilization to take place.

Notes

1. For more on Uruguayan social movements, see for instance: Bucheli et al. (2005) on the mobilization for human rights against the crimes committed by the military dictatorship; Midaglia (1992) also on the early stages of the human rights movement and on the cooperative housing movement; Mirza (2006) on the cooperative housing movement and the union movement in comparative perspective; all the articles in Filgueira (1985) on gender, student, union, neighborhood and rural movements during the democratic transition; Moreira (2011) for an updated perspective on the recent relationship of social movements with the leftist government.
2. For example, in Latin America the Polanyi (1944) pendulum moved from neoliberalism in the 1990s to a return of the left with an emphasis on redistribution in the 2000s.
3. For more research emphasizing the relationship of Latin American squatters and the state, often through politicians, see also: Stokes (1991, 1996) for the Lima case, Eckstein (1988), Özler (2003) and Cornelius (1974, 1977) for the Mexican case, Roberts (1973) for Guatemala city, Portes (1972), Handelman (1975), Castells (1983) and Özler (2003) for Santiago de Chile, Burgwal (1995) for Quito, Auyero (2000) and Merklen (1991, 2005) for Buenos Aires, and Gay (1990, 1994, 2006) and McCann (2013) for Rio. The literature is huge and I do not mean to be exhaustive but just to mention a part of the literature that were crucial to building my questions and finding my answers in the Uruguayan case. For a general perspective on housing problems and land squatting in Latin America, see Gilbert (1994) and Portes and Walton (1976).
4. According to the last available estimation (the 2011 census), there are 31.921 houses and 112.101 people living in 332 squatter settlements (PMB-PIAI 2013) in a city of 1.319.108 inhabitants.

References

Alsayyad, N. (1993). Squatting and culture. A comparative analysis of informal developments in Latin America and the Middle East. *Habitat International, 17*(1), 33–44.

Alsayyad, N., & Roy, A. (2003). Prologue/dialogue. Urban informality: Crossing borders. In N. Alsayyad & A. Roy (Eds.), *Urban informality. Transnational perspectives from the Middle East, Latin America and South Asia*. Lanham and London: Lexington.

Alvarez-Rivadulla, M. J. (2000). Asentamientos irregulares montevideanos: la desafiliación resistida. *Documento de Trabajo del IPES. Serie Monitor Social del Uruguay, 4.*

Amarante, V., & Caffera, M. (2003). Los factores determinantes de la formación de asentamientos irregulares. Un análisis económico. *Revista de la Facultad de Ciencias Empresariales y Economía, Universidad de Montevideo, 2*, 61–95.

Auyero, J. (2000). *Poor people's politics. Peronist survival networks & the legacy of Evita*. Durham, NC: Duke University Press.

Bucheli, G., Curto, V., Sanguinetti, V., Demasi, C., & Yaffé, J. (2005). *Vivos los llevaron: historia de la lucha de Madres y Familiares de Uruguayos Detenidos Desaparecidos (1976–2005)*. Montevideo: Ediciones Trilce.

Burgwal, G. (1995). *Struggle of the poor: Neighborhood organization and clientelist practice in a Quito squatter settlement*. Amsterdam: CEDLA.

Caetano, G., Rilla, J., & Pérez, R. (1987). La partidocracia uruguaya. Historia y teoría de la centralidad de los partidos políticos. *Cuadernos del CLAEH, 44*, 37–61.

Canel, E. (1992). Democratization and the decline of urban social movements in Uruguay: A political institutional account. In A. Escobar & S. E. Alvarez (Eds.), *The making of social movements in Latin America* (pp. 276–290). Boulder, CO: Westnew Press.

Castells, M. (1983). *The city and the grassroots*. Berkeley: University of California Press.

Collier, D. (1976). *Squatters and oligarchs. Authoritarian rule and policy change in Perú*. Baltimore: The John Hopkins University Press.

Cornelius, W. A. (1974). Urbanization and political demand making: Political participation among the migrant poor in Latin American cities. *American Political Science Review, 68*, 1125–1146.

Cornelius, W. A. (1977). Leaders, followers, and official patrons in Urban Mexico. In S. W. Schmidt, L. Guasti, C. H. Lande, & J. Scott (Eds.), *Friends, followers, and factions. A reader in political clientelism*. Berkeley: University of California Press.

Davis, M. (2006). *Planet of slums*. London and New York: Verso.

Dietz, H. A. (1998). *Urban poverty, political participation and the state. Lima 1970–1990*. Pittsburgh, PA: University of Pittsburgh Press.

Dosh, P. (2010). *Demanding the land: Urban popular movements in Peru and Ecuador, 1990–2005* (D. Collier Ed. Vol. Ph.D.). State College: Pennsylvania State University Press.

Eckstein, S. (1988). *The poverty of revolution. The state and the Urban poor in Mexico.* Princeton, NJ: Princeton University Press.

Filgueira, C. (1985). Movimientos Sociales en la restauración del orden democrático: Uruguay, 1985. In C. Filgueira (Ed.), *Movimientos Sociales en el Uruguay de Hoy.* Montevideo: CLACSO-CIESU-Ediciones de la Banda Oriental.

Gamson, W. A., & Meyer, D. S. (1996). Framing political opportunity. In D. McAdam, J. McCarthy, & M. N. Zald (Eds.), *Comparative perspectives on social movements.* Cambridge: Cambridge University Press.

Gay, R. (1990). Community organization and clientelist politics in contemporary Brazil: A case study from suburban Rio de Janeiro. *International Journal of Urban and Regional Research, 14*(4), 648–665.

Gay, R. (1994). *Popular organization and democracy in Rio de Janeiro. A tale of two favelas.* Philadelphia: Temple University Press.

Gay, R. (2006). The even more difficult transition from clientelism to citizenship: Lessons from Brazil. *Out of the Shadows: Political Action and The Informal Economy in Latin America*, 195–217.

Gilbert, A. (1994). *The Latin American city.* London: The Latin America Bureau.

Goodwin, J., & Jasper, J. M. (1999). Caught in a winding, snarling vine: The structural bias of political process theory. *Sociological Forum -Ithaca-, 14*(1), 27–54.

Handelman, H. (1975). The political mobilization of Urban squatter settlements. Santiago's recent experience and its implications for Urban research. *Latin American Research Review, 10*(2), 35–72.

Hipsher, P. L. (1998). Democratic transitions and social movement outcomes: The Chilean Shantytown Dweller's movement in comparative perspective. In M. G. Giugni, D. McAdam, & C. Tilly (Eds.), *From contention to democracy.* Boston: Rowman & Littlefield.

Holston, J. (2009). Insurgent citizenship in an era of global Urban peripheries. *City & Society, 21*(2), 245–267.

Holland, A. C. (2017). *Forbearance as redistribution. The politics of informal welfare in Latin America.*

Huchzermeyer, M. (2002). Informal settlements: Production and intervention in twentieth-century Brazil and South Africa. *Latin American Perspectives, 29*, 83–105.

INE-PIAI (Producer). (2006, February 2009). Relevamiento de Asentamientos 2006. Retrieved from http://www.ine.gub.uy/piai3/inepiai.htm.

INTEC. (1995). *Relevamiento de Asentimientos Irregulares de Montevideo.* Retrieved from Montevideo.

Johnston, H., & Almeida, P. (2006). *Latin American social movements: Globalization, democratization, and transnational networks.* Rowman & Littlefield.

Kaztman, R., Filgueira, F., & Errandonea, F. (2005). La Ciudad Fragmentada. Respuesta de los sectores populares urbanos a las transformaciones del mercado y el territorio en Montevideo. In A. Portes, B. Roberts, & A. Grimson (Eds.), *Ciudades Latinoamericanas. Un Análisis Comparativo en el Umbral del Nuevo Siglo.* Buenos Aires: Prometeo.

Luna, J. P. (2007). Frente Amplio and the crafting of a social democratic alternative in Uruguay. *Latin American Politics and Society, 49*(4), 1–30.

Markoff, J. (2015). *Waves of democracy: Social movements and political change.* New York: Routledge.

McAdam, D., McCarthy, J., & Zald, M. N. (1996). *Comparative perspectives on social movements: Political opportunities, mobilizing structures and cultural framings.* New York: Cambridge University Press.

McAdam, D., Tarrow, S., & Tilly, C. (2001). *Dynamics of contention.* Cambridge: Cambridge University Press.

McCann, B. (2013). *Hard times in the Marvelous city: From dictatorship to democracy in the Favelas of Rio de Janeiro.* Durham, NC: Duke University Press.

Merklen, D. (1991). *Asentamientos en La Matanza. La terquedad de lo nuestro.* Buenos Aires: Catálogos.

Merklen, D. (2005). *Pobres Ciudadanos. Las clases populares en la era democrática (Argentina 1983–2003).* Buenos Aires: Editorial Gorla.

Meyer, D. S. (2004). Protest and political opportunities. *Annual Review of Sociology, 30,* 125–145.

Midaglia, C. (1992). *Las formas de acción colectiva en Uruguay.* Montevideo: CIESU.

Mirza, C. A. (2006). *Movimientos sociales y sistemas políticos en América Latina: la construcción de nuevas democracias.* Buenos Aires: CLACSO.

Moreira, C. (2011). Movimientos populares y luchas sociales en Uruguay. In M. Mondonesi & J. n. Rebón (Eds.), *Una década en movimiento: luchas populares en América Latina en el amanecer del siglo XXI.* Buenos Aires: CLACSO, Prometeo Libros.

Murphy, E. (2015). *For a proper home: Housing rights in the margins of Urban Chile, 1960–2010.* Pittsburgh, PA: University of Pittsburgh Press.

Özler, S. I. (2003). *Squatters stand up: Political institutions and demand making in the developing world* (Ph.D.). Los Angeles: University of California.

PMB-PIAI. (2013). *Informe Técnico: Relevamiento de Asentamientos Irregulares. Primeros Resultados de Población y Viviendas a partir del Censo 2011.* Montevideo.

Polanyi, K. (1944). *The great transformation.* Boston: Beacon Press.

Portes, A. (1972). Rationality in the slum: An essay on interpretative sociology. *Comparative Studies in Society and History, 14*(3), 268–286.

Portes, A. (1989). Latin American urbanization during the years of the crisis. *Latin American Research Review, 24*(3), 7–44.

Portes, A., & Walton, J. (1976). *Urban Latin America*. Austin: University of Texas Press.

Roberts, B. (1973). *Organizing strangers: Poor families in Guatemala city*. Austin: University of Texas Press.

Rodé, P., Marsiglia, J., & Piedracueva, E. (1985). Experiencias recientes de movilización urbana en las áreas de la salud, nutrición y organización barrial. In C. H. Filgueira (Ed.), *Movimientos sociales en el Uruguay de hoy*. Montevideo: CLACSO-CIESU-Ediciones de la Banda Oriental.

Santos, C., Valdomir, S., Iglesias, V., & Renfrew, D. (2006). *Aguas en movimiento: la resistencia a la privatización del agua en Uruguay*. Montevideo: Ediciones de la Canilla.

Sassen, S. (2014). *Expulsions*. Cambridge: Harvard University Press.

Schneider, C. L. (1995). *Shantytown protest in Pinochet's Chile*. Philadelphia: Temple University Press.

Stokes, S. (1991). Politics and Latin America's Urban poor: Reflections from a Lima Shantytown. *Latin American Research Review, 26*(2), 75–101.

Stokes, S. (1996). *Clients and radicals*. [S.l.]: [s.n.].

Tarrow, S. (1998). *Power in Movement: Social movements and contentious politics*. New York: Cambridge University Press.

Tilly, C. (1974). Town and country and revolution. In J. W. Lewis (Ed.), *Peasant revolution and communist revolution in Asia*. Stanford, CA: Stanford University Press.

UN-Habitat. (2014). *Background paper. October 6, World Habitat Day. Voices from slums*. Retrieved from http://unhabitat.org/wp-content/uploads/2014/07/WHD-2014-Background-Paper.pdf.

Walton, J., & Ragin, C. (1990). Global and national sources of political protest: Third world responses to the debt crisis. *American Sociological Review, 55*(6), 876–890.

CHAPTER 2

The Case of Montevideo

Squatting and the Repertoire of Collective Action by the Urban Poor of Montevideo

The explosion of squatting in Montevideo took place later than in other metropolises of the region. Although some land invasions, dubbed *cantegriles*, existed in Montevideo before squatting peaked in the 1990s, the Uruguayan capital developed differently to other Latin American cities. Despite already starting to show signs of urban socioeconomic inequality in the 1980s (Portes 1989), Montevideo was more egalitarian than other cities of the continent. Even after the military regime (1973–1984) carried out a harsh policy of evictions and demolitions in the city center, home to many of the poor, there was no massive move to squatter settlements on the outskirts of the city. Instead of organizing land invasions, the urban poor of Montevideo gravitated toward an already familiar strategy for coping with housing problems: crowding at relatives' homes (Benton 1986).

In this section, I provide contextual features of the relationship between state and society in Uruguay, which I believe can help explain this puzzle. I do so by drawing on scholarly work on Uruguayan political history as well as on some comparative works. This enables me to identify some long-term trends in the way the poorest citizens have related to the state in this country as well as some important changes that shifted that relationship. I later describe the broad changes in land squatting in Montevideo in terms of both identity and demographics.

M.J. Álvarez-Rivadulla, *Squatters and the Politics of Marginality in Uruguay*, Latin American Political Economy, DOI 10.1007/978-3-319-54534-9_2

For this, I unearthed the few sources I was lucky to find that could reveal something about the first land invasions, including two forgotten early studies of squatter settlements between the 1960s and early 1970s. A documentary film was vital for seeing life inside one of the poorest land invasions of the city in 1958. I have tried to track the changes in the popular names for land invasions from *cantegriles* to *asentamientos,* and, finally, I attempt to follow squatters' demographic changes by comparing earlier studies with the 2006 National Household Survey.

A Stubborn Statist Tradition in a Worn-Down/Elastic State

According to Benton (1986), squatting did not happen even when the military evicted city buildings in the 1970s because economic activities, as well as neighborhood identity, connected the poor with the city center. However, she also pays special attention to the traditional paternalistic role of Uruguayan welfare policy:

> Of crucial importance was the peculiar historical-political relationship between workers and the state in Montevideo. The long tradition of state assistance to the urban poor before 1973 clearly conditioned the responses of residents in bringing pressure to bear on the state. Behavior that seemed to represent attitudes of resignation –the lack of organized protest over the destruction of *conventillos* in Palermo and Sur[1] or the wait-and-see strategy of residents housed in the city stables– quietly shifted responsibility to the state for resolving the housing "crisis" it had helped to engineer. (Benton 1986: 49)

The Uruguayan state in general and its welfare branch in particular has been noted for its singularity in the region (Filgueira 2000; Mesa Lago 2000). When Centeno (2002) classifies Latin American states in a continuum of institutional capacity, he locates Uruguay, together with Chile and Argentina, as "obvious" successful end points of the spectrum. Yet as Centeno also notes, the Uruguayan state was the latest of the three to consolidate, due to continuous civil wars during the nineteenth century. The early governments of the twentieth century in Uruguay had to face two different tasks that other countries faced at separate points in time. The first was political institutionalization and the second, the demands for political participation of the new emerging social sectors such as the urban working class (Panizza 1990).

Until 1904, the Uruguayan state did not have a centralized army that could control the country's territory, divided between the two traditional political forces, the *Colorados* and the *Blancos*, born back in the first half of the nineteenth century. The Colorados controlled Montevideo, then the fifth biggest city in Latin America. More than a quarter of the population lived in the capital, whereas other cities of the region housed an average of 3–5% of the population (Panizza 1990). The Blancos, in turn, under the leadership of the *caudillo* Aparicio Saravia, controlled the countryside.

Welfare policies were one of the tools that the Colorado President José Batlle y Ordoñez (1903–1907 and 1911–1914) used to consolidate his party's power over the country. While he spent his initial presidency first fighting the revolts of Aparicio Saravia and the Blancos and later consolidating the military control of the country, he spent his second presidency building up his state project. Batlle y Ordoñez believed in strong economic interventionism and in pro-worker legislation. He also believed in state enterprises, so much so that during his term in office, he nationalized several banks such as the *Banco de la República*. Among his progressive pro-worker legislation, he fought for the 8-h workday, unemployment compensation, workers' rights to strike, regulation of child labor, maternity leave, and the establishment of retirement and handicap pensions. Some of these projects were approved during his presidency and others right after he left office. Thus, the construction of the Uruguayan state is entirely linked to the construction of its welfare state.

Despite interruptions such as the Terra dictatorship (1930–1938), the state kept growing and generously provided progressive labor rights, universal or near-universal coverage in basic social protection services, good quality public services such as education and health, and employment in a wide range of public sector administrative and productive activities. With interruptions such as the worldwide economic crisis in 1930s, for more than almost half a century, the Uruguayan economy enjoyed times of economic prosperity. The convulsive international situation of the two world wars and later the Korean War was beneficial to Uruguay because of the great demand for products such as meat and wool. After the demand for Uruguayan goods decreased, there was a crisis of inflation, unemployment, and falling living standards. Even then, the state kept growing as a sort of countercyclical buffer. Even in 1970, when the Uruguayan model of import substitution and state-led development was already falling apart, 95.4% of the Uruguayan economically active population had social security coverage (Filgueira 2000) and almost 30% of the labor force was employed by the state (Kaztman et al. 2005).

In her study of social policy-making in Chile and Uruguay, Castiglioni (2005) poses an interesting puzzle related to this. Both countries suffered democratic breakdowns in 1973 and both had big welfare states at the time. However, while the Chilean military carried out an aggressive pro-market program of state retrenchment, the Uruguayan counterpart left social policies almost untouched. Castiglioni finds that, together with other institutional factors, the ideology of Uruguayan policy-makers during dictatorship was still permeated with the legacy of Batllismo.

But a slow reform process did take place. Following the regional trend of neoliberal reforms, Uruguay shifted toward a less regulated and more export-oriented economy. Yet the citizens have consistently and stubbornly rejected the state retrenchment reforms, especially privatization of state enterprises. The most recent sign of resistance took place in 2004 when Uruguayans, for the first time, voted the leftist coalition into office with a pro-state platform, and they approved a constitutional reform that defines water as a human right and a public good, stating that piped water and sanitation can only be provided by state enterprises. Only months before, through a referendum, Uruguayan citizens had opposed a law that attempted to end the monopoly of the state-owned oil company and opened it up to outside investors. Uruguay has also blocked significant attempts to privatize its social security system, and in 2008, it engaged in a health reform, which was at odds with privatization and, in fact, wanted to expand coverage. All this contrasts with the region's two other welfare pioneers who have privatized most of their state businesses. While Argentina and to an even greater extent Chile have experienced a market revolution, Uruguay has obstinately chosen a different path. As Filgueira (2000) puts it,

> Uruguay has gone down the market oriented road to a limited extent, but clearly not to the degrees seen in other Latin American countries. The welfare state, and the [people's, unions', the left's and corporations'] response to the decline in the quality of the public goods it distributed have been able to rescue the public dimension of those goods. (219)

According to Filgueira, the strong legacies of political and social citizenship help explain why in Uruguay those sectors with resources opted for voice rather than exit. This voice has, however, been more effective in defending the existing worn-down welfare state than in making innovations.

The results of these middle road market reforms are mixed. Uruguay continues to do better in a number of development measures when compared to most third-world countries. According to the United Nations Human Development Index, Uruguay's human development is high—above the regional average—and comes in at number 52 in the HDI. In Latin America, only Argentina and Chile are above Uruguay, but the latter has been slowly dropping in the ranking over the years. In contrast to other Latin American countries, it has been unable to improve its score (PNUD 2008). In terms of poverty, Uruguay has always outperformed most of the region's countries, in terms of its low poverty rates. However, the comparison with its own past is less hopeful. Poverty rates have tended to rise even at times of economic growth since the mid-1990s (PNUD 2008).

The conclusion of a group of scholars who studied different welfare policies in Uruguay is quite disheartening (Filgueira et al. 2005), as they find an increasing disconnection between risk groups and protected groups. According to the authors, the welfare state has not adapted itself to profound changes in the labor market such as the increase in structural unemployment and informality, or to the also profound demographic changes such as less stable families and increasing poverty among children. They identify a very vulnerable group of 40% of the population—mainly children, young women on low incomes, informal workers, and land squatters—that, despite its vulnerability, does not receive enough state attention.

The legacy of *Batllismo*, the legacy of a big state, is deeply entrenched among Uruguayans. As Panizza cleverly states, rights for Uruguayan citizens did not evolve as they did in Europe, from the political to the economic to the social. In Uruguay, economic and social rights came first and this impacted people's subjectivity since they would come to conceive citizenship in a broader sense than merely voting (Panizza 1990).[2] This legacy also had an impact on the 2004 elections, in which a coalition of leftist factions, the *Frente Amplio*, won national elections breaking two centuries of bipartidism in the country. According to Luna (2007), parties competed for this election around a state versus market opposition, with Frente Amplio on the state's side, appropriating and reinventing the ideology of Batllismo, and the traditional parties on the market side.

All these contextual features help us understand Benton's opening statement about the reliance of the urban poor on the state. With this in mind, it is completely logical that the urban poor were waiting for the state to do something for them. Yet contrary to what she implies by saying that faced with housing problems they did not squat en masse but instead hoped the state would respond to their problem, as we will see throughout this book, squatters in Montevideo still depend very much on the state. In this sense, squatting in Montevideo implies continuity more than it does rupture, in terms of relying on the state. In other words, even when they settled on vacant urban land, people in need requested state's help.

The growth of squatter settlements and their characteristics are very visible, almost like a metaphor of this eroding but still stretchable and paternalistic state. The over 300 squatter settlements in Montevideo, housing 8.5% city's population, are one of the most noticeable signs of the problems of Uruguay's economy and state (PMB-PIAI 2013). They spatially remind us that the times of the "happy country," the "fat cows," or the "Switzerland of Latin America"[3]—as people used to call Uruguay—are long gone. Extreme poverty and unmet basic needs are not exclusive of the squatter settlements. Urban poverty also exists in the city center and in other formal neighborhoods. Yet with the exception of homelessness, poverty in the formal city is camouflaged behind the European-style facades of the city center or the working-class detached housing typical of the once industrial neighborhoods. Squatter settlements, in contrast—sometimes because of poor housing, often because some are located close to polluted rivers and piles of garbage, and always because of their lack of paved streets and other public services—make poverty and suffering visible to the most oblivious passerby.

In this sense, squatter settlements provide the most noticeable evidence of the process suffered by the Uruguayan urban poor in recent decades. Using Kaztman's (2001) evocative phrase, the urban poor in Montevideo have been "seduced and abandoned" by a labor market that promised formal and stable jobs, a state that promised good services and benefits, an open education system that offered opportunities of upper mobility, and a city that promised not only shelter but also interaction with other social classes. All these promises have gone unmet for many of the urban poor. It is only in this context that we can understand why many of my interviewees, both squatter leaders and non-leaders, framed their actions in terms of rights: "It is our right to squat. Housing is a right in the Constitution."

The "structure of opportunities" available to the urban poor has shrunk in all its spheres: the market, the state, and the community (Kaztman 1999). Regarding the labor market, taking 1970 as a starting point and comparing it with 2000, jobs became scarcer and those that did exist were less stable. This happened in part because women doubled their participation in the labor force in the period—from 27.5% in 1970 to 52.5% in 1999—(Kaztman et al. 2005), but also because many industries closed, the state reduced its employees by half, and there is not enough employment generation. Moreover, positions that do open up tend to be unstable and low paid, especially if targeted at less skilled workers. Salary differentials by education are on the increase (Bucheli and Furtado 2004). Unemployment has increased and is especially high for the youth and the poorly educated. Although traditionally under 10% in Uruguay, since 1970 unemployment has reached double digits several times and it rose to 16% during the 2002/2003 economic crisis (Kaztman et al. 2005). The informal labor market has increased substantially as well. According to the 2006 National Household Survey, 36.5% of the working population in 2006 did not have social security (INE 2006).

These changes in the labor market are a product of the change in the mode of accumulation from the decaying import substitution model to an increasingly open economy since the 1970s. The opening of the economy started with the military government in 1973, and the new model has been portrayed by overall growth and overall inequality. According to economic historians, this trend of growth with a non-egalitarian distribution dates as far back as the 1960s, when the trends of GDP per capita (which measure overall growth) and real wages (which measure the well-being of average workers), convergent since the 1920s, started to diverge (Camou and Maubrigades 2005). Not surprisingly, the Gini coefficient, one of the most popular inequality measures, has followed an overall growing trend since 1960 (Bértola 2005).

The role of the state—the second dimension of the structure of opportunities analyzed by Kaztman—as an employer has diminished. However, its impact among the urban poor comes also through other avenues such as the educational system, which is unable to retain many students past the first year of secondary school. This becomes particularly worrisome when we know that a person needs, on average, 9 years of education to obtain an income above Uruguay's poverty line. Finally, in terms of the community, socioeconomic residential segregation has increased in Montevideo in recent decades (Kaztman et al. 2005).

Neighborhoods are increasingly homogeneous in terms of income, occupational status, and education. This is especially problematic for the urban poor who today have fewer resources in their neighborhoods, from information to role models, which might have helped in finding jobs or making any attempt at upper mobility.

Squatter settlements are therefore visible evidence of these changes and, as we will see below, their inhabitants are among those suffering and facing this shrinking structure of opportunities. Yet, squatter settlements also provide evidence of the run-down but still generous and stretchable state described above. Although not uniformly, the state was present in all of the 24 squatter settlements I visited in my fieldwork. While in some it was only there to, imperfectly, provide basic services such as piped water and perhaps appearing once in a while to carry out a population census, in others, it had greater presence through its regularization program, investing government and Inter-American Development Bank money to pave streets, provide urban services, give land titles, and promote participation. In most settlements, there was or had been some community organization. In all, there was or had been at least a local leader or boss. One of the main goals of these neighborhood associations or local leaders is to mediate with the state for services. Depending on how well organized and connected they are, and of course also depending on the moment in which they make their demands, some squatter settlements are able to stretch the limits of the state a little bit further. This stretching becomes literal, spatially speaking, since providing services to squatter settlements, mostly located in the periphery of the city, often implies extending services beyond the originally planned city limits.

The separation between the public and private spheres, the state and civil society, the state and the government, and parties and the state are not clear in Uruguay.[4] More than sharp divisions, it is more accurate to speak of shades of gray or permeable tissues in the Uruguayan boundaries between all these spheres (Panizza and Pérez Piera 1988) . The practical implications of this are multiple; among them is the fact that to access some goods or services, it has often been more effective to talk to a politician or a local broker than to stand in line in a public building. Many squatters, particularly those that are organized in the neighborhood associations or have a local boss available have experienced this first hand. When I first started doing research in squatter settlements, back in my undergraduate years, I was naively struck by people calling politicians or high-rank state officials by their first names or having their telephone numbers in their home directories. They knew from experience that some people can successfully mediate between them and the goods they want to obtain. They knew how to combine the use of these mediators with direct petitioning to the state, and they did either or both to get what they desperately needed: electricity, water, or any other service. They had also experienced the inclusiveness of the Uruguayan state.

Squatters move in the interstices of these shades of gray, the gray shades of welfare institutions that are neither completely inclusive nor completely exclusive and the gray shades of politics. Merklen (2003), a scholar of grassroots collective action who has studied land invasions mainly in Buenos Aires but also in Montevideo, captures this with a great metaphor. He says that squatters, rather than being like the *farmer*, who can foresee the future and plan for it, are like the *hunter*, who seizes whatever opportunity he can find. This *hunter* culture, Merklen says, is part of the popular culture of individual and collective actors.

In sum, squatter settlements in Montevideo are embedded in a broader statist tradition that has defined the relationship between civil society and the state since the creation of the latter (Filgueira 2000). This strong statist tradition is what has made the state the main target and reference of almost all collective actors (Castagnola 1989), and the tradition continues, despite the fact that the state today is only a run-down shadow of what it used to be. There is less to give away and more people that need it.

Statism and Clientelism: Continuities and Changes

In addition to the entrenched statist tradition, Uruguay's squatters are also embedded in another feature of the linkage between civil society and the state: the centrality of political parties and their factions as brokers or intermediaries. Clientelism and other forms of nonprogrammatic politics have been formative of the state–society relationships in Uruguay. Yet, there have been crucial changes in recent decades. The state is now more accountable and smaller, at least as an employer or a provider of pensions, and a new party broke the traditional bipartisanship of Uruguay. All these affected the relationship of politicians with the urban poor, especially those living in squatter settlements. In this section, I trace the historical clientelistic pattern and its more recent changes.

In their comparative study of Latin America, Collier and Collier (1991) argue that the way in which the different countries incorporated the working class in political life constituted a critical juncture that left short- and long-term legacies. In Uruguay and Colombia, the main agent of that incorporation was a political party rather than the state, as in the other countries. In fact, as mentioned earlier, it was the Colorado party that was in charge of the task in Uruguay. Because of a tradition of pacts and co-participation in government between Colorados and Blancos, "progressively both parties 'colonized' the state apparatus and become crucial brokers between society and the political system" (Luna 2006). Although the Colorado party was in power for most of the twentieth century, the Blancos always participated in government in diverse ways. From the two experiences of a Swiss style collegiate executive with participation of both parties (1918–1933 and 1952–1967) to giving some ministries or positions in state enterprises' executive boards to the minority party, the Uruguayan history is full of agreements for *coparticipation*.[5]

Coparticipation was definitely useful for pacifying the country and establishing one of the most stable democracies of the region, but this has its consequences. The Uruguayan state was never a rational-legal abstraction in a Weberian sense (Panizza 1990); it was always under the influence of the two dominant parties and their multiple factions.[6] State bureaucracy was extremely politicized and connected to both parties. Public spending followed political cycles systematically growing on the eve of the electoral year (Moraes et al. 2005). Entering and ascending in the bureaucratic career depended greatly on one's party affiliation and friendships (Filgueira et al. 2003), and getting one's pension or any other state benefit often also depended on political networks.

Besides, those networks multiplied under such a factionalized political system as the Uruguayan one (Buquet 2001; González 1991; Piñeiro 2004). Each party has many factions, each with its own leaders and strong identity. Voters are often more loyal to the factions than to the parties. All these factions compete for votes, have representation in some parts of the state, and play the clientelistic game. Thus, the meaning of neutrality in the Uruguayan state has not meant the absence of particularism but a delicate equilibrium among multiple particularisms. As Filgueira (2000: 95) puts it, "because the consolidation of the state's social programs coincided with the firm establishment of the state's authority, of the parties, and of the political system, there was an early appropriation of the state by the party apparatus. (…) Although the norms regulating the state' social programs were general in content, their application became part of the clientelistic games played by parties, their factions and their leaders."

Pensions and jobs were the most traditional commodities in the clientelistic exchange (Panizza 1990). Political clubs were the neighborhood or zonal units through which most of those goods were delivered. In his study of political clubs, Rama (1971) finds that although their explicit function is to socialize citizens into party politics—something they did in the past—their real function at that time was to exchange votes for favors. Their clientele was formed by those without resources such as economic power, union representation, or instrumental personal relationships, that is, by those whose only goods to exchange were their promise of votes and political support. He finds that the period of economic recession after 1955 had several consequences for political clubs. The first reaction was an unprecedented multiplication in their numbers. Whereas previously there was only one club per relevant political faction per electoral zone, in 1966 there were about 8000 clubs for an electorate of 523,000 people in Montevideo (p. 13). The second consequence, closer in time to the dictatorship of 1973, was the disappearance of political clubs as part of the overall destruction of the political system.

At the time when Rama conducted his fieldwork, 1969, he observed the proliferation phase. He noted a complete loss of the ideological basis of the traditional parties and their transformation into "political managers." The last link in the chain of political managers was the political clubs' runner or broker who spoke nostalgically about the clubs of the past. They complained a great deal. Demands greatly overwhelmed what they could get for their constituency. They told stories of frustration and sacrifice.

The proliferation of clubs detected by Rama mirrors a rise in public spending at the time. Although public spending in Uruguay has always followed political cycles systematically growing on the eve of the electoral year (Moraes et al. 2005), 1962 stands out for its great rise in spending. The Blancos, who presided over the *Colegiado* government[7] at the time, wanted to keep office (Luna 2006). In fact, "both major political parties reacted to the crisis by reinforcing their reliance on clientelism and patronage as a way to contain discontent and maintain their electoral share. (…) In spite of that, the electorate started to seek alternatives, shifting their electoral support between and within parties" (Luna 2006: 151).

All the clubs Rama described belonged to some faction of the Colorado or Blanco parties. Although there were various leftist parties or progressive factions within the traditional parties, they did not have clubs.[8] As the author notes, "they have not been able to penetrate into those social sectors that were more marginalized by production, consumption, politics and culture. Even today for the Frente Amplio which has a different situation [he writes in 1971, year of foundation of this newer coalition], they still have a communication problem with the sectors of the electoral forces that nurture political clubs" (Rama 1971: 35).

It took the Frente Amplio many years to win that electorate, but eventually it did. Only five years after the end of dictatorship, in 1989, it won the Montevideo city government and has been in power in the city ever since (26 years to the day). In 2004, it won the national elections, bringing Tabaré Vazquez—the former city mayor—to the presidency.[9] Many reasons underlie the success of Frente Amplio in breaking with a long history of bipartidism in Uruguay. One of them is their success in winning the increasing electoral competition for the urban poor, traditionally alienated from an organized working class and intellectuals' left. In Montevideo, where half of the electorate lives, this implied winning geographical territories that were strongholds of the traditional parties, especially of the most populist factions of the Colorado party (Luna 2007; Mieres 1994). While Frente Amplio was already strong in the west of the city by 1989, in generally traditional working-class areas, it still had to win the most deprived eastern periphery. In Chap. 6, through the story of one particular land invasion, I unveil how this worked in practice both for politicians and for local leaders.

According to Luna (2007), the greatest growth for Frente Amplio among lower-class areas of the capital occurred for the 1994 election, that is, during the first period of this leftist coalition's government of the city. His hypothesis is that the decentralization process that the Frente Amplio started within the city brought this party closer to the people, particularly people in need, and that this brought electoral returns. I will address this in Chap. 5, when analyzing the political opening that decentralization brought for squatters. But what happened to the strong clientelistic networks of the traditional parties with the Frente Amplio in the city office? They started to erode long before, since the time Rama describes, due to the increasing demands, many of which could not be met. We know little about clientelistic networks during the dictatorship. All we know is that political clubs could not be active at the time.

As developed in Chap. 4, during the military regime, churches and NGOs with international funding occupied the brokers' role at least for the very poor living in cantegriles threatened with eviction. Democratization brought a peak in social mobilization (Canel 1992; Filgueira 1985); but with the reappearance of political parties, participation was rechanneled through them. They recovered the central role. Yet, the big state that supported clientelistic networks had started to change.

Although a very gradual and moderate reformer, following the regional trend of neoliberal reforms, in the last decades of the twentieth century, Uruguay shifted toward a less regulated and more export-oriented economy and a smaller and more transparent state (Castiglioni 2005; Filgueira 2000; Filgueira et al. 2003). In particular, the number of state employees started to drop in 1990, many experts replaced politicians in high positions, and many procedures, for example, those for pensions, became computerized making personalized favors more difficult.

As Filgueira et al. (2003) suggest and Luna (2006) empirically documents, state retrenchment and decentralization (more powers to municipal governments according to the Constitutional Reform of 1996) have had an impact on clientelism in at least three ways: (a) diminishing its role (recession of clientelism due to both a push toward political accountability and to state reform and fiscal crisis); (b) moving it from the national to the municipal level (due to the mayors' greater power); and (c) changing strategies and the nature of goods exchanged (e.g., while more durable goods such as pensions or employment were exchanged through clientelistic networks in the past, today more fleeting goods such as social services or information are exchanged).

Although no quantitative longitudinal measure of clientelism is available in Uruguay, according to a recent comparative study in Latin America, levels of vote buying are very low or inexistent in the country today (Nickerson 2010). It is important to know, however, that vote buying before elections is just one particular form of clientelism and definitely just one form of particularistic politics. Yet, the regional comparison is useful. According to Buquet and Piñeiro (2016: 141) "in the Uruguay of the 1990s and beyond, clientelism became something of a dinosaur." According to the authors, clientelism came to an end in Uruguay for two main reasons: "First, no one could afford it any more. Second, a new political party, the Broad Front (...) gradually changed the political game into a contest between differing programmatic appeals."

Until at least 2004, when Frente Amplio won the national government putting an end to the rise in electoral competition for the urban poor, squatters were among those who still used political networks for particularistic exchanges as one of the strategies to get information, public services, and other goods for their neighborhood. From 1989 to 2004, the electoral competition for the urban poor grew, and this encouraged the creation of new land invasions as well as the multiplication of the demands of squatters to the different factions and parties in different positions of the government, as I illustrate in detail in Chap. 6. Whether this is clientelism or not is debatable given the lack of possible monitoring, yet it is definitely a use of long-term cultivated networks to obtain collective goods in exchange for at least the promise of political support (Alvarez-Rivadulla 2012).

Although sometimes politicians deliberately helped squatters, other times they just turned a blind eye and let them do what they wanted. They tolerated squatting. Humanitarian feelings for squatters may have motivated some politicians. Yet, they also did not want to pay the political costs of evictions, especially during a period of high electoral competition. This changed later when, in 2004, tolerance to land invasions decreased and evictions became the norm. The mechanism for such tolerance appears to be similar to that of clientelism. Electoral competition increases the chances of forbearance, that is, the chances of tolerating otherwise forbidden behavior such as street vending or land squatting (Holland, 2017).

Changing the Repertoire

Going back to Benton's (1986) surprise about the Uruguayan poor not mass squatting as in other Latin American cities, I believe land squatting was just not an option for the working poor. By the time Benton wrote, squatting was still associated with the poorest of the poor, with slums, with scavenging, with marginality. The framing of land squatting as a right and feasible option for the working class who could not afford the formal city appeared somewhere in the late 1980s or 1990s.

Planned land invasions were an innovation in the repertoire of urban poor dwellers. They became part of the set of routines that are learned, shared, and acted out through a relatively deliberate process of choice (Tilly 1993). They entered the repertoire without a significant rupture with the historical paternalistic relation between the state and civil society in Uruguay. Innovation is frequent in contentious repertoires, but usually within the established forms. In general, there are no complete breaks with the old ways (Markoff 1996; Tilly 1993). In this sense, even though, through squatting, part of the urban poor became very active in the production of their housing, neighborhoods and living conditions, doing things that had previously been done by either the state or the market, they still relied a great deal on the state. In fact, it is this very interaction between squatters and the state that constitutes the peculiar form of land squatting that we see in Montevideo (especially more recently) and in other cities of Latin America. As mentioned earlier, in other regions of the world, such as Middle Eastern cities, squatters tend to solve their collective and individual problems outside the state, resorting to social and religious networks, in what Bayat (1997) calls the "quiet encroachment of the ordinary" (see also Alsayyad 1993). And yet, in others, they are forcibly removed by the state, like they currently are in many African cities (Huchzermeyer 2002).

From Marginality to the Poor Working Class: A Change in Demographics and Identity

The first land invasions appeared in Montevideo somewhere in the 1940s. The earliest one I could track was founded in 1947 and, like most of the early invasions, it was located in a deprived area of the northeast of the city with vacant non-urbanized land. There were some invasions in the more industrial working class northwest part of the city as well. These early invasions were sarcastically dubbed *cantegriles*. In *Punta del Este*, the wealthiest seaside resort of the Uruguayan Atlantic coast and a point of reference for the regional elite and jet set, there is a very exclusive club named *Cantegril Country Club,* built in 1947. It is unknown who started using that name, but some see it as a sign of popular resistance and imagination (Bon Espasandín 1963).

Cantegriles, like most squatter settlements, were associated with rural–urban migration and with extreme poverty. They were formed by slow accretion, with one family or small groups arriving at a time. Without a sewage system, drinking water, or any other service, houses were built by residents using scrap plywood, corrugated metal, sheets of plastic, cardboard, and other found materials. Their urban landscape looked very crowded, with no streets or public places. Often, you could see and smell piles of garbage and horses and horse-carts because some of the inhabitants earned money by scavenging in the city and later classifying and selling cardboard and other recyclable materials.

In 1958, a Uruguayan filmmaker, Alberto Miller, made a documentary titled Cantegriles. It is the earliest of all sources I found on the topic. This documentary, shot in the cantegriles of *Aparicio Saravia* in northeast Montevideo, for the first time, showed the reality of the people living there. Shot in black and white, it attempted to let reality speak for itself, as stated by the director more than three decades later in an interview for *TV Ciudad*.[10] It shows very precarious houses, lots of children playing with dogs or having a bath in what looks like a very dirty little lake, people sorting garbage, more children, some men chatting, people cooking on fires outside their house, and many other details of the everyday lives of the cantegriles.

Most of Miller's cantegriles still exist in the city, and, as I point out in Chap. 3, there are many new similar ones. Yet as a general pattern, the newer land invasions after the mid-1980s tend to be more urbanistically planned, with streets, blocks, sidewalks, and sometimes, public spaces such as a community center or a square. Residents still self-build their houses, but they use more solid materials such as bricks or some sort of cement. Some of these neighborhoods are, to an outsider, indistinguishable from a poor but formal neighborhood. The only difference is land ownership. What defines a squatter settlement is that residents may own the house but they do not own the plot on which their house is built.

The word cantegril has gradually become more and more specific. From being a synonym of squatter settlement, it now refers only to those that look like shantytowns. The new word is *asentamiento irregular* (literally irregular settlement). State authorities and the bureau of statistics use asentamiento irregular or just asentamiento to refer to groups of houses on an illegally occupied plot of land, as do most people. But the word cantegril is still used informally—and rarely with a positive connotation—to refer to the poorest asentamientos. One of my interviewees, a leader from a very organized land invasion, proudly told me "some think this is a *cante* [short for cantegril] and this is not a *cante*. Here, nobody collects garbage. We all have our own *ranchito* [little hut] and we try to keep everything neat. You see the houses. They are all built with cement." Like many, this squatter settlement resident identifies cantegriles with marginality, and asentamientos with a downwardly mobile, honest, and hardworking working class. Curiously, when I asked Maria, a resident from a typical cantegril, about the difference between a cantegril and an asentamiento, she told me "none, they are the same" and she kept using the terms interchangeably during the interview and while touring me around her neighborhood.

Asentamiento is somehow a more neutral word, although that seems to be changing. Montevieans increasingly identify asentamientos with undesirable spaces, red zones, criminality, and extreme poverty. The symbolic boundaries that residents of planned invasions tried to establish to distinguish themselves from the "truly" marginal are not as powerful as those that mainstream society draws against all those living in asentamientos (Álvarez-Rivadulla 2017). According to a study, the group subject to most discrimination in Montevideo and its metropolitan area is that of people living in squatter settlements. For the general public, living in an asentamiento is becoming increasingly associated with crime, danger, and marginality. About 37% of the population said they would not want someone who lives in a squatter settlement as a neighbor, and 1 out of 4 respondents said they would not like to have an informal settler as a family member (IMM 2007).[11]

As with cantegril, it is also difficult to trace the origin of the word asentamiento and the expression asentamiento irregular. It probably came from international funding agencies, which use the term settlement a lot. But a former president of the city council, a man of the extreme left who, besides living in a squatter settlement himself, was very involved with many land invasions happening in the 1990s, had a different story to tell me:

> [it's interesting] how the term asentamiento took off. I remember when I took my seat in the City Council in 1995, there was a land invasion that January. The mass media started an ideological battle… press terrorism was trying to prevent land invasions from happening (…). And then we [he refers to his political sector within the leftist coalition] met and we finally invented the term asentamientos irregulares. We started using it in the press and people started using it too. The term has a nuance that takes some pressure out of it. Before, people talked of invasions, land seizures. And we started to use asentamientos irregulares.

Regardless of who coined the term, it is important to know that the expression asentamiento irregular or irregular settlement seems to be a politically less charged expression, than land invasions or land seizures. In this work, precisely because I am trying to recover the agency and the politics of squatting, I use these terms interchangeably.

Finally, the name and identity change also implies increasing recognition by the state. Asentamientos are now part of the "deserving poor"; that is, those that need to be helped by state policies such as titling regularization and neighborhood upgrading as developed by the Program for Neighborhood Improvement (PMB-PIAI), with IADB and national funding. State policies for squatters of the past, when there were any, had mainly been aimed at eradication by building substandard public housing for squatter dwellers. Other social actors have also recognized asentamientos in a way they had not recognized cantegriles. FUCVAM (Uruguayan Federation of Mutual Aid Housing Cooperatives), the social movement for cooperative housing, a traditional working-class movement associated with unionized workers and with the left (active since 1970), has started to pay attention to the reality of squatters. As one of the leaders of the movement reflected, "The left never really understood the phenomenon of squatters. The orthodox used to say 'these are lumpens, classless, blablabla'."[12] Yet, more recently, the movement has developed strategies to be able to work with squatter populations who do not necessarily have the fixed income to pay the small but regular fees, or the time to wait the usually long time it takes to get the plot, the loan, and the building process; and they do not initially have the collective spirit to build by self-help and organize community projects. An example of the effort to overcome these obstacles is the movement's work with a group of eleven evicted families from a city center rooming house. They invaded the sidewalk until the municipality gave them a plot and they started to work with FUCVAM to build what is now a finished housing cooperative (Fossati and González 1996; Nahoum 1999).[13]

This increasing recognition by the state, other social movements, and political parties as mentioned in previous sections can be read as a process of "certification." According to McAdam et al. (2001), certification is one of the recurrent processes or mechanisms present in diverse forms of collective action. It occurs when collective actors get validation of their performances and their claims by external authorities.

Demographics Through Historical and More Recent Studies of Squatters

The study of squatter settlements in Uruguay has proliferated in recent years, with the government's increasing attention to the social problem. The National Institute of Statistics (INE) included, for the first time, in its 2006 National Household Survey, a dichotomous variable that indicates whether or not the surveyed household is located in a squatter settlement. The slum upgrading program, PMB-PIAI, has encouraged the proliferation of "neighborhood diagnostics" (PIAI 2008). Different groups of professionals, NGOs, or associations of construction companies with NGOs compete for PMB-PIAI funds to upgrade settlements. To win and later work in the field, architects, social workers, sociologists, engineers, educators, and so on produce lots of information about particular neighborhoods. I have used some of them to compare with information from my interviews or for specific information I needed.[14] The Montevideo Municipal Government, universities,[15] and other bodies have also contributed more diagnostics and some more general works.

The most frequently cited historical work is a survey conducted in 1984 by two entities: INTEC, an NGO that has been working with regularization projects for a long time, and CIESU, a research center interested in urban studies (Cecilio 1997; Mazzei and Veiga 1985). INTEC later followed up on that study on its own (Cecilio 1997). However, I found two very interesting much earlier works that are rarely cited. These two works mimic the broader Latin American discussion about squatter settlements, characteristic of the 1960s and 1970s regarding modernization theory versus Marxist-structuralist perspectives on squatters.[16] Bon Espasandín (1963) sees cantegriles primarily from the rural–urban migration angle. His work sides with the marginality theory perspective—he quotes some of its representatives such as Gino Germani—and he is very much worried by the problems residents have in getting used to urban values. In his own words:

> The man that lives in cantegriles, besides being economically poor (…) is rootless. (…). This transplanted man, without roots in the urban environment, prefers working in independent occupations because he has learned to work on his own, depending not on a patron but on his own will or nature. (66)

Nonetheless, Bon Espasandín sees the concentration of rural land as the main cause of migrants coming to the city, some of whom become squatters. In this sense, his perspective is structural. For him, the solution is trying to keep these migrants in their places of origin through various population policies. Baudrón (1979), in turn, takes a perspective more typical of the Marxism of the time, more structuralist, more dependency-theory-oriented, and, therefore, he sees squatter settlements as characteristic of a capitalist development model that does not create stable employment for all. Replicating Perlman's (1976) study in the *favelas* of Rio, Baudrón also rejects the view that squatters have different values or aspirations to mainstream society. Criticizing marginality theory, Baudrón argues that squatters' problems are not in their heads but in the structural conditions they have to face such as the rising cost of living, especially in terms of housing.

Table 2.1 summarizes and compares the findings of these two studies as well as more recent ones. It also offers, in the last two shaded columns, an update of the information I built based on the 2006 National Household Survey (INE 2006). In the rightmost column, I present data on formal neighborhoods for comparison. Given the inexistence of comparable micro-data on squatters from their emergence until today, this is the best approximation we can have to changes in their size and demographics.

The studies summarized in Table 2.1 are not strictly comparable, yet they do show general patterns and trends. Forgetting for a moment the last column, we can see some big changes in the 43 years from 1963 to 2006. The first change is the growth, whereby from a numerically insignificant phenomenon, land squatting has today grown into the form of housing used by 11% of the city's population. Secondly, the profile of squatters changed, in that today they tend to be more highly educated, they work as employees rather than on their own, and they tend to come from other neighborhoods in Montevideo, rather than from the country's interior.[17] Third, the neighborhoods' appearance has changed, so that houses now look more like poor working-class houses than they do shacks. The main construction materials are not plastic, corrugated metal, and other found materials but more solid ones, and more houses have basic services such as running water or electricity although electricity is still, more often than not, stolen.

Some of these general trends show improvement in squatters' living conditions. For some poor urban dwellers, going to live in a squatter settlement may imply improving their living conditions, which is why a considerable percentage of respondents chose the "to improve" option when asked why they moved to a squatter settlement. Even without property rights or complete certainty that they will not be evicted, evictions have been very rare and non-existent after the settlements were consolidated. Thus, for a person that rents a tiny apartment or a very run-down house at a high price, or a young couple living with relatives, to mention just some examples, going to live in a squatter settlement might be a good option.

Table 2.1 Studies on squatter settlements, Montevideo 1963–2006 and comparison of squatter settlements versus formal neighborhoods, Montevideo 2006

		Bon Espasandín	Baudrón	Mazzei & Veiga/INTEC	INTEC	Update by Alvarez-Rivadulla	
Date of the Study		1963	1971	1984	1994	Circa 2006	
Method		Survey 40 families	Survey 85 families 6 neighborhoods	Survey 524 households	Replication of the 1984 survey study (Unknown N) Aerial pictures and city explorations for the catalog of settlements	National household survey 2006 (see notes for exceptions)	
Object		"cantegriles"	"barrios marginales" (cantegriles as one subtype of them)	"cantegriles" "asentamientos precarios" and "extreme poverty" as a synonyms	"cantegriles" and "asentamientos precarios" sometimes as synonyms and sometimes to distinguish two different types of settlements	**Squatter Settlements**	**Formal Neighborhoods**
Estimate of the Universe		7000 people	-	2541 houses, 15000 people	7013 houses	144707 people (11% of city population) 39116 houses*	1181261 People*
Origin (household head born outside Montevideo)		65%	65%	46%		16% **	
Previous housing	Other squatter settlement			34%	34%		
	Inner city slum			7%	7%		
	House or apartment		52%	49%	57%		
	Other			10%	2%		
Age: Residents 10 years old or younger		27.37%	young population	35% (16% the entire city)	34%	28%	14%
Sex: percentage of women				48%	51%	51%	54 %
Motives	Couldn't afford rent/eviction		37%	47%	30%	25%	17%
	To improve				10%	45% ***	38%
	Other		63%	53%	60%	30%	45%

(continued)

Table 2.1 (continued)

		Bon Espasandín	Baudrón	Mazzei & Veiga/INTEC	INTEC	Update by Alvarez	
Poverty: % families with an income of less than 1 minimum salary		Squatter families have $9 a day on average ****	33%	45%		17%	7%
Ocupation	Work on their own	68%	70%	62% (hh)	28% (hh)	36%	25%
	Employees			35% (hh)	56% (hh)	63%	69 %
Formal Education	Without formal instruction	38%	15% (pop>6)			2% (hh)	1% (hh)
	Incomplete elementary education	38% (pop>11)		51% (hh)	33% (hh)	24% (hh)	14% (hh)
	Finished elementary education	14% (pop>11)	50% (pop >6)	40% (hh)	37 % (hh)	36% (hh)	23% (hh)
	Started secondary education	0%	5% (pop >6)	11% (hh)	28% (hh)	36% (hh)	42% (hh)
	Started tertiary education	0%	0%	0%	0%	2% (hh)	20% (hh)
Household size		4.5 mean	5.4 mean		51% 5 or more	4.0 mean	2.9 mean
Over-crowding		3.3 people/ bedroom			40% of houses have over crowding problems	2.4 people/ bedroom	1.6 people/ bedroom
Children per family average						1.4	0.5
Houses' walls built with solid materials (bricks or similar)		7.5% (67% are shacks)		36%	63%	89%	98%
% of households with piped water inside the house		Almost none			38%	84%	97%

(continued)

Table 2.1 (continued)

		Bon Espasandín	Baudrón	Mazzei & Veiga/INTEC	INTEC	Update by Alvarez	
Sewage: households connected to the city sewage system					7%	21%	80%
Main use of buildings	Housing				95%	96%	96%
	Commercial/other				5%	4%	4%
Electricity	Paying				39%	48%	94%
	Stealing				56%	52%	6%

* Uruguay's Institute of Statistics' population count, 2004 (1st phase of the 2010 census)

**Census of selected settlements by PIAI (government's regularization program), 2001-2002

*** To be able to compare, I have grouped the categories offered by question mv11 of the 2006 National Household Survey as follows: 1-"eviction" and 2-"economic reasons" as "couldn't afford rent/eviction" and 3-"house in bad shape", 4-"get my own house" and 6- "problems of space" as "to improve"

****Minimum cost of a basic food basket for a poor family was 20 $/day at the time

Yet we should not forget that there are many more squatters than there were in the past, and that if we compare squatter settlements with formal city neighborhoods—as we can by looking at the two last shaded columns of Table 2.1—we can clearly see that squatters are an underprivileged group. They are poorer and less educated; they live in larger households, with fewer rooms per person and with more children; and they have fewer basic services. Although most households have potable water inside their houses and pay for that service, half of the households steal electricity from the street with very unsafe connections, and only a minority is connected to the city sewage system.

Interestingly, the latest report, by the slum upgrading program PMB, based on the 2011 census data, finds less squatter settlements and less population living in them than in 2006, both in the city and in the country as a whole (PMB-PIAI 2013). This relates, fundamentally, to the regularization policy. According to the report, during the 2006–2011 period, only 18 small new settlements appeared in the whole country whereas 91 settlements where relocated or regularized, which means they are not counted as squatter settlements any more (there is no information discriminated by city).[18] Thus, for each new settlement, the state upgraded and regularized five; all this in a context of economic bonanza and decreasing poverty, which made land invasions less likely.[19]

Conclusion

In this chapter, I have tried to summarize the relevant features of the Uruguayan context in relation to urban poverty and land squatting in particular. I have emphasized the historical trends and facts that might have started path dependence trajectories, and, at the same time, I have tried to account for the changes. As exhaustive as I have tried to be, this case presentation is in many ways incomplete. Yet in building it and in including the relevant references for each of the multiple intertwined topics, I have aimed at providing the reader with enough elements to understand the main questions set out in this book and to be able to agree or disagree with, or at least be suspicious about, the answers I have found.

The history of land squatters in Montevideo provides a window through which to observe larger transformations in Uruguayan politics, economy, and society during the twentieth century. The rarity of squatters during the first part of the century responds to a society with a very early high level of urbanization and to a state and a market with a great capacity to incorporate the lower classes as workers and citizens. The explosive growth of squatters in recent decades responds to the erosion of that capacity of integration of both the market and the state.

Beyond the size variation, the changing demographics of squatters show that today in Montevideo, one does not need to be a scavenger or unemployed to squat. Quite the opposite, squatters are today more educated and have better jobs than in the past. They are, in fact, part of the working class of the past who due to structural mobility accessed higher levels of education than previous generations. But unfortunately that does not guarantee them the satisfaction of their basic needs. They are, in comparison with the rest of city, a very underprivileged group. They have been "seduced and abandoned" by a model of inclusion that does not seem to work anymore. In that adjustment, "squatting" changed its past connotation as a synonym of "marginal" and became increasingly appealing as a decent housing strategy for the lower classes.

Finally, as I argue throughout this book, mediating between the structural changes and the decision to mobilize or invade a plot, there are people deciding, strategizing, and sometimes using political or other types of networks. These networks often facilitate access to the state from which squatters need a lot and whom many squatters feel should do something for them, because they have rights. These perceptions about the state are not new, rather, they come from a tradition of state proximity, benevolence and, very importantly, permeability through personal political contacts.

Notes

1. Palermo and Sur are two traditional neighborhoods of the city center. Together with Ciudad Vieja, they were the areas most affected by the urban policies adopted by the military government. Before 1973, they housed many of the urban poor in poor living conditions in overcrowded substandard buildings, popularly known as *conventillos*. Subletting and squatting in these buildings was the norm. Not only were these people affected by the deregulation of rents but also by direct eviction from some of those buildings. In 1978, a decree law authorized the municipality to institute evictions of residents of any property found to be in "imminent danger of collapse." The number of evictions rose immediately. As a consequence, some individuals resettled in other parts of the city, while others were relocated either in "temporary" shelters or in public housing (Benton 1986).
2. The Constitution of 1918 declared suffrage universal and compulsory for men over the age of 18. Women's suffrage did not happen until 1932, and it was implemented in 1938 for the first time.
3. The myth of the "Switzerland of Latin America" appeared at some point in the first part of the twentieth century, perhaps from the admiration that President José Batlle y Ordoñez (1903–1907 and 1911–1915), designer of the Uruguayan state, felt for Swiss political and welfare institutions. Costa Ricans also see themselves as the Switzerland of (Central) America.
4. A common neologism among Uruguayan scholars is to say that Uruguay is a case of *partidocracia* or political parties-rule to represent the parties' historic centrality in both the state and civil society (Caetano et al. 1987).
5. See Gros Espiell (1964) for an interesting history of the collegiate executive ideas and implementation in Uruguay.
6. High factionalization is one of the main features of the Uruguayan political system (Buquet 2001; González 1991; Piñeiro 2004). Voters are often more loyal to the factions than to the parties. All these factions compete for votes, have representation in some parts of the state and play the clientelistic game.

7. From 1952 until 1967, Uruguay had a Colegiado government that is an executive of 9 members elected by the people (6 for the majority party and 3 for the one that follows in votes). This was an idea discussed and discarded by the political elite many times. In 1913, when José Batlle y Ordóñez came back from a trip to Switzerland enchanted by their collective executive, he started advocating for it. Yet, the idea of a Colegiado did not prosper until an opportunistic time in which the Blancos, who have not been in the presidency since 1865 saw it as their chance to be on the executive and made a pact with the Colorado President at the time, Andrés Martínez Trueba, who was also interested in the Colegiado. See (Gros Espiell 1964).
8. The Socialist Party of Uruguay, for example, founded in 1910, was quite old by the time Rama conducted fieldwork in the late sixties. In 1962, several leftist groups and some people and fractions that had broken away from the traditional parties formed the first leftist coalition, FIDEL (Frente Izquierda de Liberación).
9. See Lanzaro (2004) for a collection of studies describing and explaining the growth of Frente Amplio.
10. Interview of Alberto Miller with *TV Ciudad*, 1991. I thank the staff at *TV Ciudad* for allowing me access to their archive and other digital material.
11. Other categories of undesirable neighbors were former convicts (33%), politicians (18%), military officers (15%), gay people (14%), and people with AIDS (13%). The percentage of people who said they would not like squatters as neighbors increased with the socioeconomic level of the interviewees' neighborhoods, reaching 49% among those who live in affluent urban areas.
12. Interview with Javier Vidal, Anthropologist and director of the FUCVAM's Training Center.
13. For more about FUCVAM, see Midaglia (1992).
14. As an example, I have used the neighborhood diagnostics of IPRU, an NGO that has worked in regularization programs for years. In their very thorough case studies, they collect information on the history of the neighborhood, as well as demographics and other data.
15. Some undergraduate students of Urban Sociology from the School of Architecture at Universidad de la República had conducted exploratory work in different squatter settlements of the city, visiting them and randomly interviewing one or two residents. I found some of their papers through professors I contacted and also through social workers at the Zonal Community Centers who had copies. Although they were generally very initial and sometimes naïve approaches to these settlements, they had some information I could use to compare with mine. Some were very

interesting and all offered an interesting perspective of the way in which architecture students, not usually exposed to the reality of poverty and popular housing on their courses, see the reality of land invasions.

16. Squatter settlements in Latin American cities became very sexy objects of study in the 1960s. The region's massive and rapid urbanization in the mid-twentieth century, accompanying what would turn out to be an incomplete industrialization process, has fascinated scholars from the region and abroad. In the 1960s and 1970s, social scientists found the massive migration from rural areas to urban centers very interesting. Migrants' demographics, values, behaviors, political attitudes, and neighborhoods were under continuous scrutiny. The uncertainty of the time triggered academics' imagination to think about the new reality. Two major theories developed, with contending explanations of the migration and the fate of these migrants, especially those left out of the industrialization process, those that could not become incorporated into the built city and had to find alternative jobs and alternative housing and who built the shantytowns or squatter settlements that are so characteristic of Latin American cities until this day. On the one hand, the modernization theory—with Germani (1968) as its main representative—considered migrants' shantytowns as transitory, as one stage in a longer process of change and development. Once these migrants learned urban values, and once the modernization process was more complete, squatters would get incorporated into the culture of modernity, and therefore into its institutions, such as the labor market and the formal housing market. On the other hand, Nun (1969, 2001) and his more structuralist colleagues developed a very different theory. Much more pessimistically, they predicted that shantytowns were there to stay, because the peripheral form of Latin American capitalism would never incorporate them. Squatter settlements constituted the housing of a marginal mass, whose existence was, according to Nun, functional to the whole system. It contributed to low salaries and therefore to the region's very unequal form of capitalism. These theories structured the discussion of empirical results, and have been challenged and molded by them, giving birth to a rich tradition of studies and theoretical reflections about urban poverty. Perlman's (1976, 2004) work on the *favelas* of Rio showed that in the 1960s, squatters were not that different from formal urban dwellers, and that their marginality was just a myth. She claimed that *favelados* were very much integrated into the formal economy and the values of the modern city. In the same vein, studying the case of Santiago de Chile, Portes (1972) examined "rationality in the slum." He empirically challenged the idea that slum dwellers were irrational. He also demonstrated that they were not apathetic, and that their political views and strategies could be radical

or consensual depending on the circumstances, just like citizens living in the formal parts of the city. For a review and update of this debate, see de la Rocha et al. (2004).

17. It is important to note here that squatters were never completely considered migrants in Montevideo, and they were very rarely the typical rural migrant arriving in the city and not finding a place there, or not having "urban values." Bon Espasandín (1963) already found that the majority of the population of his *cantegriles* was from the city. When he only looked at household heads, he did find a pattern of migration. Nonetheless, those migrants were not mainly from rural areas but rather from cities or towns other than Montevideo (Baudrón 1979).
18. According to this report, in 2011 there were 112,101 people and 31,921 houses in squatter settlements (8.5% of the city's population).
19. Unfortunately, there is no data on whether people who lived in squatter settlements moved to the city in this bonanza period, and if so, how many. My hypothesis is that not many. Housing and renting prices went up and, once one moves to a squatter settlement, it is then difficult to go back to the city for many reasons. There are many pull factors. Residents "own" a house that they built with effort and it is unlikely that they become owners outside the settlement, they also form ties within the neighborhood, and they save money from not paying for public services and taxes, at least until they get the titles, which can take decades.

References

Alsayyad, N. (1993). Squatting and culture. A comparative analysis of informal developments in Latin America and the Middle East. *Habitat International, 17*(1), 33–44.

Alvarez-Rivadulla, M. J. (2012). Clientelism or something else? Squatter's politics in Montevideo. *Latin American Politics & Society, 54*(1), 37–63.

Álvarez-Rivadulla, M. J. (2017). The weakness of symbolic boundaries. Handling exclusion among Montevideo's squatters. *International Journal of Urban and Regional Research*. doi:10.1111/1468-2427.12450.

Baudrón, S. (1979). *Estudio Socioeconómico de algunos barrios marginales de Montevideo*. Montevideo: Fundación de cultura Universitaria—Ciedur.

Bayat, A. (1997). *Street politics. Poor people's movements in Iran*. New York: Columbia University Press.

Benton, L. (1986). Reshaping the urban core: The politics of housing in authoritarian Uruguay. *Latin American Research Review, 21*(2), 33–52.

Bértola, L. (2005). *A 50 años de la Curva de Kuznets: Crecimiento Económico y Distribuciónn del Ingreso en Uruguay y otros Países de Nuevo Asentamiento desde 1870*. Working Paper, Instituto Laureano Figuerola de Historia

Económica. Universidad Carlos III de Madrid, Madrid. Retrieved from http://docubib.uc3m.es/WORKINGPAPERS/DILF/dilf0504.pdf.

Bon Espasandín, M. (1963). *Cantegriles*. Montevideo: Tupac Amaru.

Bucheli, M., & Furtado, M. (2004). *Uruguay 1998–2002: características de los cambios en el perfil de la distribución del ingreso*. Montevideo: Naciones Unidas, CEPAL, Oficina de Montevideo.

Buquet, D. (2001, September 6–8). *Selección de candidatos y fraccionalización partidaria en Uruguay (1942–2004)*. Paper presented at the Latin American Studies Association meeting, Washington, DC.

Buquet, D., & Piñeiro, R. (2016). Uruguay's shift from clientelism. *Journal of Democracy, 27*(1), 139–151.

Caetano, G., Rilla, J., & Pérez, R. (1987). La partidocracia uruguaya. Historia y teoría de la centralidad de los partidos políticos. *Cuadernos del CLAEH, 44*, 37–61.

Camou, M., & Maubrigades, S. (2005). La calidad de vida bajo la lupa: 100 anos de evolución de los principales indicadores. *Boletín de Historia Económica, 3*(4), 51–63.

Canel, E. (1992). Democratization and the decline of urban social movements in Uruguay: A political institutional account. In A. Escobar & S. E. Alvarez (Eds.), *The making of social movements in Latin America* (pp. 276–290). Boulder, CO: Westnew Press.

Castagnola, J. L. (1989). *Actores Sociales y Espacio Público*. Montevideo: FESUR.

Castiglioni, R. (2005). *The politics of social policy change in Chile and Uruguay: Retrenchment versus maintenance, 1973–1998*. New York: Routledge.

Cecilio, M. (1997). Relevamiento de Asentamientos Irregulares de Montevideo *Asentamientos Irregulares*. Montevideo: Ministerio de Ordenamiento Territorial y Medio Ambiente. Comisión para la normalización de asentamientos irregulares.

Centeno, M. (2002). *Blood and debt: War and the nation state in Latin America*. University Park: Pennsylvania State University.

Collier, R. B., & Collier, D. (1991). *Shaping the political arena: Critical junctures, the labor movement, and regime dynamics in Latin America*. Princeton, NJ: Princeton University Press.

de la Rocha, M. G., Perlman, J., Safa, H., Jelin, E., Roberts, B. R., & Ward, P. M. (2004). From the marginality of the 1960s to the "New Poverty" of Today: A LARR Research Forum. *Latin American Research Review*, 183–203.

Filgueira, C. (1985). Movimientos Sociales en la restauración del orden democrático: Uruguay, 1985. In C. Filgueira (Ed.), *Movimientos Sociales en el Uruguay de Hoy*. Montevideo: CLACSO-CIESU-Ediciones de la Banda Oriental.

Filgueira, F. (2000). *Economic and social development: A critique of the neoclassical perspective. The case of Uruguay, 1985–1998*. Ph.D. Thesis, Northwestern University, Evanston, IL.

Filgueira, F., Garcé, A., Ramos, C., & Yaffé, J. (2003). Los dos ciclos del Estado uruguayo en el siglo XX. In I. d. C. Política (Ed.), *El Uruguay del siglo XX. La Política*. Montevideo: Banda Oriental.

Filgueira, F., Rodríguez, F., Rafaniello, C., Lijtenstein, S., & Alegre, P. (2005). Estructura de riesgo y arquitectura de protección social en el Uruguay actual: crónica de un divorcio anunciado. *PRISMA, 21*, 7–42.

Fossati, M. R., & González, G. (1996). *Quo vadis Montevideo?: alternativas urbanas para los sectores de menores recursos: reflexiones de tres décadas*. Montevideo, Uruguay: s.n.

Germani, G. (1968). *Política y Sociedad en una Época de Transición*. Buenos Aires: Paidós.

González, L. E. (1991). *Political structures and democracy in Uruguay*. Notre Dame, IN: University of Notre Dame Press.

Gros Espiell, H. (1964). El ejecutivo colegiado en el Uruguay. *Revista de Estudios Políticos, 133*, 152–172.

Holland, A. C. (2017). *Forbearance as redistribution. The politics of informal welfare in Latin America*. Cambridge: Cambridge University Press.

Huchzermeyer, M. (2002). Informal settlements: Production and intervention in twentieth-century Brazil and South Africa. *Latin American Perspectives, 29*, 83–105.

IMM. (2007). Encuesta Sobre Percepción De Exclusión Social Y Discriminación. Rompiendo Mitos. *Montevideo en la mano 13*.

INE. (2006). *Encuesta Nacional de Hogares Ampliada*. Montevideo: Instituto Nacional de Estadística.

Kaztman, R. (2001). Seducidos y abandonados: el aislamiento social de los pobres urbanos *Revista de la CEPAL, 75*, 171–189.

Kaztman, R. (Ed.). (1999). *Activos y Estructura de Oportunidades. Estudios sobre las raíces de la vulnerabilidad social en Uruguay*. Montevideo: PNUD-CEPAL.

Kaztman, R., Filgueira, F., & Errandonea, F. (2005). La Ciudad Fragmentada. Respuesta de los sectores populares urbanos a las transformaciones del mercado y el territorio en Montevideo. In A. Portes, B. Roberts, & A. Grimson (Eds.), *Ciudades Latinoamericanas. Un Análisis Comparativo en el Umbral del Nuevo Siglo*. Buenos Aires: Prometeo.

Lanzaro, J. (Ed.). (2004). *La Izquierda Uruguaya: Entra la Oposición y el Gobierno*. Montevideo: Instituto de Ciencia Política.

Luna, J. P. (2006). *Programmatic and non-programmatic party-voter linkages in two institutionalized party systems: Chile and Uruguay in comparative perspective*. Ph.D. dissertation. University of North Carolina, Chapel Hill.

Luna, J. P. (2007). Frente Amplio and the crafting of a social democratic alternative in Uruguay. *Latin American Politics and Society, 49*(4), 1–30.

Markoff, J. (1996). *The abolition of feudalism. Peasants, lords, and legislators in the French Revolution*. University Park: The Pennsylvania State University Park.

Mazzei, E., & Veiga, D. (1985). *Pobreza Urbana en Montevideo. Nueva encuesta en "cantegriles" (1984)*. Montevideo: CIESU-Banda Oriental.

McAdam, D., Tarrow, S., & Tilly, C. (2001). *Dynamics of contention*. Cambridge: Cambridge University Press.

Merklen, D. (2003). Vivir en los márgenes: la lógica del cazador. In M. Svampa (Ed.), *Desde Abajo. La transformación de las identidades sociales*. Buenos Aires: Biblos.

Mesa Lago, C. (2000). *Desarrollo social, reforma del Estado y de la seguridad social, al umbral del siglo XXI*. Santiago de Chile: Naciones Unidas, CEPAL.

Midaglia, C. (1992). *Las formas de acción colectiva en Uruguay*. Montevideo: CIESU.

Mieres, P. (1994). *Desobediencia y Lealtad. El voto en el Uruguay de fin de Siglo*. Montevideo: Fin de Siglo.

Moraes, J. A., Chasquetti, D., & Bergara, M. (2005). *The political economy of the budgetary process in Uruguay*. Washington, DC: Inter-American Development Bank, Regional Operations Dept. 1.

Nahoum, B. (1999). *Las coopertivas de vivienda por ayuda mutua uruguayas: una historia con quince mil protagonistas*. Sevilla: Junta de Andalucía, Consejería de Obras Públicas y Transportes.

Nickerson, D. W. (2010, April 15). *Detecting vote buying in Latin America using list experiments*. Paper presented at the Presentation for the Center for the Study of Democratic Politics Seminar.

Nun, J. (1969). Superpoblación relativa, ejército industrial de reserva y masa marginal. *Revista Latinoamericana de Sociología, 5*(2), 178–236.

Nun, J. (2001). *Marginalidad y Exclusión Social*. Buenos Aires: Fondo de Cultura Económica de Argentina.

Panizza, F. (1990). *Uruguay, batllismo y después: Pacheco, militares y tupamaros en la crisis del Uruguay batllista*. Montevideo: Ediciones de la Banda Oriental.

Panizza, F., & Pérez Piera, A. (1988). *Estado Y Sociedad*. Montevideo: FESUR.

Perlman, J. E. (1976). *The myth of marginality: Urban poverty and politics in Rio de Janeiro*. Berkeley: University of California Press.

Perlman, J. E. (2004). Marginality: From myth to reality in the favelas of Rio de Janeiro, 1969–2002. In A. Roy & N. Alsayyad (Eds.), *Urban informality. Transnational perspectives from the Middle East, Latin America, and South Asia*. Lanham, MD: Lexington Books.

PIAI. (2008). Programa de Integración de Asentamientos Irregulares. Retrieved from http://www.piai.gub.uy/.

Piñeiro, R. (2004). Elección de diputados y fraccionalización partidaria en Uruguay 1942–1999. *Revista Uruguaya de Ciencia Política, 14*, 15–42.

PMB-PIAI. (2013). *Informe Técnico: Relevamiento de Asentamientos Irregulares. Primeros Resultados de Población y Viviendas a partir del Censo 2011*. Montevideo.

PNUD. (2008). *Desarrollo Humano en Uruguay, 2008. Política, políticas y desarrollo humano.* Montevideo: PNUD.

Portes, A. (1972). Rationality in the slum: An essay on interpretative sociology. *Comparative Studies in Society and History, 14*(3), 268–286.

Portes, A. (1989). Latin American urbanization during the years of the crisis. *Latin American Research Review, 24*(3), 7–44.

Rama, G. (1971). *El Club Político.* Montevideo: ARCA.

Tilly, C. (1993). Contentious repertoires in Great Britain, 1758–1834. *Social Science History, 17*(2), 253–280.

CHAPTER 3

The Cycle of Land Invasions

Snapshot 1: A Story of an Accretion Invasion (1950s)

The *Acosta y Lara* settlement, as referred to by the state, people around the neighborhood, and lately also in police reports on the news, is named after the street that borders with the edge of the neighborhood on one side. It is not a name that the settlers chose but rather one that was chosen by others to identify a settlement that did not have a name for many years. Curiously, many years ago, an NGO started working there and due to the external intervention, a neighborhood association called *La Esperanza* (Hope) was created. Although its president has insisted that this name should be used rather than the name of the street, to give the neighborhood a new more destigmatized identity, people still do not use it. Strangely enough, Hope or New Hope is the most common name for squatter settlements in Montevideo, and this perhaps illustrates squatters' need to find their place in the city. Rather than despair, for many, squatting means hope and the possibility to "aspire" (Appadurai 2004). The neighborhood is located on a thin stretch of land in between Acosta y Lara Street and a polluted stream. Crammed with houses, the only open spaces are the irregular narrow passages that run through it. Unlike most accretion invasions in Montevideo and thanks to the help of a local NGO, its houses are poor but built with solid materials. However, their quality depends on their location. Walking toward the end of the neighborhood bordering the stream, the landscape becomes denser and poorer. There is garbage everywhere,

M.J. Álvarez-Rivadulla, *Squatters and the Politics of Marginality in Uruguay*, Latin American Political Economy, DOI 10.1007/978-3-319-54534-9_3

dogs and horses eat from it, and there is a penetrating putrefactive smell that lingers in the air.

By the end of the 1950s, the settlement was made up of a group of four or five shacks; most of the rest—set up by migrants from other parts of Uruguay—arrived slowly during the 1960s. José, 48, the current neighborhood president and a temporary construction worker, moved to this neighborhood with his parents when he was very small. They used to live in a formal working-class peripheral neighborhood in Montevideo, but—he remembers—they could not pay the rent because they did not have regular jobs. His grandparents had been among the first settlers who arrived sometime in 1956–1957. In the beginning, people sold sand from the banks of the stream for construction, until it ran out. There was no neighborhood association then. As José describes it:

> There was no organization, no structure. Nobody told you this is your plot. There was no limit. So people would come and fence in the parcel they wanted. Some took too much. Many people from the interior of the country started to come. A family would come and then that family told other families "come to Montevideo. At least here you don't have to pay rent, you live in a shack, and there are some jobs" (…). My grandparents came with a plastic tent. I remember that they built a house with mud, reeds and cane, all from the swamp that used to be here. (…) People cooked on open fires (…). They found their way to survive.

José is a very articulate and empowered man and, as most of his neighbors are embarrassed to speak in public, they always rely on him to talk to the authorities. They feel they do not know how to speak.

Because it has been there for decades and because of its very poor landscape, many call it a *cantegril.* Since the settlement is located close to one of the most affluent areas of the city, there had been pressures for relocation. During the dictatorship, some of the settlers were relocated and their houses bulldozed. Outside neighbors accuse squatters of robbery, and a recent homicide in its surroundings has revived tensions. The most affluent neighbors protested with pots in the street, demanding justice and blaming the settlement. Despite the fact that many of the squatters work for the richer neighbors, class tension hangs in the air. Big ostentatious houses surrounded by barbed wire fences and equipped with security cameras coexist with horse carts entering and leaving the settlement, collecting garbage.

José recognizes that some people in the settlement do steal but he says that they also do this inside the settlement, and that it is only a small group. "They can't taint us all with the same brush," he protests. He is angry at that stigma. Denouncing the thieves is difficult—he says—because people fear retaliation against their families. "It is difficult to work together" against this problem, José adds. In fact, it has been difficult to work together for many things, for example, bringing electricity to the neighborhood. Although there have always been some neighbors willing to work for the neighborhood, in general, associations have been very fragile.

There might be changes in the future, however, as the settlement is entering the state regularization program. The state will introduce sewage and other public services, and will propose a different map of the neighborhood that will involve the relocation of many dwellers, perhaps to some place outside this plot, because there is not enough room for everybody. It remains to be seen how successful the state and the neighborhood association are in this process and whether this intervention can undo the legacy of an accretion land settlement.

Snapshot 2: A Story of a Planned Invasion (1990s)

Villa Libre (Freedom Village) was founded in December 1995. A group of about 20 young and middle-aged people had been meeting for about a month at a soup kitchen in the *El Cerro* neighborhood to plan a land seizure. El Cerro used to be a thriving working-class neighborhood; famous for its meatpacking industry as well as for the contingent of Eastern European and other immigrants it received to work, particularly during and after World War II (WWII), during the period of the country's import substitution development model. The neighborhood is now greatly impoverished. Its big closed industrial sheds are living phantoms of decay. Many of its empty fringes have been occupied by squatter settlements, mostly planned ones like Villa Libre. These planned invasions drew from the tradition of union participation in this neighborhood. As one of the early settlers who was then renting at a rooming house in the city center told me:

> The majority, who were from the FAU's (Anarchist Federation of Uruguay) soup kitchen, wanted the plot to be in El Cerro. For people like me who were not from El Cerro, we didn't care.

They also wanted a place from where they could reach their jobs easily. When they felt ready, they invaded a private plot from the iconic *Frigorífico Nacional*, once a huge meat processing plant that gave jobs to many but that is now closed like many other similar plants and industries in the area. They thought the site was safe because it had been abandoned for many years. They invaded on a Friday night, trusting nobody would notice them over the weekend. But the police came that same evening and held some of the men overnight. They freed them the following morning with a warning to leave the plot immediately. Faced with this situation, the squatters decided to cross the street and invade a public park. The police came and this time took some of the women, who tended to stay at the camp site while most of the men asked for donations in street markets or sought advice as to what to do. Settlers asked a local lawyer for help and she put them in touch with some other lawyers. The group started to shrink because some people got scared of being evicted.

After holding the group of settlers at the police station for a day, they released them the following morning telling them that they needed to leave the public plot. On January 6, a holiday in Uruguay, municipal staff arrived with an eviction order and started loading settlers' belongings onto a truck, told them they needed to go with them, and took them to another plot. Residents remember this as a confusing event, because the trucks were private and the eviction order was not signed by a judge. They felt the mayor wanted to get them out of the park and since he could not do it legally, he hired private trucks on a holiday. They also have angry memories of that day as the municipal workers were not at all careful in the handling of their belongings, throwing them onto this new plot. Now that they were on a private plot, the owner—a neighborhood soccer club—also wanted to evict them. The group started to fight with the local government asking it for a solution. If the municipality had evicted them from the park, now it had to find them a solution. The group became stronger; they decided everything in assemblies and chose a number of representatives to be in charge of talking to the authorities. Pedro, one of the representatives, was chosen because he had previous experience in a land invasion. As another settler told me, "he had contacts, and he knew how to move and whom to talk to." They started to fight with the local government and, in the end, were given another plot in which to settle. Residents remember different sectors of the leftist municipal government fighting for a decision as to whether to evict them or not. The fact that most of the invaders were leftist militants was an asset, according to Darío:

> When the local government came and saw some of us here, they said 'Wow, you were here?' It was as if they came with a position and when they saw there were people from their political sector, they changed.

After a period of confrontation with authorities, the local council assigned them another plot. It was next to two other land invasions, but rather than join either of them, the group wanted to form its own neighborhood. One early resident remembers, "We had different ways of seeing things and different ways of deciding. We stayed apart." Some of those differences were political, as the other neighborhoods had connections with the traditional rightist parties.

Early times were tough because they had to clean the plot, smooth it, and start building everything. They planned streets and blocks, with the hope that one day they would become regularized; that is, that they would receive their property titles and urban services and, in the end, become an ordinary city neighborhood. In what they remember as a time of solidarity, they started to build their shacks, they built a house for one of the residents who was a single mother, one group of settlers cooked for everybody, and so on. They got together with local authorities to discuss the criteria for selecting new residents, and although the authorities wanted to accept only families with children, the settler fought to change that criterion as some members of the group were single men. Other criteria included that newcomers' incomes could not be higher than three minimum salaries; that they had a deadline to build something with solid materials, which left out very poor people who could not build anything but a shack; they did not accept people with horses or other animals, which left scavengers out; etc. In an assembly, they decided that they did not want anybody from the military, strike breakers, or thieves. They quickly obtained services such as water and electricity by directly asking the relevant state agencies and often also asked the local council for help. They brought services for the whole area that the nearby settlements had never managed to get. They never trusted politicians and did not want to feel used. But they were very pragmatic at the same time:

> We were always rebellious with that (…). We used to go to the City Council or wherever and we talked to everybody, Blancos, Colorados,

> Frenteamplistas. If someone opened the doors to us and offered something, we were there (...). Here in the local government, we often went and told them "ok, you are closing the door on us, so we are going to go elsewhere."

After the first 2 years, participation started to decline. Some of the initial settlers had moved out. According to Pedro, "Divisions started when people began to sell parcels and leave." And he adds—"That's when the respect was over (...) it's hurtful...after all this sacrifice." Pedro and Nelly, early founders who are still in the neighborhood association, say people do not want to participate. "Everybody complains because the neighborhood association doesn't do this or that", Nelly explains, "but whenever we call a meeting to choose representatives, everybody votes for us because nobody wants to be responsible for this...and with the years you get tired." But Darío, one of the early settlers, who is not participating in the neighborhood anymore, says that the neighborhood association has sold out, that they do not confront the local government any more but rather just do what they want them to do.

The neighborhood association's main goal remains as it was in 1995: to become regularized. Although they are included among the settlements to be regularized, and they have already initiated the process, the state runs on slow time. The first time they asked for a school was in 1998. In 2007, when I conducted fieldwork, it was only just under construction. Very recently, I saw pictures of the two main leaders of this neighborhood, taken on the day they received authorities in the neighborhood because they were going to be regularized after so many years. The slow process was at least beginning. When I saw their pictures, the 20 years that had passed since I met them were evident. They were together with a microphone, crying. Their bodies, their wrinkles, and their emotions testify all these years of waiting and fighting for their neighborhood to be improved. They look older than they actually are. They are the typical patients of the state, as described by Auyero (2011). For most of their lives, they have been waiting for the state to pay attention to their demands.

Snapshot 3: A Story of a Land Invasion by Subdivision and Sale (Early 2000s)

When María and her husband saw an advertisement in one of the national newspapers for an affordable plot in *Villa García*, Northeast of the Montevideo, they decided to visit it. It was December 1988. She was quite puzzled because there was no electricity or water. It was just a plot in the middle of the countryside, but they decided to buy it. They had to make a down payment and then monthly installments. They never saw the owners. They paid everything to a notary in an office located in the city center.

María, who had a history of social participation in different organizations and political participation in the Colorado Party, become the president of the newly formed neighborhood association. Soon, she became suspicious because the plots were too small and she had the idea that the municipality required more area per parcel. One day, while waiting to pay taxes at the notary office, she overheard an argument between two men. One of them said, "If the people of Villa García knew this is a fraud, they would kill us." Her suspicion was confirmed. She went back to the neighborhood, called an assembly and told the 20 families already living there what she had heard. She went to the municipality where she had some political friends from the Colorado Party, and she found out that the bigger plot had never been formally divided. Their property titles were false. She did not find much support in the municipality, and only received a warning by one staff member, telling her to be careful, to not pursue the issue, because she would be dealing with the mafia. But the fraud was even bigger than she had thought because they had oversold parcels, meaning that there were parcels with two or three owners who, when they came to claim their land, found it was already inhabited. With the help of a lawyer they sued the sellers, but nothing happened. They were in jail for 48 h after which they were released. According to Maria, they had political connections.

When the neighbors realized they were on their own, and that they were formally squatters, they started to organize as such. Using her political contacts and her leadership skills, María got electricity and water for the neighborhood. She remembers how she got the water, after failing through the regular procedures:

It was a time of electoral campaign, so we had to use it. You needed to negotiate. You need votes, I need 80 water meters. (...) People here needed water and we didn't have it because we had already demanded it but the paperwork was sleeping somewhere. (...) I talked to the water company's president. He was Colorado. I told him 'I'm a Colorada' (...) He said they were overwhelmed with work. And I said, ok, the campaign is coming and if you want votes, come down to earth: I need water for my people.

Today, the neighborhood is in good condition. Houses have basic services and are built with solid materials. There are streets, although not paved, and I was impressed by the high-tension cables right next to the settlement. María talked about that too:

> The pollution from high-tension cables is worrisome. Kids can have cancer in 10 years or so [due to radiation exposure]. That's been proven. (...) We also have the pollution from the garbage containers. We've talked to the local council several times, but they don't care about the problems of *Villa García*, you know?

Maria's hope is that one day her neighborhood will no longer be a squatter settlement. She wishes to get land titles in order to be able to sell legally and feel more secure. Spatially, her neighborhood resembles a planned land invasion.

Snapshot 4: Eviction (from 2004 Onwards)

In January 2011, the police evicted a recently formed planned land invasion from a private plot in the Northeast of the Montevideo, very close to other squatter settlements. Two hundred and sixty families were evicted. The rarity of the event and the univocal response of all state institutions, supporting the judicial decision, meant that the news appeared in the national press for several days. The news even reached neighboring Argentina: "Dozens of families settled on an empty plot in the suburbs of Montevideo, have been were evicted. The government of Mujica [former president from the leftist party and usually prone to the popular causes] transmitted zero tolerance to usurpations," wrote the La Nación newspaper (Fernández 2011).

Despite the fact that occupants were organized and tried to negotiate with the judge with the help of a lawyer, there was no possible agreement. This was not the first time a judge opposed a land invasion or that the police evicted occupants. In fact, the procedure is a regular occurrence for land invasions. Yet, in the past, negotiation was possible, generally arguing the "state of necessity," a legal figure that exempts those who commit a crime in the Uruguayan Penal Code when the person can prove that the motive of the crime is a situation of extreme need. Legal and political changes are behind the event described in the previous paragraphs. This time, instead of the "state of necessity," the judge used the legal category of "usurpation" which leads to immediate eviction by the criminal route. In addition, this was the first time that the Executive publicly declared itself against an invasion. Land invasions "are not the mechanism to demand housing," said the Undersecretary of Housing to one of the national newspapers ("La ocupación no es el mecanismo para exigir vivienda" 2011).

Making Sense of the Snapshots

These four stories represent four moments of the history of the informal city in Montevideo. While early squatters tended to form accretion invasions, the second wave tended to seize land and plan the new neighborhoods. Fraudulent sales or "pirate invasions," as they call them in cities like Bogotá, have always occurred. Yet they became more common in Montevideo by the time planned invasions started to decrease. While historically the state has been rather permissive with squatters, at times just letting them stay, and at others bringing them services, or even encouraging them, squatting is currently not allowed. Different coordinated state agencies have systematically detained all attempts of land seizure since 2004.

Although usually subsumed under the concept of *asentamiento* in Uruguay or informal neighborhoods or other terms in the literature, these neighborhoods' different histories of settlement formation tend to have a long-lasting impact on neighborhood characteristics such as spatial design, community organization, and services. As we can see in the snapshots, they were all affected by politics, but in very different ways. Accretion invasions grew at the margins of the state. Yet, the state tolerated and did not evict them as in other parts of the globe (although the dictatorships were harsher with some of them). An exception to this was the period around 1980, when a series of evictions coincided with the political opening enabling the mobilization described in the next chapter. Occasionally, often during elections, traditional parties, often the most populist factions of the Colorado Party, reached them offering meager gifts in the hope of exchanging them for votes.

As we will see in Chap. 5, planned invasions peaked at a moment of enhanced electoral competition for popular votes, during a second wave of mobilization after democratization. "Pirate" invasions often required political ties, yet these ties were regularly more centralized in one person—the promoter—than in other types of settlements. Evictions have been rare events. The Uruguayan state, like many others, has tolerated land invasions. But, since 2004, they have become the norm in the case of new land seizures in Montevideo. While in the past, politicians could not afford the political costs of evictions, I argue that the (at least temporary) reduction of the electoral competition for the popular vote enabled that possibility. While in this chapter I describe the three types of land invasions, I analyze evictions in Chap. 5, when describing the end of the cycle of planned invasions.

When, How, and Where?

As Tarrow (1989: 13) clearly argues: "what needs to be explained is not why people periodically petition, strike, demonstrate, riot, loot and burn, but rather why so many of them do so at particular times in their history, and if there is a logical sequence to their action." As explained in the Introduction, I believe ideas and methods developed for the study of social movements can be helpful to understand other more elusive forms of collective action or contentious politics that are arguably beyond the scope of the concept of social movements, such as land squatting. Juan, the leader of a land invasion and one of my interviewees, has a more mundane way to express what Tarrow theorizes: "When the time is right, we'll ask for regularization. You need to wait until the time is right."

When looking at the evolution of land squatting in Montevideo over time, at least three striking features appear: a late start in relation to the rural–urban migration process, steady growth during the military regime, a very notorious peak in 1990 followed by a decade of high numbers of land invasions, and a decline since the end of the 1990s. Figure 3.1 illustrates the density of land squatting in Montevideo; that is, the cumulative number of land invasions per year. It is built on the 256 settlements in the city for which I found the year of settlement, for the 1947–2004 period (see Appendix B for more information on data collection and data set). It shows that land squatting was a rare event until the 1970s. It also shows a low though steady rise in land invasions, which occurred during the 1970s and 1980s. Around 1989–1991, we see a change that corresponds to the highest peak of the cycle, followed by a decade of rapid and sustained growth in land invasions. More recently, the cycle seems to have reached a ceiling with a low number of land invasions per year since the late 1990s.

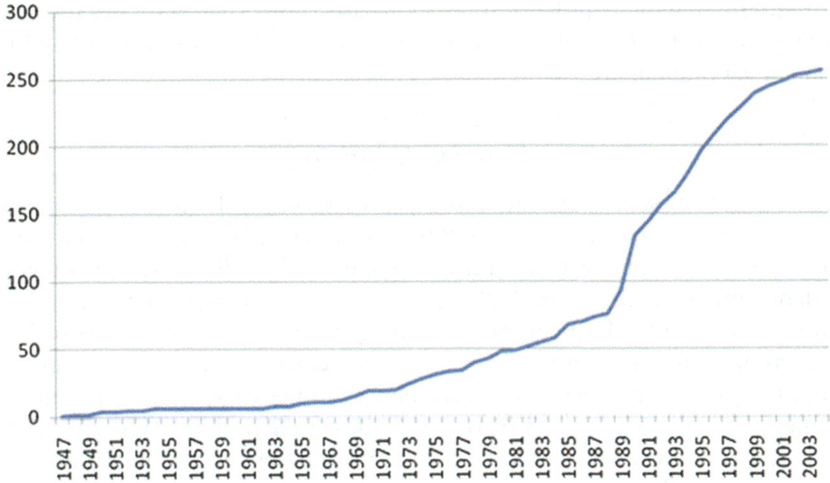

Fig. 3.1 Cumulative number of land invasions per year (density), Montevideo 1947–2004

It is important to state, however, that although new land invasions became rare events in Montevideo again, many existing squatter settlements kept growing. This happens both because of internal growth (e.g., births, grown-up children going to live independently or forming a new family and building a small room in the backyard) and because of new population coming from the formal city in search of housing. Squatters also expanded in the Montevideo metropolitan area. Yet, as stated in the previous chapter, both the number of settlements and the population living in squatter settlements have decreased in the capital and in the country as a whole (PMB-PIAI 2013).

As we can see in the opening vignettes, land invasions vary in many ways: in their landscape, area, location, size, demographics, relations to politicians, and the state and time of settlement, among other things. In this book, I emphasize the type of settlement formation because I believe it affects many other characteristics. I distinguish three types of settlement formation, based on my fieldwork in Montevideo. Accretion invasions are those that are formed gradually and without planning. Planned invasions are those that involve some degree of organization before the invasion and at least during the first days or months of settlement. Finally, subdivision and sale are those that start because an entrepreneur divides a piece of land and sells parcels in a transaction with some level of illegality.

Accretion Invasions

As in the first snapshot, the case of the Acosta y Lara settlement, in accretion invasions, land was occupied gradually, without organization or planning. After the first family or group of families invaded a piece of land, more residents gradually arrived. There was generally no political intervention at the beginning or any apparent—formal or informal—government involvement. There was no neighborhood association or local leader assigning plots, drawing blocks and streets, or selecting newcomers and this is reflected in the neighborhood outline. When I asked María, a resident of a very poor squatter settlement in the north-east of Montevideo, whose family was among the first to invade the now packed neighborhood, whether someone had told them where to build or how much land they could take, she explained:

> No, no, everyone took a piece of land. Now, there's no more land. I'll tell you. We are a big family. We must have about 40 square meters [about 400 square feet] and we have 3 houses there and we also have the sheds for the horses, because we have animals, you know?

María's family knew about this abandoned plot because they used to live opposite, in public housing. They had moved out of public housing to a town outside Montevideo but things did not go well for them financially and they moved back to their old neighborhood. As she remembers it, "we came back to the neighborhood. The only choice we had was to build a shack in the middle of the lot. In time, more people started to come and the neighborhood started to grow. I think it has more than 400 families now."

Accretion settlements are generally crowded groups of small shacks, with no public space or streets. Services are scarce. Settlers tend to provide themselves with water and electricity by "hooking" themselves to the main lines. Typical houses are very poorly built, with materials found in the garbage such as metal sheets and wood. Piles of smelly garbage, horses, carts, and other indications of scavenging are common in their landscape.

One of the main features of accretion invasions is their invisibility. As a resident of one of the settlements I visited told me, "this neighborhood was never on the map, never. When we tried to get a phone line, they couldn't find the address. The neighborhood did not exist." Invisibility derives from a lack of contact with the state, which in turn reveals negligence both from a state that does not appear and a generally nonexistent neighborhood association that does not demand.

There is generally no collective history of the neighborhood but rather a multiplicity of histories. When I asked Jacqueline, a resident of an accretion settlement who works at a scrap dealing family business, if there were any NGOs working in the neighborhood, she answered, "I can tell you about this part of the neighborhood [the one visible from her location]. Maybe someone that lives there can tell you about that part, but I can't."A telling indicator of this is that having applied the same oral history questionnaire—with adjustments—to first residents of planned and accretion invasions, interviews in the first type of neighborhood lasted on average 1 h, whereas they lasted only half an hour on average for accretion invasions, even after probing as much as I could.[1]

In general, I did not find any neighborhood associations or leaders. In the few cases in which there was one, it was because an external agent such as an NGO or the government regularization program (PMB-PIAI) had motivated the election of neighborhood representatives. Early residents are those who have some attributes of leadership, through having been there the longest. When other people arrived, the newcomers asked them if they could stay. Sometimes neighbors rely on them for help. But they do not tend to be bridges to the outside world, like leaders of other neighborhoods. Nor do they assume the task of guaranteeing the well-being of the neighbors.

Perhaps because of this lack of collective history and leadership, collective action problems are common. Residents often speak of a lack of trust, fragile neighborhood organizations that do not last long, neighbors stealing collective goods such as food from the soup kitchen, etc. This resident's appreciation of her neighborhood illustrates this:

> Everyone looks after their own interests, to find things for themselves and not to help the neighborhood. My father was about to participate in a neighborhood association but everyone wanted a bite, and that's not how it is...If you are fighting for the neighborhood, it shouldn't be because what you really want is to get a job in the municipal government. Everyone

> looks after his or her own interests. That's why it never worked. I have known at least 4 or 5 neighborhood associations, but they don't last.

Politicians did not appear spontaneously in squatters' narratives when I asked about the history of the neighborhood. When I asked, residents saw politicians as very distant, uncaring, and only wanting to use them. José, from one of the accretion invasions I visited, told me "nobody ever did anything for this neighborhood." And another resident critically answered those politicians "always came five or six months before the elections but they never came to say (…). They never give you anything! They build their fame through you. They come, they film you and then you are there [on TV] showing the poverty in Uruguay." For him, "those at the top are all a band of liars."

When asked, "which are the three persons or institutions that helped the neighborhood the most," people had trouble answering. The most common answers, after hesitating, were "nobody" or the name of some NGO working in their neighborhoods. In fact, even though some of these NGOs, if not all of them, run state-funded projects, squatters do not perceive state presence.

Planned Invasions

Planned invasions generally happened suddenly and were thought of or were brought up by either one person or a group. People may have generally happened, but a first group came together and seized the plot, generally overnight and on a weekend or holiday in order to avoid attention from police and owners. They required some prior organization at least to find out about available plots and decide which one to seize and when to do it. Research into available, safe plots, that is, state-owned land or private land whose owners had died or had not paid taxes for a while, often included contacts with politicians or state officials who had that type of information. It was not uncommon for the group to confront authorities, the police, or the owner on the first days of the invasion. Still, besides perhaps 24 h of detention at the police station and, even less likely, relocation by the authorities after some fighting, eviction was very rare. From the start, a (often self-proclaimed) leader or group started dividing the plot into smaller parcels, drawing streets, and leaving some room for community buildings or public spaces. This planning imitated the urban planning and the norms of the outside formal city. This person or group often crafted some neighborhood rules, including rules for selecting newcomers.

These rules often reflected the intention of not being like an accretion invasion or, in a resident's words, "we didn't want this to be a cantegril. (…) What we always tried, the idea was to build a neighborhood." Another resident spoke of planning the neighborhood as a collective project, a "vision."

> You have to have a certain vision. That's the difference between asentamientos and cantegriles. And there are asentamientos that turn into cantegriles. And there are others that end up being a *barrio* [neighborhood]. If you have the vision that you don't want to live in a cantegril and want to build a barrio, then you have to do what the state doesn't do. The state often plans the city. Since the state is not planning [your settlement] then you have to do some planning yourself so one day, the state can bring you some services and you can develop. If you don't have that vision, then you turn into a cantegril.

Some of the neighborhood rules had a class connotation, excluding the poorest of the poor by either prohibiting animals such as the horses used for scavenging or establishing a deadline to start building with brick or other (relatively expensive) solid materials. Explaining these rules, residents of three different planned invasions told me:

> We were all people of work. If the person had a job, we gave them a parcel. If he didn't, then we didn't. Because if you don't work, what are you going to do, man? You can't even build one room with cement.

> We were not delinquents and here there were no carts, no horses. I mean, there were no very low-income people. We were really hard working people, workers that needed a house and couldn't pay the rent (…). We are families of *workers* [her emphasis] not people that beg or rob. We are people that like to live well but don't have the means, that's it. But with dignity, that's the thing. Because I'm sure that if you now enter into any of these little houses, the humblest you can find, I'm sure it doesn't stink of dirt, rotten things or animals. [And her husband added] If you bring a dirty nigger with a cart and a horse.… We didn't want that. We didn't want to live in the dirt, you know?

> We formed a group with people like me, workers I mean, not marginal people, for instance.

The working-class identity expressed in these quotes was clearly a characteristic of most of my interviewees from planned invasions; leaders and non-leaders that have lived in the settlements since the early days. It is probably not shared by all residents, but it was part of the neighborhood project, of the idea that the early settlers had about where and how they wanted to live, and with whom. Despite the fact that most of them were in low-paid informal jobs when I interviewed them, they defended their identity as workers.

The spatial outline of planned neighborhoods tends to look like a regular neighborhood. Yet because of population pressure, especially for internal growth and also because of newcomers, sometimes the original design starts to fade. Shacks start to appear toward the fringes of the settlement, some families start dividing their parcels either because they sell part of them or because they give a piece to a family member to build a new house. Population pressure also makes it difficult to maintain public spaces or those plots originally designed for the future construction of a soup kitchen or a neighborhood plaza. The durability of the original design tends to depend on the settlers' ability to enforce the original rules.

If accretion invasions were characterized by invisibility, planned invasions are generally at the other extreme. They want visibility. They want the state to recognize them, bring services, give them an address so they can have phone and other services, pay the bills, and be able to call an ambulance in case of emergency. They went to be regularized by obtaining titles for their property. They want to be owners. That was the common answer when I asked about the neighborhood goals, even if some were starting to recognize that they might not be able to afford taxes if regularization actually takes place. This search for visibility is also a search for recognition, for belonging, and ultimately for citizenship. Elsewhere, I have called it a search to "resist exclusion" (Álvarez-Rivadulla 2007 [2000]).

The early residents together endured the invasion and the construction of the neighborhood, giving rise to a common narrative of origins among them. Of course, there are dissident voices, even among founders, but there are memories of a shared past, distinguishing the early settlers from the newcomers. The latter came at different points in time, when the plot was already seized and the most pressing needs solved, so they did not have the same experiences as the founders. They did not share the experiences and hopes of the early days. Often, this narrative includes epic accounts of how residents fought with the police; filled a swamp with their own hands; purged the neighborhood of a group of thugs by destroying their shack and then entrenching themselves for 3 days with provisions and arms in case they came back to avenge themselves; transformed a garbage dump into a clean, smooth plot; helped each other to build houses; cooked together in a soup kitchen; left their doors open; and displayed all kinds of group solidarity. As an already quoted politician that has helped many squatters put it, planned invasions go through a "stellar moment in which people feel they are the main actors of their own lives."

This real and idealized past is very difficult to transmit to the next generations of dwellers, especially because after a while, an informal market tends to appear and people start buying and selling their plots with a great rotation of settlers. As Celeste, a settler of a planned invasion nostalgically told me,

> When we came to live here, people cared if you needed money to pay the electricity, or if you needed some medicine. It was very nice, and it still is, but there are new people now that do not know the habits that we use to have at the beginning. Here, for instance, when the neighborhood started, we said, well if you open a produce store, I'll open a grocery store, but don't start the same business as me, you know? We respected each other to be able to work together, you know?

This "key theme of memory" as another resident put it, often translates into insecurity problems. Many told me, they fear to leave their houses alone when they go out. Celeste has a little store in her house but she only dares to attend to customers through the window grille for fear of being robbed. The solution of collective and individual action problems depends a lot on the persistence and legitimacy of a leader or neighborhood association. For example, I was given access to the minutes—from 1998 to 2003—of the neighborhood association meetings of a planned invasion. I was surprised to see, for example, how they controlled every land transaction in the neighborhood. People buying or selling had to be authorized by the neighborhood association. They also impeded the invasion of the neighborhood soccer field. Yet this notebook of minutes takes us to another feature of planned invasion: their close relationship with the state; in almost every meeting, the group recorded having met with some authority or having written a letter to petition something, etc.

Neighborhood associations involved in planned invasions want to reach out. Once in the plot, one of their main tasks is to reach out, especially to the state, to get the things the neighborhood needs, and they use different strategies to do so. Directly demanding something from the authorities bypassing regular bureaucratic procedures is a very common strategy among squatters of planned invasions. Sometimes they use political brokers to reach authorities or to accelerate the fulfillment of their demand. They know insisting is key. And when pressure is needed, they use the power of multitude, by going to a public office together and camping there until they are given the water pipe or the electricity service they are looking for. Only rarely do they use more disruptive strategies such as street blockades. The most successful strategy—described in depth in Chap. 6—is what I dub *market clientelism*, which consists of a very strategic use of clientelistic networks promising loyalty and votes to the best bidder. The common phrase "we are apolitical in this neighborhood" often hides these market-like clientelistic networks in which leaders do not commit to any politician or party but rather flirt with many at the same time in order to obtain services for their neighborhood.

Some of the leaders I interviewed were experts in how the state works, and where and who to ask; they had the phone numbers of the secretaries of this or that authority and some even had very high technical knowledge on issues such as water connection. Joking about their thorough knowledge of state institutions and the amount of time spent demanding, one leader told me: "We were like City Council staff members; when we entered the offices, everyone knew us. We used to go 2 or 3 times a week." Some brought this knowledge from before, from their participation in unions, housing cooperatives, or neighborhood associations, but many learned by doing once they invaded. For the latter, participating in the neighborhood association was their first politicizing experience.

When asked which three institutions or persons had helped a neighborhood the most, early residents—leaders and non-leaders—of planned invasions, in contrast to accretion invasions, tended to mention a variety of state institutions as well as politicians and authorities. The institutions varied depending on the needs of the settlement. As one resident put it:

> We went where we had to go. If you know that the Municipal Council has the competence to give you what you want, then you go to the Municipal Council. You are not going to go to the Health Ministry.

The institutions whose doors they knocked on also depended on the plot's owner. If the plot was city owned, then the municipal government was the most frequently visited by squatters. Yet those institutions also varied with time and with institutional changes. When, in 1990, the Montevideo municipal government started a decentralization process, squatters began to make demands on their closest local government (CCZ or Centro Comunal Zonal).

To conclude this characterization of planned invasions, I will discuss one very particular kind: *utopian invasions.* During my fieldwork, I found a few planned invasions whose early residents wanted more than merely solving their housing needs. Their framing of the land invasion was different. They emphasized horizontal decision-making and a great distrust for vertical neighborhood associations, for example. Decisions were to be made in assemblies and many declared themselves in a "state of permanent assembly" during the first months of the invasion. Leaders were connected to the left, had participated in one of the Frente Amplio factions, in unions, and/or in the cooperative housing movement. This is reflected in actions that make utopian invasions different, such as the distribution of plots in *Nuevo Amanecer* (New Sunrise) where instead of distributing land on a first-come, first-served basis, they first divided the plot into equal parcels and then shared them out randomly among the first 36 families. It is also reflected in critical discourses such as the one by this neighborhood leader, who received me in a living room with a huge picture of Raúl Sendic hanging on the wall; one of the founders of the *Tuparamo* guerrilla movement, and a firm believer in the need for land reform in Uruguay:

> The theory was to build an invasion clearly denouncing existing housing policies. So in a way, it was a protest. But at the same time, it tried to be effective for the people who were invading. I mean, we were not only interested in the symbolic act of invading. There was a real commitment to solving people's housing problem. And the third element was to try and somehow organize the invasion, for example, in terms of infrastructure, that could later be a bridge to other forms of organization (...) In one assembly, we even had a discussion to try to arrive at a model of collective property (...), to offer an alternative to individual property. We also thought that perhaps the collective part could come through self-help construction (...). Once we thought of producing collectively in those plots [currently invaded by a second wave of squatters] because there were a lot of unemployed people that knew how to bake, make shoes, plant (...).

> But in time, the neighborhood association started to decline. It disappeared, in fact. The most crucial needs were solved and you can have a lot of political willingness but people only move if they are prodded by necessity. Your ideas can be beautiful, but if they don't coincide with people's needs, you are done.

He nostalgically describes one particular period of 2 or 3 months as a "fulfilled utopia" because they all fought for the same thing, they all helped each other in a context of need. Sometimes the fulfilled utopia lasted longer but in none of the cases I observed, was it currently alive. It was something early residents remembered, but the idealists' projects of the beginning tended to fade in the first year of settlement.

The utopian land invasions I was able to identify all dated back to the 1990s and they were located in El Cerro or in the nearby working-class neighborhoods in the western periphery of Montevideo. Residents agree that they are more organized because they are from El Cerro or the nearby area. As one of them told me, "El Cerro is different. We are the Republic of El Cerro." A municipal official agreed with this perception but was more specific:

> El Cerro is a place, like *La Teja* [nearby neighborhood] with a working class fighting tradition. They have been fighting since the beginning of the 20th century, so they have that tradition. (...) If you walk around El Cerro you will not find many metal sheet shacks, even though there are about 60 squatter settlements there. That happens because people still have that fighting spirit. It is something that gets transmitted from generation to generation. And the person who squatted with some metal sheets and wood, you visit him two months later, and he has started to build something with bricks. You go again, and he has started to make something bigger and already has a septic tank. I mean, there is an organizing tradition. And there is a tradition of improving your house.

Despite there being a minority of planned invasions, utopian invasions epitomized the mobilization of squatters during the 1990s as described in the next chapter.

Subdivision and Sale

Besides accretion and planned invasions, Montevideo also has what we can call entrepreneurial invasions or invasions by subdivision and sale.

From the air they tend to look like planned invasions, but they differ in that their planning involves (often fraudulent) economic profit. Informal housing markets tend to develop in all types of invasions. After a while, even in utopian invasions and even the most committed leaders may sell their house and go to a formal neighborhood or to another squatter settlement. But what distinguishes this third type of land invasion is that the market component is there from the moment of the invasion. No household settles without paying something.

These are invasions that are planned, generally by one individual, in which land is subdivided and sold to residents. The individual may be the owner of the land or a designated seller, but they are sometimes bandits that claim to be the owners and cheaply sell plots they do not own. Therefore, sometimes squatters do not even know they are squatters until they discover they have been victims of fraud. Some owners of vacant and unproductive land have incited invasions to later ask the state for compensation. Land is often private and located in protected rural areas in the periphery of the city. According to the Montevideo municipality, plots cannot be subdivided for urban use, so these transactions are illegal. In addition, these areas do not have the necessary services for a new neighborhood to be constructed and so, as in planned invasions, settlers start making demands on the state for services.

During my fieldwork, I found several examples of this type of invasion and develop one in depth in Chap. 6. In yet another one, one of the residents started coming to the plot because they saw an ad in the newspaper. They bought a plot and later realized they had been victims of a fraud. The sellers had divided the plot into smaller pieces than the zoning rules permit for that area, and the property titles they gave them were fake despite being signed by a notary. Neighbors started organizing after they realized they were not owners but squatters. They were able to get water and other services, mainly through the leadership and contacts of a neighbor who has always worked for the Colorado Party. Their current goal is for the Ministry of Housing to regularize their neighborhood by giving them real property titles and providing them with services.

A lot of imagination has been put into getting around the law. As a former city councilor told me,

> [Generating squatter settlements by selling private land in rural areas] got pretty technical. The last thing that happened to us at the City Council, and we reported it, (…) was that somebody that owned rural land as a

corporation [*sociedad anónima*] would sell pieces of it as shares. [There was a case] in which after you bought a share, they calculated how much you needed to build your house. So people could go to the owner's son's construction materials store, purchase what they needed leaving the share as a guarantee. If you didn't pay for the materials, they would take your share and evict you. It was a cartel!

Prevalence, Timing, Land Ownership, and Geography: A Panorama of Land Squatting in Montevideo

Figure 3.2 shows how prevalent these types of invasions have been in the city of Montevideo, for those I have been able to classify (240 out of 427).[2] The most common type of land invasion in Montevideo has been accretion (57% of those I could find information on), about 1 out of 3 invasions have been planned, and 11% have been a product of land subdivision and sale. This variation challenges any generalization about land invasions.

Types of land invasions are not distributed randomly throughout the history of the cycle or throughout the city. Figure 3.3 shows the cycle of land invasions by type, over time.

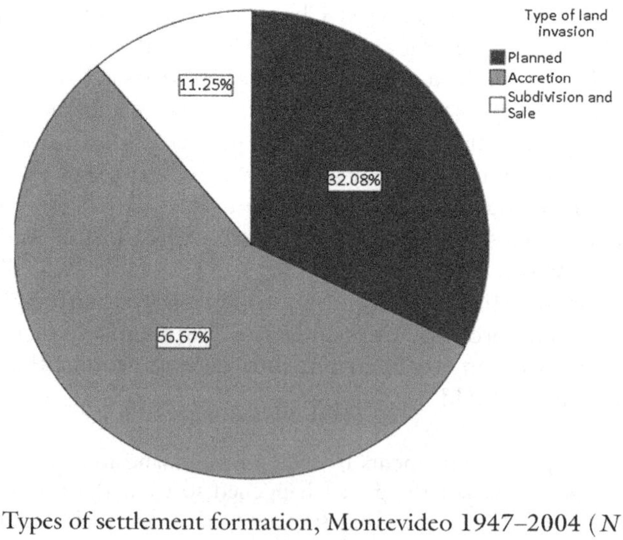

Fig. 3.2 Types of settlement formation, Montevideo 1947–2004 ($N = 240$)

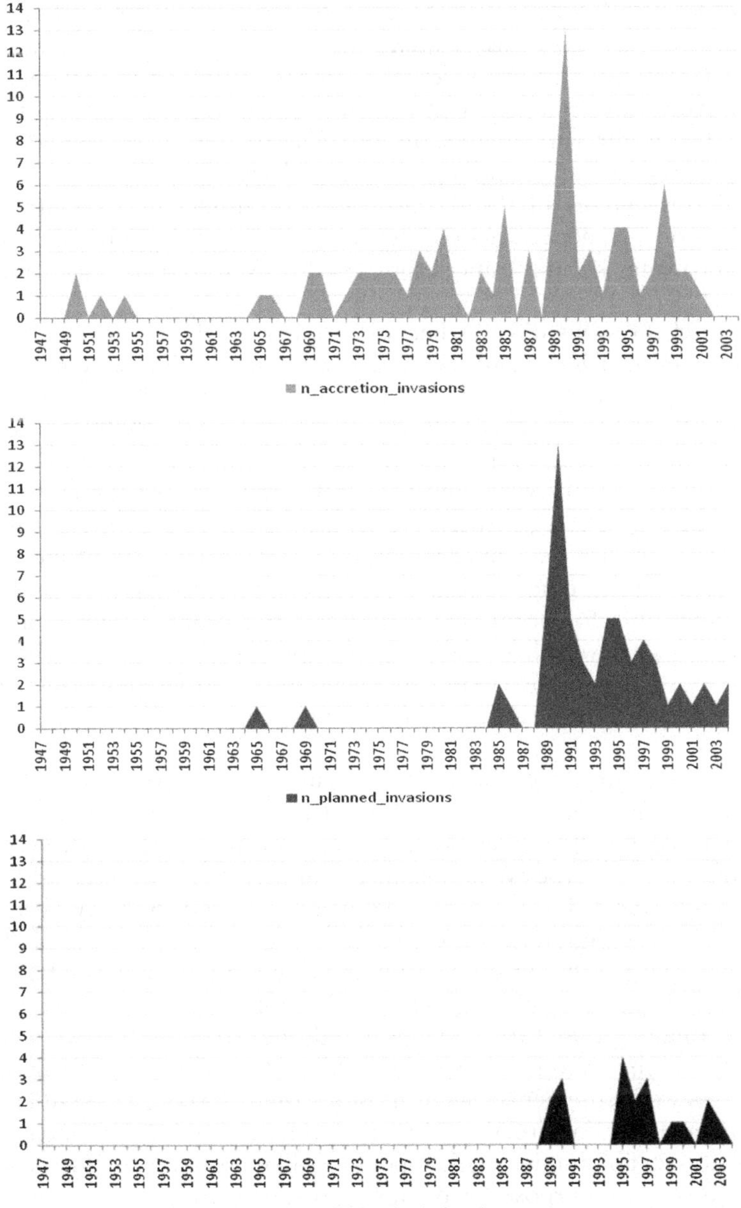

Fig. 3.3 Cycle of land invasions by type of invasion. Montevideo 1947–2004 ($N = 256$)

The first land invasions in Montevideo were of the accretion type. As stated in the previous chapter, they appeared toward the middle of the twentieth century, when the golden days of the "Switzerland of the Americas" started to crack. State-led industrialization acted as a pull factor for rural migration and successfully incorporated most of those migrants. Yet, cantegriles were always the visual sign of the limited possibilities of the developmentalist model in a country and a region deeply dependent on the international situation. They have been growing steadily since the 1950s, even during the military regime (1973–1984).

Planned invasions did not become popular in the repertoire of land squatters until 1989–1990, with one very interesting exception, the *Casabó* neighborhood, founded in 1965, very much embedded in political networks.[3] They remained popular during the 1990s, surpassing the number of accretion invasions every year from 1991 to 1997. Even today, judging by the characteristics of the cycle toward the end of the studied period (2004), if there is a land invasion, it is likely that it is a planned one rather than an accretion one. (Fraudulent) land subdivision and sale, in turn, appeared late in squatters' repertoires, as it probably took some time for promoters to perceive the profit derived from the business. Also, given that they are mostly on private land while the others are mostly on public land, it might be the case that an exhaustion of vacant and neglected public land is playing a role in this changing repertoire.

Figure 3.4 introduces the analysis of land ownership. Most land invasions have taken place on public land (61%). Occupying public land is safer because the state does not enforce its rights as private owners do. But this varies by type. While planned and accretion invasions are overwhelmingly located on state-owned land (68 and 63%, respectively, which is not a significant difference as the error bars illustrate), those invasions that started by subdivision and sale are mostly located on private land. The state, especially Montevideo's municipal government, has been strongly opposed to subdivision and sales. However, as we will see in Chap. 6, the state is never monolithic and leaves room to help even these types of settlements. Such invasions often involve a defrauding of poor people and constructing in remote areas that the government considers not fit for building either because they are reserved for productive or ecological purposes or because it is too costly to bring services to

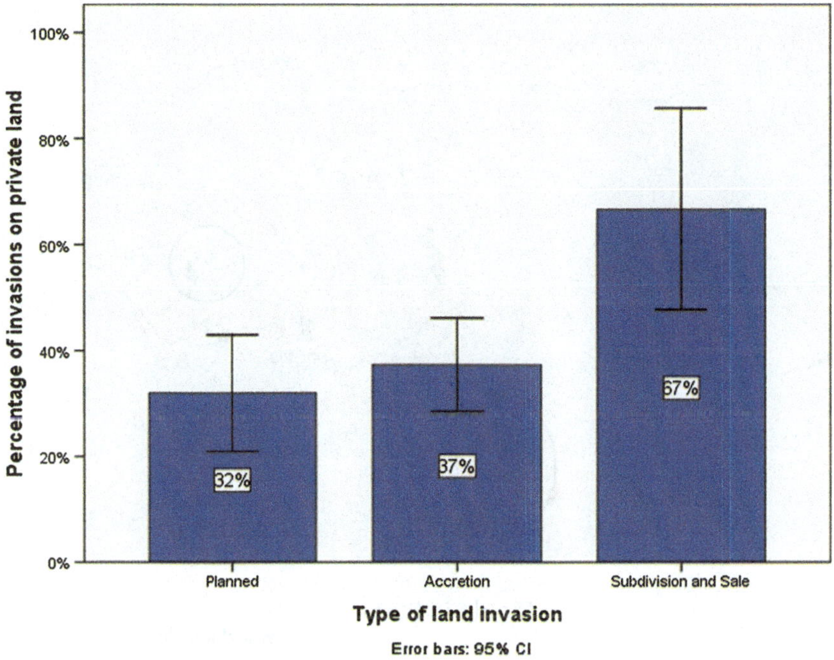

Fig. 3.4 Percentage of invasions settled on private land (vs. public land) by type of settlement formation. Montevideo 1947–2004 ($N = 217$)

them. Entrepreneurs are therefore more attracted to private land, where policing is less intense. It has been the owners of unproductive land or opportunistic intermediaries that have promoted the subdivision and sale invasions on private land.[4]

Besides the temporal description of the cycle of land invasions, it is telling to look at the geographic or spatial distribution of these land invasions. Far from being randomly located, land invasions are clustered in certain areas of the city. Contrary to what happens in a city like Rio, whose peculiar topography generates *favelas* in the middle of the city, on the hills, in Montevideo squatter settlements are on the periphery, circling the urban city center. Figure 3.5 shows a map of Montevideo, superposing the approximately 400 squatter settlements onto the 18 administrative units into which the city is divided.

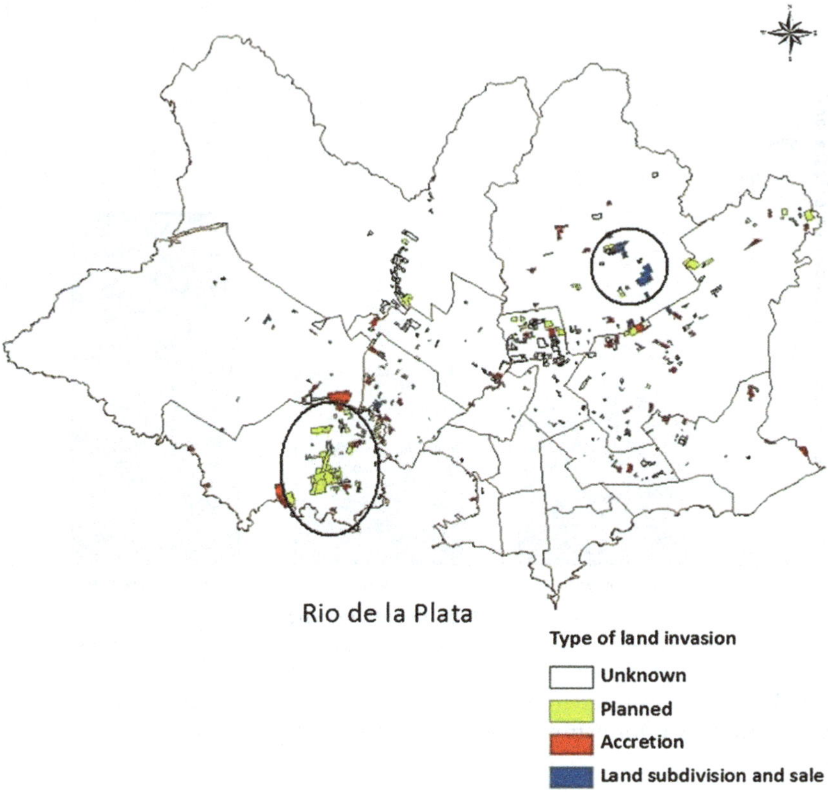

Fig. 3.5 Location of land invasions by type of settlement. Montevideo map

The areas of the city with the most squatter settlements are traditionally the most deprived. There are very few land invasions in the coastal southeast of the city, a highly urbanized area and the most affluent part of the city. A combination of higher population density, high land values of the relatively scarce vacant land, and pressure from affluent neighbors who would not like to see their properties depreciated have provoked, on the one hand, fewer land invasions to begin with and, on the other, the relocation of those squatter settlements that were already there.

For example, the few squatter settlements that were still in the old city (the commercial and historical center) in the 1990s were relocated to the periphery. The northeast and northwest of the city are home to most of the squatter settlements. These were areas that were already deprived even before the peak in land squatting, but they had available land and, importantly, they are not far away from avenues or streets that could get people to their jobs. More recently, however, even more remote areas have been occupied (e.g., see the more isolated spots in the east and west of the city). Some of them are land subdivisions and sales located on what the city government considers non-urbanizable rural land. In fact, Fig. 3.5 shows them in a different color.

I have circled two clear clusters: in the west of the city (left) there is a group of planned invasions, in the post-industrial, working class, leftist Cerro area, and in the east, there is a smaller cluster of settlements that started by subdivision and sale, located on what the city considers rural land. There is no clear pattern for accretion invasions, other than what they share with all invasions: they tend to be in the periphery of Montevideo.

Putting all these characteristics together concisely, we can see three main constellations of settlement formation. Table 3.1 organizes information by political period and shows the distribution of land invasions according to land property, type of invasion, and region of the city. Prevalent types per political period are highlighted in grey.

The first wave of land invasions in Montevideo occurred between around 1950 and the first years of democracy in the late 1980s. These land invasions were formed by accretion and settled on public land, especially city-owned land, located in the eastern periphery of the city. The second configuration was formed by a boom of planned invasions, which took place throughout the 1990s in the western periphery of the city, although, in time, they diffused to the eastern periphery. Despite the first planned invasions being on public land, they increasingly started considering private land as well. Toward the end of the considered period, planned invasions tended to be on private plots. Finally, the last configuration identified in the table refers to the very few land invasions that are either planned or land subdivisions and sales, located overwhelmingly on private land in the eastern periphery of the city.

Table 3.1 Distribution of squatter settlements by land property, type of invasion and location, per political period (percentages)

	Land Property					*Type of Land Invasion*					*Region of the City*				
	Private	*State City*	*State Other*	*Total*	**N**	*Planned*	*Accretion*	*Subdivision & Sale*	*Total*	**N**	*Center*	*East*	*West*	*Total*	**N**
Before 1974	29.7	51.4	18.9	100	**37**	12.1	81.8	6.1	100	**33**	4.0	60.0	36.0	100	**50**
Dictatorship	31.4	43.1	25.5	100	**51**	2.8	86.1	11.1	100	**36**		66.1	33.9	100	**59**
1985–1989	18.6	55.8	25.6	100	**43**	34.3	57.1	8.6	100	**35**	2.1	29.2	68.8	100	**48**
1990–1994	36.0	37.1	27.0	100	**89**	53.4	39.7	6.9	100	**58**		42.3	57.7	100	**97**
1995–1999	52.5	23.7	23.7	100	**59**	39.5	39.5	20.9	100	**43**		54.8	45.2	100	**62**
2000–2004	83.3	11.1	5.6	100	**18**	50.0	18.8	31.3	100	**16**		77.8	22.2	100	**18**

Conclusion

This chapter has emphasized that time—especially if divided by political periods—seems to be related not only to the *number* of land invasions but also to the *types* of land invasions in Montevideo. While accretion invasions are related to periods of low electoral competition for popular votes, including the dictatorship, the peculiar context of the 1990s with great political competition and the Frente Amplio in the municipal government appears to be connected to the emergence of a wave of planned invasions. Geography has some explanatory power as well. Most of these planned invasions are located in the west of the city, especially in the traditional working-class neighborhood of El Cerro and its surroundings.

This heterogeneity defies most generalizations about squatting. As mentioned in the Introduction, in an interesting comparative analysis of land squatting, Alsayyad (1993) suggests that while in Latin America the most common types of squatting are of the generated (i.e., planned and incited by some person or group) and mobilized type, in the Middle East, gradual and spontaneous processes of squatting are more typical. Although probably true in general terms, there is great variation between cities in Latin America, and, as I explore here, there is great variation even within the same city, depending on the location and timing, and, fundamentally, on the relationship between squatters and authorities. When squatting started in Montevideo, neighborhoods were more similar to what Alsayyad and other authors like Bayat (1997, 2004) describe for the Middle East: a "quiet encroachment of the ordinary" to use Bayat's term, that is mostly invisible to the state, growing and surviving at the margins of the state.

While these accretion invasions did not establish early relationships with the authorities, planned invasions are fundamentally built on those relationships. It was through them that squatters often obtained information about available plots to occupy, or public services such as water or electricity. Land subdivision and sales are different in that they are born in the informal land market. Otherwise, they are very similar to planned invasions both in spatial outline and in relation to authorities (see Chap. 6 for a description of one invasion that started as a hybrid between subdivision and sale and planned). This descriptive chapter has prepared the terrain to better understand two very different moments of mobilization among Montevideo's squatters, which I describe and analyze in the next two chapters.

Notes

1. Visits lasted longer. Averages only refer to the recorded part of the interview. See the questionnaire in the Appendix.
2. I was able to classify 56% of all of Montevideo's settlements. At first I thought those unclassified were most likely accretion cases, but after checking with the data I realized they do not follow a pattern different from the whole. Unclassified invasions do not resemble one type more than they do the other. They tend to be on public land (67%) just like most invasions of any type (63%). They are not clustered in one area of the city but distributed throughout the city periphery, although there is a slight tendency toward the east of the city rather than the west (56% of unclassified invasions are located in the east vs. 51% of all invasions). Finally, although unclassified invasions started throughout the period of study, they peaked in 1990–1994, just like all invasions. See Appendix A for information on how I built the data set.
3. The squatter settlement known as *Casabó*, located in the traditional working-class neighborhood of *El Cerro*, is a big portion of land that in fact includes three different smaller squatter neighborhoods. It was one of the settlements I studied in depth. All the stories of early residents coincided in the role of the Colorado Party in this invasion. A local broker, who would later be a city councilor (1985–1990) and who at the time worked for a politician who would soon be presidential candidate (i.e., *Vasconcellos* would run for election in 1966) and senator, was the one who distributed the parcels, selected the first residents, and created the original neighborhood association, whose president was also a Colorado. This squatter settlement would show unusual signs of urban planning and mobilization that ended up with the treatment of this case in the Parliament and the approval of a law, designed by a Colorado Party politician, which gave settlers ownership of their plots and guaranteed services (Ley 14006).
   The discussion of this bill in the House of Representatives is very interesting for many reasons (Diaro de Sesiones de la Cámara de Respresentantes 605 (1593–1613), March–April–May 1971, Uruguay). First, the great majority of representatives supported the law (41 of 47 voted affirmatively for the bill in general). All representatives from all parties agreed they wanted to guarantee the rights of the inhabitants of Casabó. In that discussion, one Colorado representative expressed what seemed to be a consensus in the chamber by saying: "At the moment, about 200 families or about 1000 people live there. They are hard working and of good habits. They have not only built their own houses, which are very different from those in cantegriles, but they have also built a clinic, a sports plaza, a soup kitchen, things that speak of a great spirit of solidarity. These people

deserve the support of the State." The second interesting thing derives from this quote. The opposition is clear. While inhabitants of Casabó are "deserving poor" those who live in cantegriles are not. A third interesting aspect of the discussion is that representatives enter into a discussion on the concept of marginality that I will not analyze here but that deserves its own treatment. Fourth, a delegation of neighbors from Casabó was present at the discussion. The transcription includes some moments in which neighbors applaud and the chamber's president threatens to remove the spectators. Finally, although the bill dated back to 1967, this discussion and the final approval occurred in August 1971, right before the November elections. Although the state has provided Casabó with many services, property titles were never given out. Yet, squatters in Casabó were never evicted and feel somehow backed by this law, even if many would like the titles to be real. Neighborhood associations still fight for the implementation of the law.

4. I found a small group of squatter neighborhoods that were settled on pieces of land from different owners. For the cases in which the owners were two different public institutions, I simply considered the settlement to be on public land. Yet, I have excluded from this analysis those settlements located on public and private land at the same time. Those were mostly accretion invasions (9 out of 10) that probably started in one plot and slowly expanded toward a neighboring plot from a different owner.

References

Alsayyad, N. (1993). Squatting and culture. A comparative analysis of informal developments in Latin America and the Middle East. *Habitat International, 17*(1), 33–44.

Álvarez-Rivadulla, M. J. (2007 [2000]). Asentamientos irregulares montevideanos: la desafiliación resistida. *Cadernos metrópole PUC/SP & IPPUR/UFRJ, 18*, 207–249.

Appadurai, A. (2004). The capacity to aspire: Culture and the terms of recognition. In V. Rao & M. Walton (Eds.), *Culture and public action* (pp. 59–84). Stanford, CA: Stanford University Press.

Auyero, J. (2011). Patients of the state: An ethnographic account of poor people's waiting. *Latin American Research Review, 46*(1), 5–29.

Bayat, A. (1997). *Street politics. Poor people's movements in Iran*. New York: Columbia University Press.

Bayat, A. (2004). Globalization and the politics of the informals in the global south. In A. Roy & N. Alsayyad (Eds.), *Urban informality. Transnational perspectives from the Middle East, Latin America, and South Asia*. Lanham: Lexington Books.

Fernández, N. (2011). Un argentino buscó liderar una toma de terrenos en Uruguay. *La Nación*.

La ocupación no es el mecanismo para exigir vivienda. (2011, January 19). *El Observador*.

PMB-PIAI. (2013). *Informe Técnico: Relevamiento de Asentamientos Irregulares. Primeros Resultados de Población y Viviendas a partir del Censo 2011*. Montevideo.

Tarrow, S. (1989). *Democracy and disorder*. Oxford: Clarendon Press.

CHAPTER 4

Accretion Invasions. A Story of an Unlikely Contention (1979–1990)

In 1988, an independent radio collective led by journalist Graciela Salsamendi, who had arrived back in Uruguay after 14 years of exile, recorded a series of radio programs about the city's *cantegriles*. They wanted to portray both the extreme deprivation and the expressions of solidarity and organization present in those informal neighborhoods. Like many leftist professionals of the time, overrun by the violence of 11 years of dictatorship, they found some fascination in the cantegril and their characters. In them, they saw, on the one hand, the extreme inequalities of the capitalist system and, at the same time, an anarchist or grassroots way of resistance not contaminated by the instrumental and hierarchical logics of political parties and the state. Many of those interviews centered on the epic figure of Father Cacho, a Catholic Priest who in 1979 took a radical preferential option for the poorest and went to live in a cantegril in the outskirts of Montevideo changing the life of many dispossessed individuals, families, and neighborhoods. He was an exceptional being, as biographers and residents remember him. Yet, he was also part of broader changes and tensions within the Catholic

This chapter is mostly based on historical material, and some interview material. I had the fantastic help of Historian María José Bolaña in the collection of relevant press material both at the Archive of the Center of Interdisciplinary Uruguayan Studies (CEIU), School of Humanities, Universidad de la República, and the archive of the Legislative Palace Library.

M.J. Álvarez-Rivadulla, *Squatters and the Politics of Marginality in Uruguay*, Latin American Political Economy, DOI 10.1007/978-3-319-54534-9_4

Church in Latin America before and during the military regimes of the Southern Cone. He was part of those committed priests that felt the Church should not tolerate social injustice and that its main role was to be with the poorest. Even if not an open member of the Liberation Theology himself, he was part of the branch of the Catholic Church that gave some spaces for mobilization when the state repressed them everywhere.

In one of the interviews Salsamendi recorded, an eloquent cantegril resident, Esther, summarized her perceived effect of Father Cacho on individuals and collectivities:

> Father Cacho made us wake up to life. We were asleep, as if we had a blindfold on. (...). Before I was selfish, I was stingy (...) The Father made us feel more like Christians. The only thing you get by being selfish is being locked up in your house and isolated. (...) We are also part of MOVIDE, the Movement for a Decent Life, and we presented a plan to the Netherlands [for funding]. (...) People participate and they are happy. It's a different thing now (Esther, from the Santa María "community" 1988).[1]

Although the NGO Cacho founded, San Vicente, still works and has many projects and great presence in the neighborhood, the level of organization cantegriles reached around 1980 and until 1987–89 remains unparalleled. Accretion invasions have been invisible to the state and to politicians, with the exception of sporadic visits around election times or violent police patrols as part of the neighborhoods' everyday life (*razias*). Yet, they came to the forefront of the political arena, turning into an unlikely political actor toward the end of the military regime and during the beginning of the democratic years. As a movement, they became so important during the transition that they were one of the civil society organizations invited to participate in the 1984–85 multiparty consultations, known as National Conciliatory Program (*Concertación Nacional Programática* or CONAPRO).

The return of political parties after 11 years of dictatorship, in such a party-centered society, made other actors fade. The spring of mobilization that started in 1980, with the plebiscite against dictatorship, started declining around 1985, the first year of the democratic government. Besides, a concrete policy implemented by the first Colorado Party municipal government, had demobilizing consequences for neighborhood organizations (Canel 1992), and with the return of democracy, many NGOs that had been active in grassroots organizations lost their external funding. Finally, and this is particularly relevant for the mobilization of cantegriles mobilization in the early 1980s, the Church changed gears. Its preferential option for the poorest lost strength with the retirement of the Archbishop of Montevideo Carlos Parteli in 1985.

In this chapter, I describe the mobilization of the cantegriles of Montevideo around 1980. A particular configuration of causes aligned making this unlikely mobilization possible. I call it unlikely because it was unique in the history of the informal city, it involved the poorest of the poor with little resources to mobilize, and it transcended individual neighborhoods to become an umbrella organization or social movement that managed to sit with other more traditional social movements and political parties at the negotiation table during the democratic transition.

Different triggering factors were crucial in enabling and channeling this mobilization: the combination of threat, a series of evictions from cantegriles in different parts of the city, a political opportunity, the relaxation of dictatorship, and the beginning of the democratic transition. Yet, it would not have happened without the resources and the structure provided by the Catholic Church and some associated NGOs. This chapter recovers the story of this mobilization, led by nontraditional political actors such as Church organizations and NGOs at a time of political opening in the Uruguay of the 1980s. However, to put this into context, it becomes crucial to understand a longer history of the informal city.

Late Start in Relation to the Rural–Urban Migration Process

The first striking characteristic about the cycle of land invasions in Montevideo is its late start in comparison to other Latin American cities but, more importantly, its late start in relation to Montevideo's early urbanization. In most of the region's and the world's cities, squatter settlements house rural migrants trying to find a place in the city and this was definitely the case with earlier squatter settlements in the city of Montevideo. Yet this was not a generalized phenomenon as most original rural urban dwellers found a place in the formal city.

Esther, the same woman from the previous quote, is a clear example of the early cantegril dwellers. She came to live there at 6, when her father lost his job and they could no longer pay rent in the working-class neighborhood they use to live in. As described in Chap. 2, despite the myth of the rural migrants, many came, expelled from the city or from other cities in the country, and not directly from rural areas (Baudrón 1979).

Uruguayans from rural areas or urban areas in the country's interior started migrating to Montevideo very early on, and by 1960, the capital had already stabilized its population at about 45% of the country's total. Uruguay also experienced its demographic transition early on, reaching fecundity rates in the 1950s that the rest of Latin America would reach only in around 2000 (Kaztman et al. 2005). Thus, Montevideo is an odd case as it shows no correlation between population growth and the rise of land invasions, the first of which appeared around 1950. The first one I could track dates back to 1947. Yet it is not until the late 80s that land invasions started to multiply, at a time when the city had already stopped growing.

As already mentioned, other forces were in action. The economic downturn of the country since the 1950s and liberalizing policies, including liberalization of rent prices and state reduction, appear as the main suspects. These economic forces interacted with political ones to shape the number and types of settlement formation and their waves of mobilization.

Steady Growth During the Military Regime

The second salient feature of the early squatters is a steady growth during the military regime (1973–1984). This might have a lot to do with the liberalization of renting prices by a 1974 law, consistent with the monetarist policies implemented by other Southern Cone military regimes. Many of the key informants I talked to, such as architects, social workers, and so on, think so, and it was a recurrent reason in the narrative of all residents I interviewed both from this period and throughout the cycle. They claim they could no longer afford to live in the city. Benton (1986) states that with prices that had been artificially kept down for years, suddenly opening up to market forces, housing prices spiked and became the goods category with the steepest price increase.

But these were not the only transformations to the urban environment of the poor that the military brought about. Besides liberalizing rent, the authoritarian government also "cleaned" the city center of poor people living in tenement houses. Central neighborhoods like Palermo and Sur housed many *conventillos,* the term for generally large old buildings with many rental rooms overlooking an internal patio. Besides offer ing a relatively cheap way of remaining in the city, conventillos were also related to *candombe* music, an Afro-Uruguayan rhythm originally associated with slaves and later with the popular classes. The government evicted and destroyed many of those buildings. Some people offered resistance but probably much less than they would have in a democratic regime. According to Benton (1986) who studied precisely this period,

> The transformation of Montevideo's central city must be understood above all as part of a process of political change. The advent of the bureaucratic-authoritarian regime simultaneously disrupted traditional forms of political integration of the urban poor and dismantled the legal and institutional apparatus that had permitted the survival of stable working-class neighborhoods in the city center. The new housing policies were not explicitly directed at removing the poor from desirable areas or otherwise facilitating the escalation of real estate investment and construction. They were inscribed instead in a general policy of deregulation of the housing market and were implemented through locally directed measures according to supposedly technical criteria.

What puzzles Benton the most is that people's response was not to invade lands en masse, but rather resort to other strategies such as going to live at relatives' houses or rent at a different place in groups. She attributes this to the residents' willingness to remain in the city and to their hopes that the state might do something for them.

Yet, despite Benton's surprise about them not invading lands collectively, as pointed out earlier, there was indeed a steady growth of land invasions during the military regime. According to my estimates, about five new land invasions appeared every year from 1973 to 1984. Given that other military regimes, such as the Chilean one, were very repressive with new land invasions and with the old ones that showed any kind of mobilization (Schneider 1995), I was struck to find steady growth in this period. The secret might be in the type of invasions characterizing this period, which began by accretion, with each family arriving separately. Apparently, these slow forming and extremely poor neighborhoods did not represent a big threat to the military government. However, the relationship between cantegriles and the military was far from harmonious. During the period, it was the Church that helped them the most and acted as a shield from state repression.

politica

REPROCHA EL PRESIDENTE A LA IGLESIA DAR ALOJAMIENTO A LOS DESVALIDOS

ANUNCIARON DETALLES DE LA REMODELACION DE LOS HOSPITALES

EROGACION SUPERIOR A LOS 6 MIL MILLONES

CHIAPPE VISITO A RACHETTI

Fig. 4.1 Article published in the weekly *Ahora* on April 26, 1973. The headline reads: President accuses the Church of housing the underdog. *Source* Archive of Observatorio Obsur. Picture taken by María José Álvarez-Rivadulla

A Powerful Ally: Squatters and the Catholic Church During Authoritarian Times

A difficult relationship between squatters and the military government became evident even before the dictatorship started. Two months before he dissolved the General Assembly in June 1973, President Bordaberry showed his discontent with the Catholic Church for housing a group of people that had occupied the newly built social housing next to their cantegriles in Cerro Norte, a very poor area of the city until today. Affected by flooding due to a period of heavy rain, they decided to seize the empty new buildings and the police evicted them by force. A nearby parish gave them shelter and the President called the Archbishop of Montevideo to show his discontent (see the press article in Fig. 4.1).

Police raids became commonplace in cantegriles during this period, and evictions without housing alternatives became much more common than before. The Catholic Church became a powerful ally in this context.

As an institution, the Catholic Church was going through a great transformation, which began after the Second Vatican Council in 1962 and later, the Medellín Conference in 1968, which declared that the Church should take a preferential option for the poor. In Latin America, this turned into the Liberation Theology, a very important movement that changed the way the Church related to the poor. In Uruguay, this materialized in, among other actions, the search for a better relationship with squatters, who epitomized the excluded urban dwellers. The Archbishop of Montevideo, Carlos Parteli, was a main character in this movement (Clara 2012; Ricci Cabrera 1993). He had participated in the Pact of the Catacombs, a document signed in 1965, during the Vatican Council, by a group of mainly Latin American archbishops, in which they committed themselves to a simple life, without material possessions, and to working with the poor. He also developed the concept of structural sin, referring to the social dimension of sin, to the institutional basis of poverty and marginality and to how those institutions served the status-quo (Sánchez 2010). It was he who President Bordaberry scolded in the previous anecdote, and it was under his wing that Father Cacho from the opening vignette was allowed to go and live with the very marginalized, leaving his tasks as a traditional priest assigned to a parish. According to historian Mario Cayota, former ambassador to the Vatican who had access to its recently opened archives, the dictatorship wanted to fire Parteli and the government's ambassadors in the Vatican actively tried to do so, but Pope Paul VI never allowed it (Correa 2016).

There is surprisingly little research on the relationship between the Church and politics during the military regime in Uruguay. Klaiber's (2009) comparative work on the Church and dictatorships in Latin America is an exception. In his Uruguayan chapter, he argues that while the role of the Catholic Church in promoting human rights was "modest and at times ambiguous" (p. 110) during most of the dictatorship, it became crucial during the democratization period. In fact, the Church was divided and Klaiber describes the conflicts between Parteli and others (such as bishop Marcelo Mendiharat, expelled by the military in 1972) and its conservative wing allied with the government.

The best-known Church role was through SERPAJ, an independent yet religious-based transnational Latin American organization that promotes nonviolent action in defense of human rights, which opened a chapter in Uruguay in 1981 (Pagnucco and McCarthy 1992). Catholic priests, such as Luis Perez Aguirre (best known as Perico) and Jorge Osorio and Methodist pastors such as Ademar Oliveira, some laity and some other professionals were among the founders and early members. SERPAJ Uruguay offered a safe space for the movement of relatives of the disappeared under the military regime to meet in parishes and organize to search for their relatives and for their rights (Bucheli et al. 2005). It also denounced torture globally after the detention, torture, and incarceration of a group of members of the Communist Youth in 1983. This obfuscated the military which wanted to close the organization and which started to harass its members. In response, Aguirre, Osorio, and Oliveira started a hunger strike and many people supported them demonstrating and banging pots (Se cumplen 30 años de la primer "caceroleada" contra la dictadura 2013). The political opening that started in 1980 was in danger and the hunger strike of these priests and pastors attempted to unlock the situation (Olivera 2009). It did not take long for repression to kick in; the dictatorship soon ordered the closure of SERPAJ. Its members kept fighting for human rights and the organization was reopened in 1985, already in democracy. SERPAJ is still active today and keeps fighting for justice in cases of human rights violations under dictatorships and for the generation of a culture of peace that respects human rights more generally, particularly in relation to the prison system (SERPAJ 2016).

Montevideo • Jueves 23 de Diciembre de 1982 OPINAR POLITICA NACIONAL • 11

Con Pérez Esquivel

Se agrava la situación de los Derechos Humanos

El martes visitó nuestra ciudad el **Prof. Adolfo Pérez Esquivel, Premio Nóbel de la Paz 1980.** En su breve estada de 24 horas desarrolló una intensa actividad: visitó [illegible] sindical de FUNSA, estuvo en el Servicio Paz y Justicia y por la noche entregó los premios "Paz y Justicia", de cuyo otorgamiento informamos aparte.

En horas de la tarde iba a realizar una Conferencia de Prensa, pero ésta fue suspendida por resolución policial.

OPINAR siguió los pasos del Premio Nóbel argentino y también logró conversar con él. Este es el diálogo mantenido.

—Pérez Esquivel ¿cuáles son los motivos de su visita?

—El motivo de mi visita a Montevideo es reunirme con el Secretariado del Servicio Paz y Justicia de Uruguay para ver el trabajo hecho y las tareas del año próximo. Y también para tomar contacto con distintos sectores del pueblo uruguayo. Hoy los problemas que vivimos son comunes, lo que ocurre en un país repercute en otro.

—Usted estuvo aquí hace un año y muchas cosas han pasado desde entonces. ¿Qué nos puede decir sobre la historia de este tiempo reciente?

La historia del '82 en América Latina muestra la intensificación de puntos críticos en algunos países, en otros éstos disminuyen o se estabilizan. Pero en general se han agudizado los problemas. Se han agudizado en el sentido de un deterioro de la vida de los pueblos: la falta de participación, de libertades y de autodeterminación. Pero también vemos signos de esperanza, la democracia en Bolivia, la respuesta en las elecciones brasileñas, los procesos que se están generando en [illegible]

Pérez Esquivel y Pérez Aguirre, dos pacifistas rioplatenses.

para que nuestros pueblos no se conozcan, para que no sean solidarios. Primero debemos conocernos. Sólo avanzaremos en los procesos sociales en la medida que crezca nuestro esfuerzo de solidaridad. A veces se piensa que los problemas se centran en la situación económica. Pero además de solucionar lo económico, debemos desarrollar la comprensión, la fraternidad, la humildad de los pueblos. Partimos de las diferencias y no de los acuerdos con los demás. Un espíritu nuevo nos acercará entonces a una realidad también novedosa y más justa.

—¿En qué piensa al encarar la tarea que aún resta por delante?

—Pienso en todas las contradicciones que vive el continente. La falta de distribución de los verdaderos valores, la distorsión de las cosas. Vemos los campesinos sin tierra, el hambre, la miseria. Cuando hablamos de los derechos humanos nos referimos a los derechos individuales de las personas, pero también a los derechos de los pueblos. Y vemos la loca carrera armamentista, cuando los pueblos latinoamericanos no necesitan armas, necesitan medios para la salud, la vivienda, la educación. Todo esto nos angustia y tratamos como organismo cristiano de encontrar alternativas. Y pensando que hay un derecho de los pueblos a vivir en libertad y democracia.

—Para terminar ¿cómo define la situación de los derechos humanos en América Latina y cuál es su mensaje para esta Navidad?

—La situación de los derechos humanos se está agravando. Vemos falta de vivienda, salud, de participación. Todo eso es parte de los derechos humanos.

Muchas veces nos quedamos con una idea vacía de los derechos humanos. Nos quedamos sólo con los efectos del problema, las muertes, las desapariciones, el dolor. Tenemos que ver las causas que generan la situación de una injusticia estructural y que son las que provocan las violencias. Debemos desterrar la violencia que tanto afecta nuestros pueblos, violencia que se da en muchas formas.

Como mensaje para Navidad, creo necesaria la unidad de los pueblos, superar los miedos y vivir el mundo con esperanza. A veces se nos presenta el futuro a [illegible]

Fig. 4.2 Article published in the weekly *Opinar* on December 23, 1982. The headline reads: The Human Rights situation is exacerbated. Archive of the Center of Interdisciplinary Uruguayan Studies (CEIU), School of Humanities, Universidad de la República. Picture taken by María José Bolaña

Figure 4.2 shows priest Pérez Aguirre with Argentine Human Rights activist and Nobel Prize winner Pérez Esquivel.

Yet, more invisible Church actions took place throughout the military regime organizing the poorest of the poor.[2] During this time, Catholic parishes and NGOs "were like islands"[3] in which people could participate while avoiding repression. Two experiences stand out in relation to squatter settlements: *La Calera* and *San Vicente,* which were the seed of what later became MOVIDE.

La Calera

La Calera was a housing cooperative organized by the Catholic Church and an NGO (CIDC) working with Catholic-based communities, liberation theology, self-help cooperative construction, and participatory methodologies based on the popular education paradigm of Paulo Freire.[4] The imminence of an eviction of a very underprivileged settlement that had grown in the outskirts of the state and the city, located on private land in the *La Teja* working-class northwestern neighborhood of Montevideo, detonated the experience. Harassed by a threat of eviction by the government due to the construction of Route 1, in 1980, the inhabitants of *La Calera Vieja*, an accretion invasion, a group of recyclers, domestic servants, and other types of informal workers, went to the local parish for help. It was the local parish, which asked a local NGO, CIDC, to intervene. Together, they started a relocation process with those families willing to engage in a self-help transforming experience (28 houses were built on the new plot).

La Calera was the first housing cooperative born of a cantegril. Although the general framework was oriented by the experience of the cooperative housing movement, FUCVAM, residents, and technicians made a lot of changes to adapt rules and the manner of work—typical of the Uruguayan working classes—to these extremely poor populations, distrustful of formal organizations. In a very well-documented history/testimony of this cooperative, written by one of the main characters, a member of the group that accompanied the process, the author carefully describes all the tensions that arose, as well as the learning experience for both technicians and volunteers on the one hand, and residents on the other (Ricci Cabrera 1993). Funding was an important problem, but not the only one. Although residents organized raffles and paid quotas, a loan from a Dutch organization (CEBEMO) was decisive for the project's success. State help was not an available option at that time and in fact only made its presence felt through evicting the neighborhood as a triggering factor for mobilization.

San Vicente

Another important example of Church activity with squatters during the military government is the case of *San Vicente* in northeastern Montevideo, located more precisely in *Casavalle,* the poorest neighborhood of the city. This nongovernmental organization was founded in 1979 by a Catholic priest, known to all neighbors as *El Padre Cacho* (from the opening vignette) and is today, after the death of its founder, the most significant institution for many of the area's residents. For example, when I asked Luisa, a resident from *Plácido Ellauri,* a very poor squatter settlement in that area, about the three people or institutions that have helped her neighborhood the most, she simply said "I would name just one, the San Vicente Organization." This is hardly surprising, since Plácido Ellauri was, in fact, the first neighborhood in which Cacho first worked in the area with a group of young residents, and it was the neighborhood that he later moved into.[5] Luisa, like many nearby residents, works in one of the organization's garbage-recycling projects, which is her first relatively stable job. Like many people in her neighborhood, she had always worked as a scavenger. Her answer is nonetheless significant, since in many other interviews, elsewhere in the city, people tended to mention a politician, or the municipal government or some state institutions such as the water company.

When Cacho decided to move into the neighborhood, as a part of his radical option for the poor, the main state presence in the neighborhood was through police raids (*razzias*). And this reality has not changed much. In an interview in 1988, a resident laughed when the reporter asked whether ambulances came to the neighborhood.[6] He said that the only people that came to the neighborhood were the police and politicians in election season. The presence of a priest in the neighborhood, and this particular priest, changed some dynamics among the forgotten of Montevideo. As the opening vignette testifies, many felt acknowledged, respected, and listened to.

In the same way as in La Calera, the community started organizing itself under the threat of eviction in 1979 (Clara 2012).[7] It was a cantegril two blocks from Plácido Ellauri. Cacho helped by acting as a broker, finding information about the situation of the land, and obtaining resources and volunteers from a parish in the wealthiest neighborhood of the city. They were able to buy the plot, and this was the beginning of a longer process of neighborhood organization that involved self-help construction of brick houses, a soup kitchen, a community center, and other forms of collective grassroots organizing. The social worker of the local parish, Alicia Martirena, the architect Américo Médici (Meco) and other professionals and volunteers were also crucial in this enterprise. The community calls itself *Nueva Esperanza* (New Hope). The mythical figure of this rather shy priest summoned many people and resources, including international ones and press attention, as the articles in Figs. 4.3 and 4.4 testify.

TEMAS DE INTERES

Un cantegril que quiere transformarse

Fig. 4.3 Article published in the weekly *Aquí* on June 7, 1983. The headline reads: A cantegril that wants to transform itself. The picture shows the recently built community center and some of the brick houses. Archive of the Center of Interdisciplinary Uruguayan Studies (CEIU), School of Humanities, Universidad de la República. Picture taken by María José Bolaña

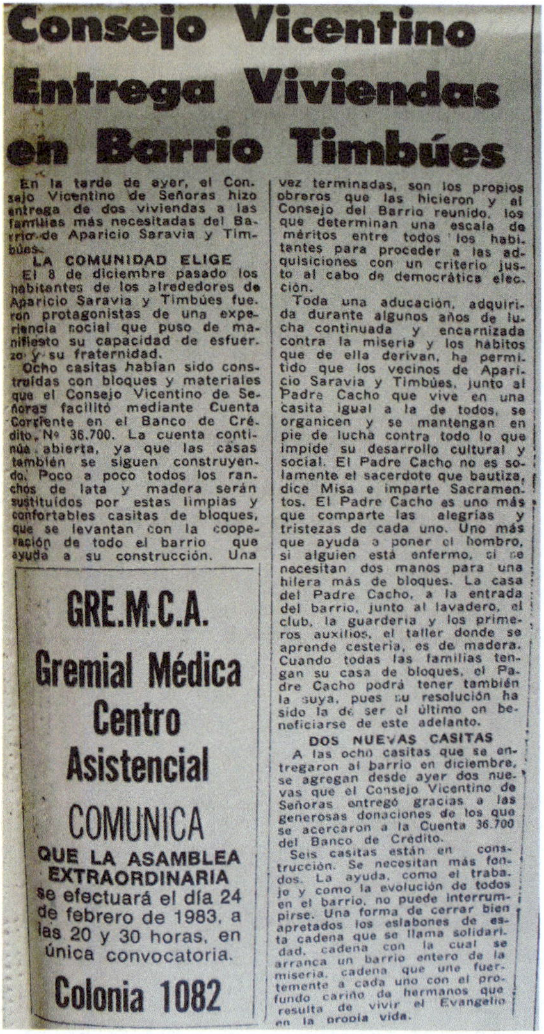

Consejo Vicentino Entrega Viviendas en Barrio Timbúes

En la tarde de ayer, el Consejo Vicentino de Señoras hizo entrega de dos viviendas a las familias más necesitadas del Barrio de Aparicio Saravia y Timbúes.

LA COMUNIDAD ELIGE

El 8 de diciembre pasado los habitantes de los alrededores de Aparicio Saravia y Timbúes fueron protagonistas de una experiencia social que puso de manifiesto su capacidad de esfuerzo y su fraternidad.

Ocho casitas habían sido construídas con bloques y materiales que el Consejo Vicentino de Señoras facilitó mediante Cuenta Corriente en el Banco de Crédito, Nº 36.700. La cuenta continúa abierta, ya que las casas también se siguen construyendo. Poco a poco todos los ranchos de lata y madera serán sustituídos por estas limpias y confortables casitas de bloques, que se levantan con la cooperación de todo el barrio que ayuda a su construcción. Una vez terminadas, son los propios obreros que las hicieron y el Consejo del Barrio reunido, los que determinan una escala de méritos entre todos los habitantes para proceder a las adquisiciones con un criterio justo al cabo de democrática elección.

Toda una aducación, adquirida durante algunos años de lucha continuada y encarnizada contra la miseria y los habitos que de ella derivan, ha permitido que los vecinos de Aparicio Saravia y Timbúes, junto al Padre Cacho que vive en una casita igual a la de todos, se organicen y se mantengan en pie de lucha contra todo lo que impide su desarrollo cultural y social. El Padre Cacho no es solamente el sacerdote que bautiza, dice Misa e imparte Sacramentos. El Padre Cacho es uno más que comparte las alegrías y tristezas de cada uno. Uno más que ayuda a poner el hombro, si alguien está enfermo, si se necesitan dos manos para una hilera más de bloques. La casa del Padre Cacho, a la entrada del barrio, junto al lavadero, el club, la guarderia y los primeros auxilios, el taller donde se aprende cesteria, es de madera. Cuando todas las familias tengan su casa de bloques, el Padre Cacho podrá tener también la suya, pues su resolución ha sido la de ser el último en beneficiarse de este adelanto.

DOS NUEVAS CASITAS

A las ocho casitas que se entregaron al barrio en diciembre, se agregan desde ayer dos nuevas que el Consejo Vicentino de Señoras entregó gracias a las generosas donaciones de los que se acercaron a la Cuenta 36.700 del Banco de Credito.

Seis casitas están en construcción. Se necesitan más fondos. La ayuda, como el trabajo y como la evolución de todos en el barrio, no puede interrumpirse. Una forma de cerrar bien apretados los eslabones de esta cadena que se llama solidaridad, cadena con la cual se arranca un barrio entero de la miseria, cadena que une fuertemente a cada uno con el profundo cariño de hermanos que resulta de vivir el Evangelio en la propia vida.

Fig. 4.4 Article published in the daily *El País* on February, 1983. The headline reads: The Vicentine Council delivers houses in the Timbúes neighborhood [One of the neighborhoods in which Father Cacho intervened]. Archive of the Center of Interdisciplinary Uruguayan Studies (CEIU), School of Humanities, Universidad de la República. Picture taken by María José Bolaña

SCALING UP: MOVIDE

Although at opposite extremes of the periphery of Montevideo, La Calera in the west and San Vicente in the east, these two experiences connected. They started as two separate projects but toward the end of the military regime, they came together to form MOVIDE (*Movimiento Pro Vida Decorosa* or Movement in Promotion of a Decent Life), together with another seven cantegriles.

MOVIDE emerged from a threat posed by a wave of evictions of settlements on private land, caused by speculation by owners and by the urban restructuring caused by the construction of the new access routes to Montevideo from the northwest. The movement was formed by two very different types of actors: on the one hand, the poorest squatters of the city and people evicted from buildings in the city center, and, on the other, a number parishes and NGOs, with professionals and priests with radical views about making the voice of the poor heard and improving their living conditions.

The first meeting took place in the newly inaugurated community center of San Vicente on November 14, 1982.[8] Nine neighborhoods threatened with eviction participated (*La Calera, 19 de abril, San Vicente de Manga, Corralón Municipal, Oficial 2-Camino Maldonado, 17 metros-Piedras Blancas, Hogar Martínez Reyna, Emancipación y Aldao*, and *San Vicente*). Some of these evictions appeared in the press as shown in Fig. 4.5. Initially dubbed just Coordination Board of the nine Neighborhoods *(Coordinadora de los 9 barrios)*, it soon became the Movement for Decent Housing to later articulate broader claims and change its name to Movement for a Decent Life (see Fig. 4.6 for an initial appearance in the press). As a movement, they managed to sensitize the broader public to the reality of many families living in extreme poverty. They were also able to reach the state. For example, the *19 de abril* cantegril was able to obtain its plot through expropriation by the state after it had an audience with ESMACO, the executive power. After this precedent, other neighborhoods, *17 metros,* for example, asked for the same (Fig. 4.7).

MOVIDE was exceptional because through the few newspapers and radio stations that were not repressed and were sympathetic to the cause, it gave the poorest of the poor a voice. It challenged the left's prejudices about squatters. Leftist militants used to dub them the lumpenproletariat and they did not feel they were members of the same class. And there they were, these people coming from the bottom of society giving

La otra cara de la gran ciudad

Un joven amigo nos entregó un extenso documento, suscrito por nueve personas que así lo hacían en representación de nueve barrios distintos de Montevideo, con el pedido de que lo incluyéramos en la página de los lectores. Era muy largo para eso. Además, era muy importante. Le dijimos que con ese material escribiríamos una nota. Pero la nota se escribió sola. Lo que sigue es, con muy pocos retoques —de forma y no de contenido— el documento de referencia. Plantea, nuevamente, un tema del que más de una vez se ha ocupado OPINAR. Pero en el que hay que seguir insistiendo. Habrá que hacerlo hasta que los sordos oigan y hasta que quienes se tapan los ojos con las manos se animen a bajarlas.

Esta nota revela el drama de miles de personas, que son nuestros compatriotas y nuestros conciudadanos. Y que viven una situación de penuria —no ya de pobreza— que compromete la misma condición humana. ¡Si precisará "cambio" la sociedad uruguaya, para que éstos pasen, de una buena vez, a ser los primeros y principales problemas y, por tanto, los primeros y principales a tratar de solucionar!

Más de 3.000 personas, de las cuales 2.000 son niños y jóvenes, se encuentran en una difícil y angustiosa situación, por la falta de viviendas decorosas, luz, agua y servicios higiénicos adecuados. La mitad de ellos están desalojados por ser considerados como habitantes precarios o de casas ruinosas.

Los barrios donde viven son: el Barrio 19 de Abril, ubicado en la zona de Nuevo París; el Barrio 17 Metros, de Piedras Blancas; el Barrio San Vicente, de Manga; el Barrio de Emancipación y Aldao, de Nuevo París; el Barrio de Virrey Elío y Cno. Maldonado; el Barrio La Calera, de La Teja; el Centro San Vicente, de Aparicio Saravia; además los desalojados de viviendas ruinosas del Hogar Martínez Reina, en el Paso Molino y el Corralón Municipal en la calle Cuareim y Gonzalo Ramírez.

Todos juntos, a través de sus respectivos delegados, los habitantes de estos barrios pobres, han solicitado y siguen solicitando a las autoridades competentes resuelvan, con la urgencia del caso, su situación.

LOS DESALOJADOS POR VIVIR EN VIVIENDAS PRECARIAS

19 de Abril, 17 Metros y San Vicente se encuentran desalojados. Allí viven 1.388 personas: 923 son menores. Los vecinos indican que han realizado gestiones en forma independiente y ahora lo harán con el apoyo de todos los barrios. Fueron al ESMACO, la Junta de Vecinos y la Defensoría de Oficio. Al no tomarlos en cuenta, comenzaron idénticas gestiones ante la Intendencia Municipal de Montevideo, el Ministerio de Educación y Cultura, el Comando General del Ejército, la División Ejército 1, y nuevamente en el ESMACO. Además concurrieron al Consejo de Estado, a Casa de Gobierno, etc. En todos estos lugares, dicen que van a ayudar, pero en los Juzgados de Paz los dos primeros barrios ya perdieron el pleito [illegible] los cedulones de desa-

Fig. 4.5 Article published in the weekly *Opinar* on December 23, 1982. The headline reads: The other side of the big city. [A group of evicted neighborhoods went to the military government for solutions. They didn't find answers. This is the beginning of MOVIDE]. Archive of the Center of Interdisciplinary Uruguayan Studies (CEIU), School of Humanities, Universidad de la República. Picture taken by María José Bolaña

hot discourses using spontaneous phrases such as "our heads aren't just for lice, they can think,"[9] mesmerizing every listener. They claimed their character as workers as well as their right to decent housing, health, jobs, and so on. Their name change showed a more profound change, from single issue demands after the threat of eviction to a more radical discourse, with a more ample platform, a critical analysis of their situation, and the ability to make some external alliances (Filgueira 1985).

Coordinadora barrial analiza situación

La coordinadora popularmente conocida como la "de los 9 barrios desalojados", transformada o rebautizada en "Movimiento Pro-Vida Decorosa" (MO.VI.DE.) dio a conocer un comunicado en el que se analizan los pasos dados recientemente.

Fechada a fines de junio, la comunicación va dirigida a la opinión pública y a las autoridades de gobierno y dice textualmente:

"En diciembre de 1982 realizamos un planteamiento a la Presidencia de la República y a toda la prensa como Coordinadora Pro-Vivienda Decorosa (también conocida como Coordinadora de los 9 barrios desalojados), sin obtener hasta el presente ninguna respuesta a nuestras solicitudes. Ante este hecho queremos hacer algunas puntualizaciones:

1) Agradecer a los medios de comunicación que apoyaron nuestro pedido de difusión de la Coordinadora. Estas publicaciones han calado hondo en la opinión pública y esto nos reconforta.

2) Queremos dejar claro que también existió un aprovechamiento de nuestra situación por parte de algunos medios de comunicación y de algunas personas, planteando proyectos diferentes al nuestro. En ningún momento

sideran nuestra participación en la creación de los nuevos barrios y no tienen en cuenta la realidad de nuestras familias, habituadas a tener un terreno para huerta y jardín y para mantener animales, muchas veces nuestra única fuente de subsistencia.

5) El Barrio 19 de Abril, que comparte y participa de nuestro Movimiento, ha logrado, luego de tres años de lucha, que las autoridades anuncien la expropiación, por parte del Banco Hipotecario, de los predios que ocupan desde hace más de treinta años. De esta manera el esfuerzo de los vecinos logró detener un lanzamiento que hubiera significado la expulsión de todo el barrio.

Si bien nos alegra este paso hacia una alternativa al problema de 19 de Abril, estamos a la espera que los planes del Banco contemplen la necesaria participación de los vecinos en la discusión, planificación y gestión de las posibles soluciones. Por otra parte reiteramos que hay otros barrios en la misma situación que 19 de Abril, entre ellos el Barrio 17 metros en Piedras Blancas, que tiene anunciado el lanzamiento para el próximo mes de julio.

6) Exigimos que cuanto antes se resuelvan nuestros problemas y en especial el del barrio 17 me-

Fig. 4.6 Article published in the weekly *Aquí* on July 12, 1983. The headline reads: Neighborhood Coordination Board analyzes the situation. Archive of the Center of Interdisciplinary Uruguayan Studies (CEIU), School of Humanities, Universidad de la República. Picture taken by María José Bolaña

They held a clear anti-politician discourse; politicians who they blamed in part for their marginalized situation. In one of the movement's documents, written to be presented at a seminar of popular organizations in October 1984 (a month before the first post-military elections), we can read phrases such as "politicians used us and deceived us," "when politicians were governing, life was very difficult," "some politicians saw that the situation was difficult and they got together with the military," "with the coup, our situation worsened, we became

Un barrio entero ante un probable desalojo

De no mediar alguna solución por parte de las autoridades gubernativas, el próximo 29 de agosto serán desalojados los habitantes del Barrio 17 Metros, en la zona de Piedras Blancas.

En terrenos baldíos ubicados sobre la calle 17 Metros se fueron asentando, hace más de una década, algunas familias que, no pudiendo acceder a una vivienda propia por otros medios, comenzaron a construir sus hogares allí.

riormente, les permitiera comprar los terrenos.

Con ese propósito, el Centro Vecinal comenzó su interminable recorrida por distintas dependencias estatales, principalmente la Intendencia, y también la Casa de Gobierno. Cartas pidiendo la expropiación de los terrenos fueron llegando a la Comuna capitalina pero, ante la consulta de qué trámite se le deba a la solicitud, se encontraban los vecinos con un

Fig. 4.7 Article published in the weekly *Aquí* on July 19, 1983. The headline reads: An entire neighborhood faces likely eviction. [The article says that the first MOVIDE achievement was to avoid the eviction of the *19 de abril* neighborhood and that they are trying to do the same with another neighborhood, *17 metros*]. Archive of the Center of Interdisciplinary Uruguayan Studies (CEIU), School of Humanities, Universidad de la República. Picture taken by María José Bolaña

even poorer," "some politicians appeared in our neighborhoods making promises they never fulfilled," "the state doesn't provide enough resources for everybody to have good health (...) It gives more resources to the military."[10]

It was a successful movement in many ways. It protected the originally threatened neighborhoods from eviction by finding alternatives. It made its issues visible to the general public. It resisted other types of evictions in the city and connected with other organizations around the issue of housing (see Figs. 4.8, 4.9). It marched with the more traditional FUCVAM movement on International Homeless Day (*Día de los Sin Techo*), which has been taking place worldwide every October, since 1987 (see Figs. 4.10, 4.11). As stated earlier, MOVIDE became so important during the transition that it was one of the movements invited to participate in the 1984–1985 multiparty consultations, known as

MOVIDE expresó a la IMM su desacuerdo por desalojos de Tres Cruces

MOVIDE (Movimiento Pro Vivienda Decorosa) envió una carta el intendente capitalino Jorge Elizalde, en la que expresa su desacuerdo con la notificación de lanzamiento judicial a 118 familias del barrio Tres Cruces, las que serían desalojadas para poder construir allí una terminal de ómnibus.

"Queremos aclarar que MOVIDE fue integrante de la mesa redonda de la Concertación Nacional Programática, donde se presentó como prioritario el lanzamiento de otro barrio del Movimiento (17 Metros, de Piedras Blancas) y se llegó a un consenso entre los integrantes de esa Mesa acerca de que no se darían más lanzamientos hasta tanto no hubiera soluciones habitacionales" sostiene la carta. "Hoy a dos años de la concertación, estamos igualmente esperando la participación de los usuarios de MOVIDE en todas las etapas y el respeto a las organizaciones barriales".

"No hay que olvidar que se ha dado como prioridad el construir una terminal de ómnibus, pero no se ha hablado nada de solucionar antes el problema de estas 118 familias".

MOVIDE culmina su carta planteando su negativa rotunda a los desalojos y señalándole al Intendente que "la modernización empieza por la construcción de viviendas dignas, decorosas y respetando a quienes se merecen tranquilidad y estabilidad de acuerdo a la Constitución".

AQUI informó en su edición del pasado 9 de setiembre sobre este caso, que comprende a los habitantes de la zona comprendida entre las calles Goes, Galicia, Acevedo Díaz y Bulevar Artigas.

SALUD PARA TODOS
UN DERECHO A LA VIDA

Fig. 4.8 Article published in the weekly *Aquí* on November 4, 1986. The headline reads: MOVIDE expressed its disagreement with the *Tres Cruces* eviction. [These were not squatters' evictions but evictions from the city center to make way for the construction of a bus terminal and a shopping center]. Archive of the Center of Interdisciplinary Uruguayan Studies (CEIU), School of Humanities, Universidad de la República. Picture taken by María José Bolaña

Comisión del Senado Comienza a Estudiar Ley de Alquileres; se Pronuncia COVIP

La Comisión de Constitución y Legislación del Senado dará entrada hoy al proyecto de Ley de Emergencia para Arrendamientos, que viene sancionado por la Cámara de Representantes. La comisión sesionará integrada con diputados de la comisión especial de la Cámara Baja que estudió el tema. En tanto, la Coordinadora de la Vivienda Popular (COVIP), ha emitido la siguiente declaración que reproducimos:La Coordinadora de la Vivienda Popular (COVIP), integrada por: Sociedad de Arquitectos del Uruguay, FUCVAM, Centro Cooperativista del Uruguay, SUNCA, Grupo de Estudios Urbanos, Frente de Inquilinos, FECOVI, CODECOHA, CEDA, CIDC, INTEC, CIESU, MOVIDE,

3) Que el trámite de aprobación de los mismos se ha enlentecido, cuando se debería, por el contrario, otorgar tratamiento urgente a éstos.

ATENTO:

A la imperiosa necesidad de que estos proyectos sean aprobados en los plazos más breves posibles, en pocos días si fuera posible, como así lo aspiran cientos de miles de familias de arrendatarios y cooperativistas de menores recursos, la COVIP

DECLARA:

1) Que reitera su fraternal apoyo a las justas reivindicaciones del FRENTE DE INQUILINOS - CASA DEL INQUILINO; FUCVAM Y FECOVI.

2) Que reclama la inmediata

Fig. 4.9 Article published in the daily paper *El País* on June 25, 1985. The headline reads: Senate Commission starts to study the Rents Law; COVIP speaks up. [COVIP is the Popular Housing Coordinating Organization integrated by MOVIDE and other groups and movements. They wanted to derogate the law that had liberalized renting prices during the military regime]. Archive of the Center of Interdisciplinary Uruguayan Studies (CEIU), School of Humanities, Universidad de la República. Picture taken by María José Bolaña

National Conciliatory Program (*Concertación Nacional Programática* or CONAPRO).

But that fame did not last long. Around 1989, it disappears from press accounts. With democratization, MOVIDE started dismembering for many reasons specific to the movement[11] and one general reason that affected many of the instances of the mobilization boom toward the end of the military regime: the traditional political actors reappeared (Filgueira 1985). Political parties and unions recovered the centrality

Los sin techo exigen vivienda

Hoy martes 6 de octubre se conmemora el "día mundial de los sin techo", en el marco del año internacional de la vivienda declarado por las Naciones Unidas. Con este motivo habrá de realizarse una concentración frente al Palacio Legislativo ·a la hora 18, convocada por la COVIP (Coordinadora de Vivienda Popular).

El hecho adquiere un carácter histórico en virtud de que es la primera vez que en el país se llevará a cabo una actividad de semejante naturaleza con la participación de todas las organizaciones que integran la COVIP.

Entre esas organizaciones se destacan MOVIDE, MOVEMO, FUCVAM, Frente Nacional de Inquilinos, FECOVI, CODECOA, COPENCO, Comisión para el área de la vivienda del PIT-CNT y el PIAT (Plenario de Instituciones de Asistencia Técnica).

La concentración culminará con la entrega de un documento central a cada bancada parlamentaria, en el que se detallarán las reivindicaciones particulares de cada organización, exigiendo una solución para los gravísimos problemas de la vivienda en el país. [illegible] los datos que se manejan por la [illegible] VIP, se calcula que más de 10.000 [illegible] milias habrán de ser desalojadas en [illegible] año y que alrededor de 60.000 [illegible] viven "tugurizadas" en distintas [illegible] infrahumanas de vivienda. [illegible] según las mismas fuentes, [illegible] Montevideo 110 cantegriles y [illegible] mente se les incorpora un [illegible] cinco familias, lo que supone [illegible] anual de 7.200 personas.

Fig. 4.10 Article published in the weekly *Aquí* on October 6, 1987. The headline reads: The homeless demand housing. [MOVIDE participated in this first celebration of Homeless Day, together with FUCVAM and other organizations]. Archive of the Center of Interdisciplinary Uruguayan Studies (CEIU), School of Humanities, Universidad de la República. Picture taken by María José Bolaña

they had before the military regime and with only a few exceptions, the more heterogeneous forms of mobilization slowly vanished through cooptation, neutralization, or some other mechanism.

Like an urban mirror of the decline of the movement, today La Calera, the emblematic experience of self-help among the poorest of the poor, looks just like any other of the most deprived squatter settlements. The population has grown and the infrastructure deteriorated. Finally, it is important to note that MOVIDE did not encourage new land invasions. On the contrary, it was a movement that defended people from

ARQUITECTO MEDICI

"La vivienda no puede esperar"

Si alguien creyó que habría "vivienda para todos los uruguayos en el año 2000", puede ir bajándose del caballo.

POR LUIS UDAQUIOLA

Fig. 4.11 Article published in the weekly *Aquí* on October 11, 1988. The headline reads: Housing can't wait. [The article is an interview with architect Medici, a delegate of MOVIDE to COVIP. He says that the housing problem remains after democracy. The picture is from the second Homeless Day. The sign hanging from a recycler's horse cart reads: The government only wants money. We want to live decently]. Archive of the Legislative Palace Library. Picture taken by María José Bolaña

evictions, which despite its reactive origins it switched to a more proactive platform, and was not a promoter of new land invasions.

MOVIDE from an International Perspective

Although I dub MOVIDE an unlikely movement for the particular context of the extremely poor cantegril dwellers in Uruguay, the movement was part of broader local and regional trends. Catholic communities were very active in working with squatter settlements toward the end of the military regimes of the Southern Cone, and, in some contexts, squatters became crucial actors in the fight for democracy. Moreover, in Uruguay and other places, squatters were part of the spring of grassroots mobilization of the time,[12] which made many interpret them through the European framework of the "New Social Movements" (Evers 1985; Melucci 1980). This vision highlighted the autonomous and horizontal nature of the grassroots movements of the time, as well as their focus on territorial (or other types of) identities rather than party ones. With the return of democracy, however, many of those movements started to fade or turned to political parties for different forms of representation, questioning their autonomous nature, as well as the whole interpretative framework (Roberts 1997).

In Rio, for example, McCann (2013) describes a harsh relationship between favelas and the military for many years that ended with the successful resistance of one favela (Vidigal), which, in turn, started a surge of favela resistance to the military and their contribution to democratization. Catholic parishes and NGOs working with liberation theology were a crucial part of the resistance movement helping squatters with lawyers and other resources. While "between 1962 and 1978, dozens of favelas were razed and tens of thousands of *favelados* were forcibly relocated, usually to distant housing projects" (5), "between the late 1970s and the mid-1980s, favela activists led a movement to bridge the long-standing divide between favelas and the formal city in Rio de Janeiro (…). In a rush of Mobilization, they built a movement that redrew the political map of the city and helped push the nation toward redemocratization" (15). The favelados' movement, together with other political allies, supported and helped elect a left-wing governor that had helped them and promised to keep doing so. He in fact designed a program to bring services and titling to favelas. Yet, external forces such as hyperinflation and national recession as well as increased drug trafficking and decreased favela mobilization conspired against this turning into a success story.

Thus, as McCann beautifully and sadly summarizes, "things got worse before they could get better" (15).

In Chile (Oxhorn 1995; Schneider 1995) and Argentina (Prévôt Schapira 1999), the Catholic Church also had an important role in popular organizations during the military regime, promoting horizontal, self-help forms of collective action among the poorest. With political parties suppressed, the Catholic Church was a refuge for organizing and solving everyday needs. In the context of democratizing societies, those most affected by the hardships of deindustrialization and liberalization, mobilized with the help of Church organizations and NGOs. Their brokerage role was key to access the few resources they could in a context of great economic deprivation.

Even though the Church kept working with some of these communities after democratization, political parties recovered their crucial role. Thus, in Argentina, for instance, Peronist networks became crucial brokerage structures for survival among squatters during liberalization in the 1990s (Auyero 2000). Although often common sense and even academic work associates political networks with demobilization, empirical cases such as the Argentine or the Uruguayan one tell a different story. Political networks can sometimes be useful for mobilization (Auyero et al. 2009). The next chapter, tells the story of a second wave of mobilization among Montevideo squatters, peaking around 1990, more closely related to political parties and the state than the first wave described here.

Notes

1. Radio Program *Testimonios*, interview with Esther by Graciela Salsamendi, around 1988. Archive of the Center of Interdisciplinary Uruguayan Studies (CEIU), School of Humanities, Universidad de la República (Cantegril I, bloque 1).
2. The experience of *La Huella* community, of which the same Pérez Aguirre of SERPAJ, a Jesuit Priest, was an active member, is iconic of the time. In 1975, a group of young Jesuit priests and former students of the Jesuit school in Montevideo, founded a communitarian home in the rural area of Montevideo. In the context of a harsh dictatorship, they still wanted to resist, and they founded a farm in which they could live as a community, without private property and consumerism, and take care of orphan kids (Sans and Agostino 2014).

3. Expression of Inés Giudice, one of the professional founders of MOVIDE, who taught me about the history of the movement, and told me her current reflections about why it vanished with redemocratization.
4. Interviews with Susana Regent, then Local Secretary of the 14th Zonal Community Center, administrative municipal unit where this settlement belongs, and with Inés Giudice, social worker at the Ministry of Housing at the time of the interview, who had worked directly with this settlement, through the NGO CIDC.
5. Based on the intervention of the historian and then city councilor, Mario Cayota, on September 5th, 2002, on the 10th anniversary of the death of *Padre Cacho*. Session 1037. Minutes available at http://www.juntamvd.gub.uy.
6. Radio Program *Testimonios*, interview with Juan by Graciela Salsamendi, around 1988. Archive of the Center of Interdisciplinary Uruguayan Studies (CEIU), School of Humanities, Universidad de la República (Cantegriles II, bloque 1).
7. I took the date and some other information about the history of the organization from a comic book with the oral history of the neighborhood from the Archive of the San Vicente Organization (Basanta et al., s.d.). The archives are available online at http://www.osvpadrecacho.org.uy.
8. Ibidem.
9. Interview with Inés Giudice, social worker who worked with the movement.
10. Cited by Rodé et al. (1985).
11. Among the specific reasons, Inés Giudice mentions frictions between delegates and their base in the neighborhoods, especially when the movement starts having more visibility and delegates participate in the negotiations for democracy. This contrasted with the movement's principles of horizontal participation. She also mentioned some cooptation of leaders by the traditional political parties. Besides, there were also some tensions between professionals and the people from the neighborhoods. They were part of the same movement, but the former earned a salary and the others did not. There were also tensions between the major organizations in the movement. On the one hand, *San Vicente*, and, on the other, the NGOs such as CIDC and Aportes, which were responsible for the *La Calera Vieja* cooperative mentioned in the text. The two groups had different perspectives about the work they were doing. *San Vicente* was much less politicized whereas the professionals in the other NGOs were mostly leftist militants as well. With democratization, tensions grew stronger. People at CIDC and Aportes put great emphasis on popular education, and they wanted to transfer this methodology to the political parties. *San Vicente* did not have these broader goals beyond raising the quality of life and the awareness of those in their area of action. And,

finally, she referred to cooptation of the whole project by the first democratic municipal government (*Colorado* administration). The *Plan Aquiles Lanza* aimed, among other things, at transforming *cantegriles* into better neighborhoods using self-help construction by the dwellers. According to Giudice (and this also appears in other interviews with key informants), they took the self-help working strategy but they did not promote any other participation by residents or any coordination among the different neighborhoods. The plan acted in seven neighborhoods and it did not go very well. Many families quit, the population grew, and plots were subsequently subdivided, taking over public spaces. Today these seven neighborhoods look like any other of the less planned squatter settlements of the city. According to Giudice, this plan took some ideas from MOVIDE but, contrary to it, the plan had a clear demobilizing goal.

12. In Montevideo, besides MOVIDE, there were a variety of grassroots movements in the peripheral neighborhoods, such as soup kitchens and neighborhood health clinics (Rodé et al. 1985).

References

Auyero, J. (2000). The logic of clientelism in Argentina: An ethnographic account. *Latin American Research Review, 35*(3), 55–81.

Auyero, J., Lapegna, P., & Page Poma, F. (2009). Patronage politics and contentious collective action: A recursive relationship. *Latin American Politics and Society, 51*(3), 1–31.

Basanta, M., Larrosa, M., Ripa, R., & Olveyra, G. (s.d.). *Mis vecinos de San Vicente (Padre Cacho). Una comunidad barrial con memoria.* Montevideo: San Vicente Organization.

Baudrón, S. (1979). *Estudio Socioeconómico de algunos barrios marginales de Montevideo.* Montevideo: Fundación de cultura Universitaria—Ciedur.

Benton, L. (1986). Reshaping the urban core: The politics of housing in authoritarian Uruguay. *Latin American Research Review, 21*(2), 33–52.

Bucheli, G., Curto, V., Sanguinetti, V., Demasi, C., & Yaffé, J. (2005). *Vivos los llevaron: historia de la lucha de Madres y Familiares de Uruguayos Detenidos Desaparecidos (1976–2005).* Montevideo: Ediciones Trilce.

Canel, E. (1992). Democratization and the decline of urban social movements in Uruguay: A political institutional account. In A. Escobar & S. E. Alvarez (Eds.), *The making of social movements in Latin America* (pp. 276–290). Boulder, CO: Westnew Press.

Clara, M. (2012). *Padre Cacho. Cuando el otro quema adentro.* Montevideo: Trilce.

Correa, J. P. (2016). Vaticano liberará archivos sobre dictadura uruguaya. *El País.* Retrieved from http://www.elpais.com.uy/informacion/vaticano-liberara-archivos-dictadura-uruguaya.html.

Evers, T. (1985). Identity: The hidden side of new social movements in Latin America. In D. Slater (Ed.), *New social movements and the state in Latin America*. Amsterdam: CEDLA.

Filgueira, C. (1985). Movimientos Sociales en la restauración del orden democrático: Uruguay, 1985. In C. Filgueira (Ed.), *Movimientos Sociales en el Uruguay de Hoy*. Montevideo: CLACSO-CIESU-Ediciones de la Banda Oriental.

Kaztman, R., Filgueira, F., & Errandonea, F. (2005). La Ciudad Fragmentada. Respuesta de los sectores populares urbanos a las transformaciones del mercado y el territorio en Montevideo. In A. Portes, B. Roberts, & A. Grimson (Eds.), *Ciudades Latinoamericanas. Un Análisis Comparativo en el Umbral del Nuevo Siglo*. Buenos Aires: Prometeo.

Klaiber, J. (2009). *The church, dictatorships, and democracy in Latin America*. Eugene: Wipf and Stock.

McCann, B. (2013). *Hard Times in the Marvelous City: From Dictatorship to Democracy in the Favelas of Rio de Janeiro*. Durham, NC: Duke University Press.

Melucci, A. (1980). The new social movements: A theoretical approach. *Social Science Information, 19*(2), 199–226.

Olivera, A. (2009). *Forjando caminos de liberación: la Iglesia Metodista en tiempo de dictadura*. Montevideo: Trilce.

Oxhorn, P. (1995). *Organizing Civil Society. The popular sectors and the struggle for democracy in Chile*. University Park: The Pennsylvania State University Press.

Pagnucco, R., & McCarthy, J. D. (1992). Advocating nonviolent direct action in Latin America: The antecedents and emergence of SERPAJ. In B. Misztal & A. Shupe (Eds.), *Religion and politics in comparative perspective: Revival of fundamentalism in east and west* (pp. 125–147). New York: Praeger.

Prévôt Schapira, M.-F. (1999). From Utopia to pragmatism: The heritage of basismo in local government in the greater Buenos Aires region. *Bulletin of Latin American Research, 18*(2), 227–239.

Ricci Cabrera, M. (1993). *Historia de la calera. Una cooperativa distinta*. Montevideo: Obsur.

Roberts, K. M. (1997). Review: Beyond romanticism: Social movements and the study of political change in Latin America. *Latin American Research Review, 32*(2), 137–151.

Rodé, P., Marsiglia, J., & Piedracueva, E. (1985). Experiencias recientes de movilización urbana en las áreas de la salud, nutrición y organización barrial. In C. H. Filgueira (Ed.), *Movimientos sociales en el Uruguay de hoy*. Montevideo: CLACSO-CIESU-Ediciones de la Banda Oriental.

Sánchez, G. (2010). La esperanza del Concilio. Retrieved from Redes Cristianas website: http://www.redescristianas.net/la-esperanza-del-conciliogabriel-sanchez-montevideo-uruguay.

Sans, I., & Agostino, A. (2014). *Historia de la Huella*. Montevideo: Trilce.

Schneider, C. L. (1995). *Shantytown protest in Pinochet's Chile*. Philadelphia: Temple University Press.

Se cumplen 30 años de la primer "caceroleada" contra la dictadura. (2013). *República.com.uy*. Retrieved from http://www.republica.com.uy/se-cumplen-30-anos-de-la-primer-caceroleada-contra-la-dictadura/374193/.

SERPAJ. (2016). Servicio Paz y Justicia América Latina: Uruguay. Retrieved from http://serpajamericalatina.org/web/sedes/uruguay/.

CHAPTER 5

Planned Squatting and Politics

The city of Montevideo changed drastically during the last decade of the twentieth century. The number of informal neighborhoods increased in an unprecedented manner and changed, beyond mere numbers, to involve the repertoire of land invasions. Many of the new neighborhoods started as organized land invasions, with a group identifying a piece of land, invading it, outlining streets and plots, negotiating with authorities, and organizing itself to demand for public services. While the previous chapter studies the effect of democratization as a political opening for grassroots civil society organizations, including some very poor *cantegriles* or traditional accretion invasions, this chapter tackles a second and different wave of mobilization, which occurred around 1990 and constituted a surge of organized land invasions.

Besides the previously mentioned general effect of political opening on all types of mobilization, I argue that democratization triggered land squatting, particularly planned land squatting, through at least three specific political opportunities: electoral competition for the votes of the urban poor, the leftist orientation of the city government, and the decentralization policy implemented by the leftist coalition after it assumed the municipal government in 1990. So, besides the relaxation of repression and subsequent increased freedom of organization, democratization brought

Parts of this chapter were published before as a book chapter and are reproduced here with the permission of Springer: (Álvarez-Rivadulla 2015).

M.J. Álvarez-Rivadulla, *Squatters and the Politics of Marginality in Uruguay*, Latin American Political Economy, DOI 10.1007/978-3-319-54534-9_5

at least two other important political opportunities usually mentioned in the literature on political processes: influential allies and institutional access (Almeida 2010; McAdam et al. 1996). While electoral competition and the left in the city government provided squatters with influential allies through political networks with different political parties, decentralization increased their institutional access to the municipal government.

The effect of these opportunities on squatters was not homogeneous and varied depending on social networks and other resources. Thus, leaders of the more precisely planned squatter settlements—who had usually participated in other forms of collective organization such as trade unions, the cooperative housing movement, or political parties—were better able to seize both these opportunities and transfer them to neighborhood organization.

As I mentioned in the introduction, looking at political opportunities and squatters seems particularly relevant in Latin America, where the relationships between squatters and the state have often been intense, but with great variation across cities and times. Although rooted in political process theory, I also acknowledge the tremendous importance of cultural frameworks (McAdam et al. 1996). It was not until squatting became a decent alternative for the structurally downwardly mobile Montevideans that planned land invasions entered their repertoire of collective action (Tilly 1978). Planned squatting became a strategy to resist exclusion for the "seduced and abandoned" urban poor, who, having incorporated expectations of full citizenship and stable jobs, were being expelled to the city outskirts and ousted from the labor market (Kaztman 2001). It was for this reason that squatting needed to be re-signified (Álvarez-Rivadulla 2017). Organized squatters engaged in a spatial and symbolic fight that required them to distinguish themselves from the poorest of the poor, those that squatted by accretion, and those associated with scavenging and with very precarious living conditions. The degree to which this fight succeeded is dubious in most planned invasions. Only a few were able to become just "regular neighborhoods" as the squatters framed it. Yet, many conditions that were beyond their control, such as rising poverty in the early 2000s economic and social crisis, conspired against their hopes.

A New Form of Squatting

Accretion invasions have been the prevalent type of land invasions in Montevideo. However, after democratization and, fundamentally in the late 1980s and early 1990s, there was a shift in the number and type of land invasions established by the urban poor: they peaked in number and planned land invasions became the most frequent type (see Fig. 5.1). As explained earlier, planned invasions began as organized collective action. A group seized an empty plot after finding out its legal status and then divided it into plots, marking streets and, sometimes, common spaces such as squares or community centers. The squatters then negotiated with the authorities, first, to be able to stay and later to be provided with public services and, eventually, to obtain the legalization of land titles. After at times having to resist police eviction, especially in private plots, they immediately started to negotiate with the authorities presenting a list of residents and justifying their right to stay on the basis of "necessity," a figure in the Uruguayan legislation explained below. Residents still self-built their houses, but they used more solid materials such as bricks or some sort of cement. Some of these settlements are, to an outsider, indistinguishable from a poor but formal neighborhood. The only difference is land ownership.

As described in greater detail in Chap. 3, at least to begin with, the intentions behind a few of these planned invasions were utopic. Early residents wanted more than merely to solve their basic housing needs. They wanted to form a horizontal grassroots organization, without

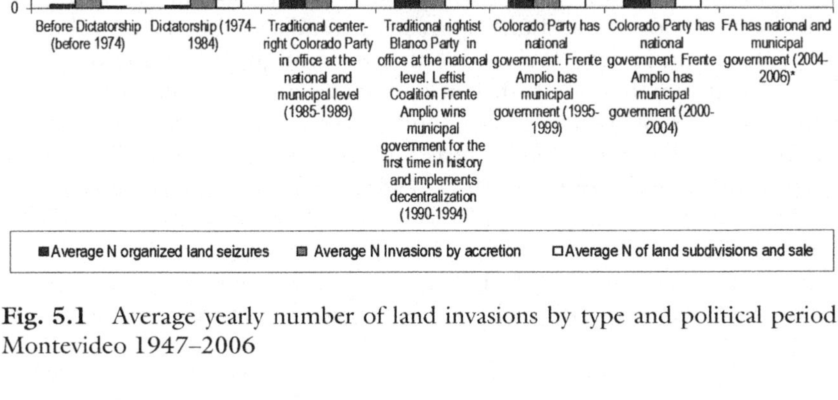

Fig. 5.1 Average yearly number of land invasions by type and political period. Montevideo 1947–2006

representatives. Other planned invasions, even if less utopic, did organize themselves to various degrees to seize land or improve their neighborhood. In the same way as in the rest of the region, squatter settlements in Uruguay are the most vital manifestation of political action by the urban poor (Portes and Walton 1976).

Uruguay's economic changes are undoubtedly behind the explosion of land invasions, which took place in the late 1980s and 1990s. Deindustrialization, state retrenchment, and increasing wage differentials by education, brought about by increasing economic liberalization, reduced the number of protected, stable, and decently paid jobs available, particularly for those with low qualifications (Álvarez-Rivadulla 2000; Cecilio 1997; INTEC 1995; Kaztman et al. 2004). More specific factors associated to housing such as insufficient and ineffective housing policies and urban policies in general, failures in the land market, skyrocketing rent prices, the excessive guarantees needed to rent housing in Uruguay, and the lack of coordination among land titling programs, were also behind the wave of new land invasions (Amarante and Caffera 2003; Cecilio et al. 1999; Nahoum 2002; Semanario-Voces 2011; Viana et al. 2006; Villamide, s.d.).

However, these economic- and policy-based explanations leave some variations unexplained. Why did squatting peak around 1989–1990 and not at other times with similar or greater levels of poverty, unemployment, and housing problems? In particular, the peak of 41 new land invasions in 1990 needs to be better explained (This figure becomes even more surprising if we consider that the 2 years with the next highest number of land invasions had only 17 each and that the annual average for the studied period was 4.4). Moreover, why was there another (lower) peak around 1994–1995? Figure 5.2 shows the wave of planned land invasions in Montevideo since the democratic opening in 1984 vis-à-vis the city's poverty and unemployment trends. It also shows a shorter series of renting prices.[1] We can see that need might be a necessary condition but definitely not a sufficient one for squatting to take place. Years with high rates of unemployment and poverty, such as the first half of the 2000s, did not produce a peak of new land invasions. To explain the peaks in 1989–1990 and 1984–1985, we need to look beyond the important factors associated with housing and labor needs. We need to look at politics.

Following Tarrow (1989: 13) again, "what needs to be explained is not why people periodically petition, strike, demonstrate, riot, loot

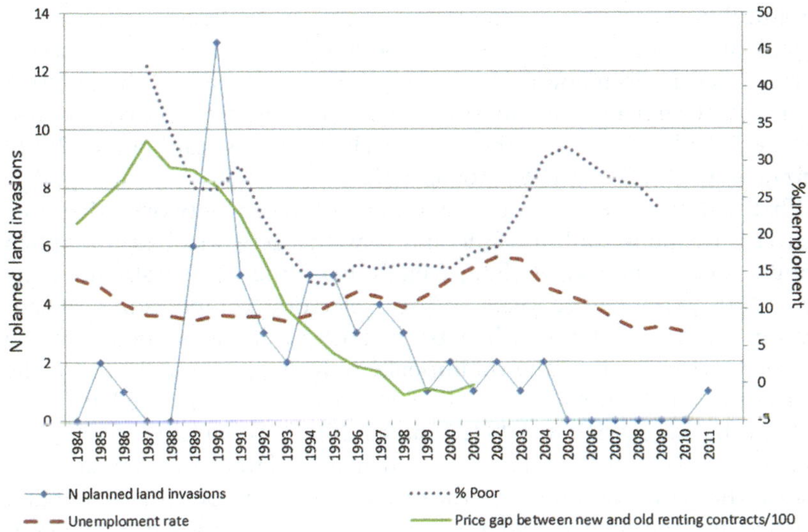

Fig. 5.2 The evolution of planned land invasions vis-à-vis well-being indicators (1984–2011)

and burn, but rather why so many of them do so at particular times in their history, and if there is a logical sequence to their action." To better understand squatting, we need an interactive theory of how grievances interact with specific political opportunities at particular moments. Below, I analyze how democratization transformed the number and type of land invasions in a context of growing inequality.

Electoral Competition as Political Opportunity

During my fieldwork, one of the most recurrent features in the squatters' stories, particularly the most organized ones, was the close contact with politicians from different political parties and their factions. It was usually through these politicians that squatters managed to obtain information about which plot to seize, services such as water and electricity, or help in building and maintaining their gravel roads. Although certainly not the only strategy for neighborhood improvement (they combined political networks with direct petitioning and self-help and, more rarely, with disruptions such as road blockades or sit-ins at state offices), the use of political ties seemed to be the fastest and most successful. This was not particularly surprising given both the body of literature that documents the role of clientelism among Latin American squatters[2] and the one that documents Uruguay's clientelism as a rooted institution that has historically linked civil society and a relatively generous state (Luna 2006; Panizza and Pérez Piera 1988; Rama 1971).

What did surprise me was the variety of those networks that one squatter settlement could include and how the networks had multiplied during a specific period of time, namely from the mid-1980s until the early 2000s. Those were years of great electoral competition, particularly for the votes of the urban poor. Historically strongholds of the most populist factions of the traditionally right wing Colorado Party, the popular areas of Montevideo slowly started to drift toward the left (Luna 2006, 2007; Mieres 1988, 1994; Moreira 2005). Squatter settlements as spaces of localized poverty became particularly relevant for campaigning. Besides, the goods and services they needed were among the few that a reformed and retrenched state could still deliver, as opposed to the pensions and jobs that circulated through the political networks of the past (Filgueira et al. 2003; Luna 2006).

This was not easy for many Frente Amplio politicians. The party's typical traditional voter belonged to the middle class or organized working class, and now had to learn how to approach a different type of popular local leader that it was not used to. As a socialist faction broker active in helping different land invasions told me, these leaders had "different codes" that the "sectarian left" couldn't easily understand. Before, they had merely seen them as the lumpenproletariat, unable to organize themselves. As recalled by a Frente Amplio campaign advisor, while in the 1984 campaign, the left could not enter into a squatter settlement, 10 years later in the 1994 campaign and after the left governing the city for its first 4 years, "everything exploded. You entered and it was like deification. I remember an image in the *Tres Ombues* settlement: Arana [twice Mayor and later Housing Minister] and Astori [Economy Minister and current Vice President] on a scavenger's cart, and people were taking them as if they were carnival queens…it was unbelievable. And they were followed by a huge parade. Unbelievable. That was definitely a turning point that still has its effects, even today."

Electoral competition for the popular vote was exceptionally high in the 1989 election, and 1990 was a very peculiar post-electoral year. It was a historical juncture for the city since Frente Amplio assumed the city government for the first time ever. In fact, it was the first time that a party other than the traditional Blanco and Colorado parties won an executive position in Uruguay since 1830 (first elections). The entire history of bipartidism was questioned, and land invasions spiked. Yet, even beyond that particular juncture, according to my quantitative analysis of the whole studied period (1947–2006), post-electoral, and to a lesser degree electoral years have been the ones most likely to witness land invasions (see Appendix 2 for the models I ran for the years 1947–2006).

Beyond campaigns, electoral competition continued from the government offices in post-electoral times. Traditionally, the Blanco and Colorado parties had a pact of co-participation that guaranteed that when any of them won, the other would still hold some positions in government. Thus, for example, during the Colorado presidency of Sanguinetti between 1995 and 1999, two relevant agencies for squatters, the Housing Ministry and the Presidency of the Water Bureau, were in the hands of the Blanco Party, and the municipal government was held by Frente Amplio. Thus, the three main parties held some office that was relevant for squatters.

Many squatter leaders made use of this favorable context skillfully managing different political networks at the same time (Álvarez-Rivadulla 2012). They did so in different ways. Some changed parties from the Colorado Party to Frente Amplio once the latter won the municipal government. Others worked with a division of labor with members of the neighborhood association. While one leader, a leftist militant, asked the municipal government for help, another got the water through contacts with the Blanco Party through his own political networks. A recurrent strategy consisted in declaring "we are a-political here," by which what they really meant was that they were hyper-political; this was made clear in another recurrent phrase, "we open our doors to everybody."

Electoral competition constituted a political opportunity that increased squatters' room for agency. Contrary to the portrayal of clientelism as a synonym of manipulation and passiveness, many scholars have shown how poor people's political networks, including clientelism, leave room for agency (Burgwal 1995; Gay 1994; Walton 1998) and even more, for mobilization (Auyero et al. 2009). It is my contention that in contexts of electoral competition there is more room, as I detail in greater depth in the following chapter.

In the same way as in Chile before the dictatorship, when different factions of the left were fighting to win *pobladores'* votes (Handelman 1975; Hipsher 1998; Schneider 1995; Özler 2003), land invasions in general and, in particular, planned invasions spiked in Montevideo during these years. Frente Amplio broadened and sharpened electoral competition, which benefited squatters giving them more elite allies. Nobody wanted to say no to potential voters. The growth of the left in the city and its consolidation in the municipal government altered the incentives of all political actors to support squatters. It is only when the left consolidated itself in the city and nationally that the electoral competition diminished, along with tolerance for new land invasions.

The Leftist Orientation of the Rising Contender in the Electoral Race

Besides the general effect of increased electoral competition, Frente Amplio was not just any political party breaking bipartidism and increasing electoral competition for the poor. It was a leftist party and this had connotations both for politicians and people who influenced land invasions. My fieldwork suggested that, on the one hand, some politicians and militants from Frente Amplio actively promoted land invasions and, on the other, some people assumed that a leftist government was going to be amiable to squatters, especially organized ones. Because of the relevance of this turning point in the history of land squatting in Montevideo, I will zoom in on the relationship between squatters and the left:

Squatters and the Left from the Politicians' Perspective

Politicians may help squatters for strategic reasons. I have found examples of this throughout the cycle of land invasions in Montevideo and from the whole political spectrum. Yet what happened during the first years of the Frente Amplio city government within this party was different. Some helped squatters also for ideological reasons. Once in the city government, there were different perspectives about how to administer the city, and specifically about what to do with those in need. While some promoted centralized city planning, with great control of the expansion of the city—the official position—some explicitly promoted land invasions. For the latter, invading was giving good use to vacant land. It was a sort of *sui generis* land reform.

The clearest exponent of this vision has been Jorge Zabalza, once a member of the *Tupamaros* guerrilla movement.[3] He was imprisoned during the Uruguayan dictatorship, when he was a member of Frente Amplio's *MPP* faction (the most radical faction). The former city councilor and president of the City Council (1995–2000), he is now independent and lives in a squatter settlement in the west of Montevideo. Unlike many elusive references to the role of politicians in squatting, Zabalza spoke to me upfront and proudly about his role:

> I was very much involved with squatter settlements because we [his political faction back then, the MPP] had defined it. We had the idea that it was good that people self-managed their own problems. And the problem of housing was very important and massive around 1987-88 in Montevideo (...). And squatter settlements were the concrete form of that idea of people self-managing themselves. There was something like a peak in which people organized themselves, occupied land, divided the individual plots... all in assemblies. You worked in assembly. You marked the streets, the places for common use like the soup kitchen, or the field for baby-soccer, according to the willingness of each settlement. And then you would start trying to get light, water and so on. (...) I can even today walk around some squatter settlements and find people that remember something like a stellar moment in their lives, in which they felt that they were the main characters, doing things, fighting. (...) But the result was very good, because the figure I read some time ago was that 11% of Montevideo's population is on occupied land.

The centrality of Zabalza in the wave of land invasions around the 1990 peak and during that decade appears in multiple other voices. He is remembered by politicians and squatters as one who "organized land invasions." During my fieldwork, he was one of the most frequently mentioned individuals.

A very active militant from the Socialist Party I interviewed, smiled as he remembered the 1990s in which he helped organize a number of settlements together with Zabalza, despite their political differences. "We divided Montevideo in two"—he tells me remembering that while Zabalza worked more with squatters in the west of Montevideo, he worked more in the eastern periphery of the city. Squatters also remembered Zabalza. He directly helped at least five of the 25 squatter settlements in which I conducted ethnographic fieldwork. When I asked Beatriz, the astonishingly articulate leader of a squatter settlement, why they had settled in 1991 and not earlier or later, she told me:

> Well, we have to acknowledge that Zabalza had started to organize squatter settlements. He would come and have talks with me. He used to come to my house or we would meet somewhere. He had a *comité de base* (local party committee) nearby around 1988-89 and, well, I was involved with them [she voted for the MPP in the last few elections]. And he always gave us guidelines about how to organize ourselves, how to organize people, how processes were going and we had information about which pieces of land where city owned and which were not.

According to Garcé (2006), this support for squatters was part of broader tensions between the official Frente Amplio position and that of the Tupamaros at the beginning of the leftist administration. It was part of the Tupamaros' "insurrectional view," their attempts to radicalize the popular classes, and their contempt for "bourgeois institutions" such as private property. Yet Zabalza and other Tupamaros were not the only ones criticizing the official government position against land invasions as too technocratic and far from people's real needs. I also found some other individual politicians who were city councilors or local councilors in the first Frente Amplio city government who held this vision.

In time, this ideological defense of squatters disappeared within Frente Amplio. The experience of more than 25 years of city government taught everybody that land invasions bring a lot of problems to the administration. This may be related to the decline of land invasions in the last years, the final striking feature of the cycle analyzed here.

Squatters and the Left from the Squatters' Perspective

According to one of the social workers I interviewed, this was "a time of hope" for many, especially for social movements. People with housing needs were not an exception and some also saw an opportunity in the Frente Amplio municipal government. In 1990, and throughout the first two periods of the Frente Amplio administration, there were expectations that a leftist government would be more permissive and generous with squatters and that it would attend to their demands for titling and services, particularly in a context of great deprivation for the urban poor, many of whom could not continue paying rent in the formal city.

For the leader of a squatter settlement that started in 1990, a man of the left himself, his group's land invasion was directly associated with the new Frente Amplio administration. As he remembers it:

> The municipal government of Tabaré [he refers to the first leftist city major, Tabaré Vázquez, later elected president of Uruguay in 2004 and 2014] was in its full peak. There was a very special enthusiasm. They supported the people who approached the city government with a good project, people that wanted to do things the right way.

This perception that if they were "doing things the right way" the municipal government was going to be on their side, was present in many of my interviews with the early residents of invasions of that first period of leftist city government. By that, they meant such things as being organized as a group, planning the invasion, and only including people who were going to live in the neighborhood (rather than speculators). Another leader of a land invasion from 1993 remembers:

> The fact that the left won the municipal government generated in one way or another conditions in the sense that people a priori had some guarantees of not being repressed, some framework for negotiation that maybe they wouldn't have with other governments. So, I think that's why in those years the process of land squatting accelerated, and I think that was a good thing.

In fact, those expectations were more than fulfilled for him and other young friends from the Communist Party who organized this particular land invasion. After an initial month of uncertainty, in which the initial group started to clean the abandoned plot, discuss the rules, and select the newcomers among many that came hoping they could squat there, they asked for and were conceded a meeting with the mayor. Given that the plot was privately owned, their goal was to have the municipal government expropriate it so that they could then negotiate directly with the government. Sebastián remembers being a bit scared when he went to that meeting, but it turned out to be better than he could ever have imagined.

> It was a working meeting. Tabaré [Vazquez] received us with a map of the plot that we had squatted and he even told us the plot was bigger than what we had thought. We didn't have accurate information. We just had

> oral information; we didn't have any documents. (…) We asked him if we could accept more people from our waiting list. We agreed and went back with the news that we could increase the family. So, I think that the history of *Youth 14* has been (…) relatively easy. It involved a lot of sacrifice from the people, but that happened everywhere. But we had great advantages. We presented ourselves, our situation and the families' profiles well…we had a survey of the number of kids, I mean…I think in some ways if there was political willingness, those things matter a lot.

Thus, the leftist orientation of the new contender in the electoral competition for the popular vote had an impact not only on the increasing number of land invasions but also, and fundamentally, on the type of land invasions which became increasingly planned.

Decentralization as a Political Opportunity

Following broader Latin American trends, Montevideo entered the 1990s with the left in the city government and a municipal decentralization process (Canel 2010; Chávez and Goldfrank 2004; Goldfrank 2002; Myers and Dietz 2002; Veneziano Esperón 2005). According to the electoral platform that took Frente Amplio into the city administration, decentralization was aimed at bringing the government closer to the citizens, especially the poorest citizens and making it more accountable and efficient. Akin to the new discourses on development, this decentralization program had strong faith in the participation and transformative power of civil society. It consisted of dividing the city into 18 zones, each with its local government (dubbed *Centros Comunales Zonales* (CCZ) or Zonal Community Centers). The original project was resisted by the opposition and, in the end, decentralization ended up being more administrative than political or financial and, thus, far less ambitious than the famous Porto Alegre experience in participatory budgeting (Baiocchi 2005). Still, every CCZ had an executive board and a local council that made suggestions to the mayor about big issues such as spending priorities in the area and some administrative decisions such as small resource allocations within the zone.[4]

The results of decentralization are not written in stone. Some emphasize how its negotiated institutional design "failed to boost civic engagement among city residents because the channels of participation offered did not convince average citizens that their input in public forums would have a significant impact on governmental decisions" (Goldfrank 2002: 51). Others, in contrast, emphasize the positive effects on participation, particularly in changing traditional clientelistic relationships with the municipal government into more accountable ones (Canel 2010; Veneziano Esperón 2005). Some, in turn, highlight how decentralization served Frente Amplio electorally both by allowing it to enter into poor areas of the city and by raising its credibility as a governing party rather than only as an opposition party (Luna 2007). Most analysts, however, stress the role of decentralization in bringing the city government closer to citizens.

This institutional opening was particularly relevant for squatters. Many of the squatter leaders of planned invasions mentioned the CCZ or the local executive (Junta Local) when asked about the person or institution that helped them the most. The CCZ often became the first actor they called once they occupied. To a head of the local executive (Secretaria de la Junta Local) of the La Teja neighborhood, what distinguished the land invasions of the 1990s was their willingness to legalize and guarantee land titling as well as their negotiating attitude. They saw the state, and particularly the local state, as an ally.

> [Land invasions during the nineties] were like the García Márquez story, "a foretold death." Normally you knew there was going to be an invasion and normally you knew more or less where. There was a negotiating attitude from the beginning. Ok, we occupy here but we call the Junta so they come and legitimize our land invasion saying we are all workers from x place and we want to negotiate to get this plot or, if this one is not available, then we can see which one is. The attitude, more than anything, was to occupy and to accelerate bureaucratic times.

Many squatters, especially those established in municipally owned land, rapidly incorporated themselves into the proposed participatory mechanisms as city councilors or members of local land or health committees. Through that participation, they obtained quicker access to information and services for their neighborhood. But that process was not easy. As Canel (2010) vividly describes, older residents of impoverished areas of the city were not always happy to have squatters in their neighborhoods and city councils. They perceived them as an invasion, as a threat to their working, cohesive, and militant culture, as people with different values and traditions who do not even pay taxes, which they perceive as unfair. At the same time, local governments could never fulfill the hyperinflation of demands based on the multiple severe needs of an increasing number of squatters. This was frustrating for squatters and it discouraged their participation.

Decentralization constituted a particular type of institutional opening, one that promoted mobilization at neighborhood level. Frente Amplio's decentralization project included a pedagogical branch, incarnated by an army of social workers, which aimed at generating more participatory local decisions. Electing representatives, holding frequent meetings, taking minutes, listening to everybody, and prioritizing needs considering other equally needy communities were part of the learning experience. Although some squatter leaders of planned invasions had previous experience participating in trade unions, neighborhood associations, the cooperative housing movement, or other types of collective action, for many squatters participation in their neighborhood associations, local councils or committees was their first experience of taking part in politics. Decentralization was, for them, a school of grassroots political participation and squatting in general, a politicizing experience.[5]

Squatters learned about the convenience of collective and formal organization at neighborhood level through interaction with other institutions. As one squatter leader put it:

> Having legal personality enables us to sign agreements with INAME [National Institute for Childhood] to create a daycare center. Besides, you can also be helped by INDA [National Institute for Nourishing]. We can sign contracts and sign everything...you can even organize festivals. Because all the institutions require that you have legal personality. Besides, it gives a much more serious image to the neighborhood. By having it, you can represent the neighborhood in a different way.

For many state officials, being organized meant that a squatter settlement was disciplined and deserving. In an interview in 1998, the first director of the mainly IADB funded government program for titling and upgrading in informal neighborhoods, told me:

> We have an implicit slogan: "we are going to help those that want to be helped". (...) The number of people that ask for help is so huge, that we cannot start searching for more demands (...). For a project to be sustainable it is necessary to have the will of the population and you know there are great conflicts within squatter settlements. In one of them, there was an empty space to build a common building for meetings and so on, and a

> person took it and built a grocery store there. How this can happen? How can it be that we say "we are going to build your streets, we are going to give you this and that" and there are still people that resist or do not cooperate?

Institutions require a level of organization that is difficult to reach in a neighborhood of "strangers" (Roberts 1973). What strikes this official as unbelievable is the most common situation in squatter settlements: problems with organization and enforcement of collective norms among a population of newcomers that also rotates a lot. The most repeatedly heard phrase among leaders is, "people do not participate" and this is corresponded by mistrust by the nonleaders, apathy, or simple lack of time. Thus, multiple agencies gave squatters a consistent message about the benefits of disciplined participation at the local level which fits in with the broader global change in the development discourse which replaces the state for civil society as an agent of development (Hyden 1997).

Yet, as Roberts and Portes (2006) point out in their analysis of fin de siècle urban participation in Latin America, decentralization can be a double-edged sword in the sense that by encouraging local participation, it may hinder scaling up; that is, taking the fights to broader territorial levels by coordinating with others. There was never a citywide movement of squatters in Montevideo. Most organization has been constrained at settlement level, with some interesting exceptions. In at least three cases, there has been coordination among various squatter settlements within decentralized areas.[6]

Finally, it is important to mention that the opportunities for decentralization opened for squatters varied across the city. In his careful study of Montevideo's decentralization, Canel (2010) shows how the local experiences of decentralization were quite different depending on each of the associational cultures of the 18 areas, the impact of socioeconomic conditions on the populations' willingness to organize and participate in community initiatives, and the ability of individual local officials to nurture trusting and cooperative relations with community activists. By looking at the spatial distribution of squatter settlements in Montevideo, we start to see a nonrandom pattern. Planned land invasions are clustered in the deindustrialized historically working-class neighborhoods of the west of the city, whereas in the traditionally poorer northeast, there are mostly accretion invasions. While the local government in the *Cerro* neighborhood had to negotiate with many organized invasions, the local government of the 11th zone had to assist a growing number of accretion squatters with excruciating needs.

A traditionally working-class and increasingly deprived area of the city surprised me for its capacity to care for public land, for its few land invasions, and for its experience in establishing cooperatives as an alternative for people with housing needs. When a group of young neighbors from Brandi—one of the neighborhoods of the 13th Zone—invaded the neighborhood soccer field and started to divide the plot and build tents, neighbors reacted quickly. They called the local authorities, who, despite it being a weekend, acted rapidly enough to evict the people in less than 48 h. A former city councilor remembers this event with pride. The city council mediation avoided both the invasion and a violent eviction.[7] Not surprisingly, it is this area of the *Peñarol* neighborhood and surroundings that has best been adapted to decentralization according to Canel (2010). Local associations, he argues, had a greater experience in negotiating with the state through different political networks and in conflict resolution, than other areas of the city.

Variation Depending on the Neighborhood and the Leader'S Resources

The effect of the two political opportunities that I have mentioned, increased electoral competition for the urban poor and the novel decentralization program, did not affect all squatters in the same way. Those with more political networks and other resources such as organizational cultures, pragmatic and recursive leaders, or relatively less poverty were better able to seize those opportunities and transform them into collective goods for their neighborhoods. They did so by skillfully using a variety of strategies, most of them to reach the state, and others to organize themselves internally.

Many have emphasized the role of organizational dynamics on collective action, but the perspective that I find most useful is the political process perspective because it puts them into dialog with broader contextual political factors (McAdam 1982; McAdam et al. 1996; Tilly 1978). Other scholars have described differential strategies and organizational types for squatters in the same city and time. Gay (1994) and Stokes (1996), for example, divide squatters into clientelistic and rebellious for Rio and Lima, respectively. More recently, Dosh (2010) shows us, by comparing squatter settlements in Lima and Quito, how some neighborhood organizations change strategies throughout their lives, adjusting themselves to different contexts choosing between conformist, militant, bootstrap, or rogue strategies to obtain neighborhood services, while others stay tied to one of these types. Those that are more flexible, he argues, are generally the most successful. This finding resonates with what I found in Montevideo. Yet, we need to add one more possibility, which is the non- or minimal use of strategies to obtain neighborhood services, as in the case of many accretion invasions.

Even though accretion invasions were the most common type of invasions during and before the dictatorship, and planned invasions were the most common after the democratic opening, accretion invasions kept growing in times of high electoral competition and decentralization. This puzzle can only be solved by looking at the settlements' differential resources. For example, around 1990, two very different settlements started up in the west of the city. One, *Victoria Nuevo*, was an accretion invasion that started to grow out of the sons and daughters of nearby old-time cantegriles. Located next to a polluted stream, piles of garbage surround very precarious houses. When I asked a local official about this neighborhood, she had a hard time identifying it. These squatters, despite settling on a municipally owned plot, did not have a history of any kind of relationship with the local government. They did not have a neighborhood organization or representatives to the local council, and they remained invisible for the most part.

The other, *Nuevo Amanecer*, had a very different story. It was started by a group of people that knew each other from their militancy in unions and that could not sustain the cost of living in the city any longer. Through political networks with city councilors, they found out about a state-owned plot in the El Cerro neighborhood that they could occupy, the councilors warned, as long as they did it in an organized way. They occupied only after having planned every detail. They were going to function like a cooperative (some had experience in the cooperative housing movement). Instead of each individual only looking after his or her own house, a number of the tasks were going to be collectively operated. They received no eviction threat and quickly started to do what Luis, one of the founders and still leader of the neighborhood association, describes as the "real hard work." Through direct petitioning, they were able to access water and electricity services. They also obtained building materials from the recently inaugurated leftist municipal administration.

Luis started to participate in the recent decentralization program as a city councilor. Yet, Luis' contacts were not enough to build roads. They needed contacts with the national government. Another neighbor, from the Colorado Party—who worked side by side with Luis—brought the Transport Minister to the neighborhood, and he built them the roads. It was through political networks and lobbying that they managed to change their plot from rural land to land that could potentially be developed and eventually entered the regularization program. *Nuevo Amanecer* then became the first settlement to be regularized in the city.

Although *Victoria Nuevo* and *Nuevo Amanecer* emerged at the same time, the latter was much more endowed to seize the opportunities of electoral competition and decentralization. Relatively better off residents, with experience in other social movements and political parties, were able to skillfully use various political networks and the recently opened decentralized spaces of participation in their favor. Yet, as mentioned earlier, they also used other strategies, from self-help to direct petitioning to the state and lobbying. Their success depended on this eclectic combination of strategies.

Variation in the ability to seize political opportunities did not only occur between accretion and planned invasions. Planned invasions also varied in their resources and their spectrum of strategies. More militant organizations, for example, that did not want to establish networks with traditional parties, were less able to seize the opportunities of electoral competition in a context of divided government. In fact, those that only had connections with one political party of any color were not as successful as the more flexible ones.

The End of the Cycle

Since about 2000, land invasions in Montevideo became rare events, almost as rare as before the 1990s.[8] Moreover, the fact that land invasions did not explode with the 2002 Uruguayan economic crisis is rather remarkable. It is, in fact, one of the main reasons behind my hypothesis that land invasions have been fuelled by more than economic hardship. If poverty skyrocketed in 2003 and 2004 reaching 40.9% of Uruguayan households, almost doubling the percentages for the 1990s (Arim and Vigorito 2007), why did land invasions dwindle rather than increase?

One could imagine many factors that could plausibly explain this decline. Perhaps the most obvious one is the simple fact that most mobilization cycles tend to have an inverted U shape. Mobilization does not last forever, but that does not explain why decline happens at specific times. Another simple hypothesis is that vacant land is scarcer now than it was in the past. Yet according to some of the experts I interviewed, there are still many free spaces in the city, especially in the periphery. Something related to the management of that vacant land is perhaps closer to reality. Two changes regarding land management better explain the decline in land invasions: legal changes that made it harder to squat, and increasing government responsibility for vacant urban land. Underlying these two causes, however, is the reduction of electoral competition for the votes of the urban poor. Frente Amplio won those votes at least until I finished writing this book.

Legal Changes

The first change is a recent harshening of property laws that makes evictions more likely and therefore increases the costs of invading.[9] The wave of land invasions that started with the peak in 1989–1990 encountered legislation and weak policing of vacant land that made it difficult for landowners to evict squatters. This slowly changed, first in practice and recently more formally.

First of all, even though property is a constitutional right, the Uruguayan Constitution includes "decent housing" as a right as well (Article 45). Squatters are located in the legal limbo between these two rights. They might have violated property rights but they are exercising their housing rights. More practically, until recently, once an invasion occurred, it was legally and bureaucratically difficult to evict settlers. Unless the owner—either the state or a private owner—filed a report in the first 48 h of the land invasion, the police could not evict settlers. After that time, and especially after settlers had started to build, it became difficult to evict them. After the first 48 h, the owner needed to start a legal eviction trial procedure, which could take a long time. If a year passed and settlers never used violence, they acquired "possession rights." The Uruguayan Civil Code legislates over "possession" by saying "one that has possessed a good [including land] quietly and publicly without interruption acquires the right of possession." Since squatters do not tend to use violence to access a plot,[10] if a year passes because the owner did not realize her plot had been invaded or because after realizing she spent too long in legal paperwork, then squatters have the right to own the plot. Besides, in an eviction trial, squatters could argue a "state of necessity," one of the excuses for breaking the law and being exempt of responsibility in the Uruguayan Criminal Code. Defined as a situation in which the person is acting "to defend her life, physical integrity, freedom, honor or patrimony," the "state of necessity" was argued for by lawyers and judges who defended squatters in eviction cases.

During my fieldwork, I found these legal interstices reflected in squatters' practices. To mention just some examples, when asked whether they thought they were breaking the law when they squatted, most residents answered "no." Some referred to their right to housing, such as a woman who argued they were not breaking anything "because housing is a right by law," or another resident who was conscious of his going against other people's property but justified it by saying "you feel you are breaking a rule, but you also feel that the rule is wrong"—and he added—"there's also the use value of the plot…before we invaded it, it was a garbage dump." There were also some who did not even understand the question, because they did not perceive the practice of squatting as something outside the ordinary.

Many of the planned land invasions occurred on weekends or holidays. Far from random, the choice of days to invade on responded to their intention of letting 48 h pass without a report, and to start building to make it difficult for the owner to evict them. Even if the police came and wanted to evict them, bureaucratic paperwork made it difficult. As one leader of an invasion on municipal land remembers:

> The municipality came several times with trucks and the police and we entrenched ourselves and often three or four ended up at the police station. I was always among them. (…). They came and wanted to destroy the tents; some of us fought to stop them taking down our houses and some of us went to the police station. They put us in the waiting room, because someone had to go and sign a report saying that we were intruders. Given that sometimes nobody went and 12, 24 and even 48 h passed, the captain started asking himself what to do with us. Without somebody filing a report, they could not send us to a judge. And we fought because… what was the solution?

Politicians, in turn, remember being constrained by the legal procedures. For example, when I asked the current Housing Minister, Mariano Arana, and former Montevideo mayor for two periods (1995–2004), what they used to do when they knew of a new land invasion, he said:

> We tried to avoid it, but it wasn't easy. If they were organized, it wasn't easy. Besides…legislation…. You had to be previously informed to be able to proceed in the first 24-48 h. After that, eviction was difficult.

Some lawyers and judges helped squatters by judging squatting under the realm of civil rights rather than for the crime of usurpation, and arguing the mentioned state of necessity. Yet, this favorable situation for squatters has changed. According to Helios Sarthou—a lawyer who has helped many squatters with legal advice, who is also a former senator and representative for Frente Amplio, and who I interviewed because his name kept appearing in my fieldwork—since about the year 2000, it has been more difficult to defend occupations of land, buildings, or individual houses. He pointed out two different moments in the legality of squatting.

> What makes the difference? I remember it perfectly. It was an instruction they gave to all attorneys. And it coincides with the government of Jorge Battle [president from 1999 to 2004, belonging to the *Colorado* party]. Attorneys started to prosecute squatters with an absolute insensitivity to their social condition. They give them 48 h [to evict] (…) Until this decision, which was made in the political sphere and reflected itself in the attorneys' decisions, we had room for judicial debate, for invoking the "state of necessity" which is true…What more "state of necessity" is there than a person being left on the street from night to morning and has to occupy somewhere? There's such insensitivity.[11]

This perceived harshening of the legal procedures against squatters, crystallized recently with a 2007 reform to the Criminal Code. A new law not only makes it easier to denounce cases of property *usurpation* but also broadens what is considered usurpation. Whereas before only a judge could denounce usurpation in the first 48 h of it happening, now any witness can, anytime. Also, while previously only clandestine or violent invasions were considered usurpation cases, now any invasion of property, even if it occurs during the day and without any use of force, is considered usurpation of someone else's property and therefore a crime. This new law, originally intended for invasions of houses in the prestigious *Punta del Este* seaside resort, has in practice also affected the land invasions studied here.[12]

In sum, the legal interstices on which squatters could rely to invade a plot without being evicted have shrunk significantly. However, besides the changes in the legal management of land, I believe that the political management of the land has also changed. This constitutes the second and last hypothesis for the recent decline in the number of land invasions.

Increasing Government Responsibility for the Land

Another important change was the government and ordinary citizens' increasing responsibility for vacant land. A new squatter settlement is a problem for the city government, which has to spend money, taking services to remote places. Helping them now will probably bring problems later. Besides, when vacant land is perceived by citizens as an important space, it becomes more likely that they denounce its invasion quickly and that eviction occurs. I will illustrate these two ideas with two examples.

The case of the *El Cambio* land invasion illustrates the increasing awareness of the city government, and of the Frente Amplio government in particular, that helping squatters can be problematic. This invasion occurred in October 2004, right before the election that put the leftist coalition in the national government for the first time in Uruguayan history. In fact, the invasion was named after Frente Amplio's campaign that year: El Cambio (The Change). Located in one of the areas of the city with the largest number of land invasions, El Cerro, with a tradition of working-class organization and with a permissive local government, the squatters of El Cambio were not evicted immediately. Yet, in contrast to what happened to most land invasions in this area, after a period of hesitation and after a change in local authorities, the local council this time decided to oppose this invasion. Moreover, it wrote a formal declaration opposing any new land invasion in the area.

This case marks the beginning of a new stage in Frente Amplio's city government. The case of an eviction in 2011 described in Chap. 3 shows that this stage persists even today. Perhaps because of the responsibility or the learning gained over the 25 years of being in charge of the city government, or perhaps because of the leverage gained by also winning the national government for the first time, the leftist administration is working hard to avoid new land invasions, even if that disappoints part of its constituency. As one of the former local authorities of the El Cerro local council told me when I asked him about this specific event: "We made many mistakes. It's impossible to govern without experience. Governing means knowing, understanding, and we used to make many stupid mistakes."

In sum, the responsibility for and the policing of vacant land has increased both by local governments and citizens and this might explain at least part of the recent decline in the number of land invasions in Montevideo. However, it is important to point out that this only happened once the electoral competition for popular votes decreased in the city.

Concluding Remarks

Drawing from this case and going beyond it, this study contributes to the literature on contentious politics in at least three ways. First, it suggests an interactive relationship between political opportunities and hardships or grievances, rather than an additive or competitive one. The idea is that political opportunities constrain and enhance/moderate hardships but do not tend to be the sole cause of mobilizations. Second, these findings suggest that political opportunities are as important for Latin American mobilization, as they have been proven to be for wealthier contexts. Even for the most aggrieved and relatively loosely organized, politics do matter in their participation in collective action. Finally, by delving deeply into the case and the actors involved, focusing on squatters, politicians, and state officials, it shows specifically how political opportunities matter. In particular, it shows the specific mechanisms through which democracy mattered: the leftist orientation of the city government, the decentralization policy implemented by the leftist coalition after assuming the municipal government in 1990, and an increased electoral competition for the urban poor. The last and following chapter focuses on these latter mechanisms showing exactly how electoral competition mattered for planned land invasion through political brokerage and multiple political networks.

Notes

1. This is a series calculated by a realtor magazine (Propiedades). It is the gap between current renting prices (constrained by the lease) and the new ones. When that gap is large, the possibilities of old renters to renew a lease is low, indicating problems in the renting/housing market.
2. (See for instance: Auyero 2000; Burgwal 1995; Cornelius 1977; Gay 1994; Gilbert 1994; Merklen 1997; Portes and Walton 1976; Stokes 1991).
3. This urban guerrilla movement, active in Uruguay in the 1960s and 1970s, was also known as MLN (*Movimiento de Liberación Nacional* or National Liberation Movement). When, after the dictatorship, they

entered into Frente Amplio as an electoral force, they formed a coalition with other groups and changed their name to MPP (*Movimiento de Participación Popular* or Popular Participation Movement).

4. More recently, in 2009, and following a national legislation, the decentralization structure became more complex. Besides the CCZs, eight municipalities were created, each with elected local authorities including a local mayor. It remains to be seen how this process is altering local and particularly squatters' politics.
5. The impact of decentralization on democratizing neighborhood associations was by no means limited to squatter settlements. In her census of Montevideo's neighborhood associations a year after decentralization had been implemented, González finds that, in comparison to her previous census during the *Colorado* city administration right after democratization (Gonzalez 1989), "there were higher percentages of associations that held regular meetings, that elected their leaders, that held meetings in public places, that applied for legal status, and that had regular contact with other organizations in their area" (Goldfrank 2002: 71–72).
6. For example: *Comisión de Tierras* in the CCZ 17, *Coordinadora de Asentamientos* in the CCZ 9, *Coordinadora de Asentamientos* CCZ 12. I interviewed members of these three umbrella organizations of squatters. None of them was actively meeting at the moment of my fieldwork. All interviewees explained how hard it is to coordinate actions. In general, coordinating efforts have been organized from above, from the municipal government. To be fair, however, in the case of the CCZ 17 (Cerro neighborhood), the committee preceded decentralization.
7. Interview with Delia Rodriguez, city councilor from the Socialist Party from 2000 to 2005 and later vice-director of the Program for the Integration of Squatter Settlements (PIAI).
8. To add to the graphical representations of the cycle, the average yearly number of land invasions per decade is perhaps enlightening: 0.4 land invasions per year for the 1950–1959 period; 0.9 for 1960–1969; 2.8 for 1970–1979; 5 for 1980–1989; 14.6 for 1990–1999; and 3.4 for 2000–2004.
9. The literature on Land Economics emphasizes the importance of the costs of squatting for the likelihood of people doing so. The probability of eviction increases those costs. For an economic analysis of land invasions for the Uruguayan case, see: (Amarante and Caffera 2003). Unfortunately, the authors did not have the data to test their model, but they suggest interesting avenues for analysis.
10. Since squatters take over empty plots they do not need to use violence. During my fieldwork, some squatters emphasized that they had not even broken the wire fence, which can be legally considered violent usurpation

of another's property. None of my informants in the 25 cases I studied more in depth, recalled deaths or injuries in the process of squatting nor did I find any reports of deaths or injuries in the Uruguayan press. The most hostile situations were those in which the police appeared at the invasion site. In 8 out of the 25 cases, I found a police presence at the invasion. These were all planned invasions. In five of these cases, the police came and held a group for some hours and then freed them, leaving the issue to a judge. Sometimes, a police officer stayed at the invasion site for weeks or months to prevent more squatters from joining. But squatters tend to remember a police presence as threatening ("they came with their clubs"), but only two of the stories were traumatic. In one case, a squatter remembers resisting the police officers trying to destroy their tents. In another case, squatters remember officers and municipal staff besieging the group of early settlers to prevent their building or leaving until authorities came up with a solution to the situation. One of these squatters remembers that if you dared to leave the seized plot, the police would beat you. She was pregnant and with two children at the time, and her friends would come and bring her milk and diapers. When another organized group invaded a plot owned by the navy, thinking it was an abandoned private plot, the military reacted immediately. As one leader remembers, "It was a very harsh eviction. It was a military owned plot so the codes there were military codes. People were shocked but, in reality, the procedure was not something unexpected if you consider we were invading the plot, you know? But yes, they besieged the area with navy trucks in the main roads, and marines entered with dogs and clubs. There was no chance of dialog." Even so, no one spoke of injury. The group left the plot without resisting but got together at a nearby bus station and planned the invasion of another plot the following morning.

11. Besides Dr. *Sarthou* I interviewed another two lawyers who have helped squatters with legal advice. Dr. *Sarthou* was the most frequently mentioned among residents, however. In two neighborhoods, squatters told me he helped them directly. In one case, he gave advice to one of the leaders when she got notified that she and her family were going to be evicted. She was from his same political party and faction and he was a representative at the time. In a different case, one of the leaders told me that they had invited all political parties to an assembly when they settled and that *Sarthou* had come and advised them to divide the plots and leave ample streets so that they could get an early state regularization since, even though they were on private land, the owner owed too much money to the state. "He gave us the strength—this leader remembers—to build houses with solid materials and so people started building." *Sarthou* was a senator then. In two other oral histories, he appeared as someone who helped squatters in general but

not them in particular. Finally, the day I interviewed him, while waiting in the very old law office in the center of Montevideo, I noticed something curious. Hanging from the faded walls of the tiny waiting room, there were lots of brass plaques from different unions or groups of workers thanking him. There was one little plaque thanking Dr. *Sarthou* "for his selfless work for the neighbors of the *19 de Abril* neighborhood," a squatter settlement that started in 1990, the year of the greatest peak.

12. Law No. 18116, which substitutes Article 354 of the Criminal Code, approved unanimously by all legislators on April 10, 2007. It was a change triggered by some occupations of houses in the luxurious seaside resort *Punta del Este*. Since these houses tend to be used only over the summer and remain empty the rest of the year, they are difficult for owners to police. (The old and new texts as well as the justification of the project and the discussions in both chambers are available at www.parlamento.gub.uy). Although the law states the usurpation happening in a seaside resort as an aggravating factor, it technically applies to the entire country. Thus, it applies to invasions such as those for squatting, for cooperative housing building, or for production by rural workers. Because of this, the law has received criticism from social movements and some sectors of the left. In an article published by FUCVAM, the movement for cooperative housing, titled "Will there be land for the poor?" they severely criticize the law by pointing out its consequences, "criminalizing land invasions of workers that are just using a survival strategy under conditions of gradual de-industrialization and recent cyclical crisis and had to choose between eating or paying rent." They call for looking at the causes of land invasions rather than prosecuting them (Accessed May 26, 2007 http://www.fucvam.org.uy). Apparently, these dissident voices have been heard since legislators from the *Frente Amplio* have developed a project to modify this article again going back to considering it usurpation only if it is violent and clandestine and allowing only owners, or people that prove to be related to them, to report it. This, in turn, has received criticism from the opposition, but the issue has not been formally treated in the legislature.

References

Almeida, P. (2010). Social movement partyism: Collective action and oppositional political parties. In N. Van Dyke & H. J. McCammon (Eds.), *Strategic alliances: Coalition building and social movements*. Minneapolis: University of Minnesota Press.

Álvarez-Rivadulla, M. J. (2000). *Asentamientos irregulares montevideanos: la desafiliación resistida* (p. 4). Serie Monitor Social del Uruguay: Documento de Trabajo del IPES.

Álvarez-Rivadulla, M. J. (2012). Clientelism or something else? Squatter's politics in Montevideo. *Latin American Politics & Society, 54*(1), 37–63.

Álvarez-Rivadulla, M. J. (2015). Squatters and politics in Montevideo at the turn of the century. *Handbook of social movements across Latin America* (pp. 205–220). Springer.

Álvarez-Rivadulla, M. J. (2017). The weakness of symbolic boundaries. Handling exclusion among Montevideo's Squatters. *International Journal of Urban and Regional Research.*

Amarante, V., & Caffera, M. (2003). Los factores determinantes de la formación de asentamientos irregulares. Un análisis económico. *Revista de la Facultad de Ciencias Empresariales y Economía, Universidad de Montevideo, 2*, 61–95.

Arim, R., & Vigorito, A. (2007). *Un análisis multidimensional de la pobreza en Uruguay. 1991–2005.* Documentos de Trabajo Instituto de Economía. Montevideo. Retrieved from http://www.iecon.ccee.edu.uy/publicaciones/DT10-06.pdf.

Auyero, J. (2000). The Logic of clientelism in Argentina: An ethnographic account. *Latin American Research Review, 35*(3), 55–81.

Auyero, J., Lapegna, P., & Poma, F. Page. (2009). Patronage politics and contentious collective action: A recursive relationship. *Latin American Politics & Society, 51*(3), 1–31.

Baiocchi, G. (2005). *Militants and citizens: The politics of participatory democracy in Porto Alegre.* Stanford, CA: Stanford University Press.

Burgwal, G. (1995). *Struggle of the poor: Neighborhood organization and clientelist practice in a Quito Squatter Settlement.* Amsterdam: CEDLA.

Canel, E. (2010). *Barrio democracy in Latin America. Participatory decentralization and community activism in Montevideo.* University Park: The Pennsylvania State University Press.

Cecilio, M. (1997). Relevamiento de Asentamientos Irregulares de Montevideo *Asentamientos Irregulares.* Montevideo: Ministerio de Ordenamiento Territorial y Medio Ambiente. Comisión para la normalización de asentamientos irregulares.

Cecilio, M., Couriel, J., Spallanzani, M., Bombaci, O., & Medina, M. (1999). *La gestión urbana en la generación de los tejidos residenciales de la periferia de Montevideo: areas acupadas por los sectores de población de bajos y medios ingresos.* Montevideo, Uruguay: Universidad de la República, Facultad de Arquitectura.

Chávez, D., & Goldfrank, B. (Eds.). (2004). *La izquierda en la ciudad.* Amsterdam Transnational Institute: Participación en los gobiernos locales de América Latina.

Cornelius, W. A. (1977). Leaders, followers, and official patrons in Urban Mexico. In S. W. Schmidt, L. Guasti, C. H. Lande, & J. Scott (Eds.), *Friends, followers, and factions. A reader in political clientelism.* Berkeley: University of California Press.

Dosh, P. (2010). *Demanding the land: Urban popular movements in Peru and Ecuador, 1990–2005* (D. Collier Ed. Vol. Ph.D). State College: Pennsylvania State University Press.

Filgueira, F., Garcé, A., Ramos, C., & Yaffé, J. (2003). Los dos ciclos del Estado uruguayo en el siglo XX. In I. D. C. Política (Ed.), *El Uruguay del siglo XX. La Política*. Montevideo Banda Oriental.

Garcé, A. (2006). *Donde hubo fuego: el proceso de adaptación del MLN-Tupamaros a la legalidad y a la competencia electoral (1985–2004)*. Montevideo.

Gay, R. (1994). *Popular organization and democracy in Rio de Janeiro. A tale of two Favelas*. Philadelphia: Temple University Press.

Gilbert, A. (1994). *The Latin American city*. London: The Latin America Bureau.

Goldfrank, B. (2002). The fragile flower of local democracy: A case study of decentralization/participation in Montevideo. *Politics and Society, 30*(1), 51–83.

Gonzalez, M. (1989). *Las comisiones vecinales en el departamento de Montevideo: Elementos para su discusión a partir de los resultados de una encuesta*. Montevideo: CIESU.

Handelman, H. (1975). The political mobilization of Urban Squatter Settlements. Santiago's recent experience and its implications for urban research. *Latin American Research Review, 10*(2), 35–72.

Hipsher, P. L. (1998). Democratic transitions and social movement outcomes: The Chilean Shantytown Dweller's Movement in comparative perspective. In M. G. Giugni, D. McAdam, & C. Tilly (Eds.), *From contention to democracy*. Boston: Rowman & Littlefield.

Hyden, G. (1997). Civil society, social capital, and development: Dissection of a complex discourse. *Studies in Comparative International Development, 32*(1), 3–30.

INTEC. (1995). *Relevamiento de Asentimientos Irregulares de Montevideo*. Retrieved from Montevideo.

Kaztman, R. (2001). Seducidos y abandonados: el aislamiento social de los pobres urbanos *Revista de la CEPAL, 75*, 171–189.

Kaztman, R., Corbo, G., Filgueira, F., Furtado, M., Gelber, D., Retamoso, A., & Rodriguez, F. (2004). *La ciudad fragmentada: mercado, territorio y marginalidad en Montevideo*. Paper presented at the Latin American Urbanization in the Late 20th Century: A Comparative Study.

Luna, J. P. (2006). *Programmatic and non-programmatic party-voter linkages in two institutionalized party systems: Chile and Uruguay in comparative perspective*. Ph.D. dissertation. University of North Carolina, Chapel Hill.

Luna, J. P. (2007). Frente Amplio and the crafting of a social democratic alternative in Uruguay. *Latin American Politics and Society, 49*(4).

McAdam, D. (1982). *Political process and the development of Black insurgency, 1930–1970*. Chicago: University of Chicago Press.

McAdam, D., McCarthy, J., & Zald, M. N. (1996). *Comparative perspectives on social movements: Political opportunities, mobilizing structures and cultural framings*. New York: Cambridge University Press.

Merklen, D. (1997). Organización comunitaria y práctica política. Las ocupaciones de tierras en el conurbano de Buenos Aires. *Nueva Sociedad 149*(Mayo-Junio), 162–177.

Mieres, P. (1988). *Cómo Votan los Uruguayos*. Montevideo: CLAEH & Banda Oriental.

Mieres, P. (1994). *Desobediencia y Lealtad. El voto en el Uruguay de fin de Siglo*. Montevideo: Fin de Siglo.

Moreira, C. (2005). El voto moderno y el voto clasista revisado: explicando el desempeño electoral de la izquierda en las elecciones de 2004 en Uruguay. In D. Buquet (Ed.), *Las Claves del Cambio*. Montevideo: Banda Oriental-Instituto de Ciencia Política.

Myers, D. J., & Dietz, H. A. (Eds.). (2002). *Capital city politics in Latin America*. Boulder: Lynne Rienner.

Nahoum, B. (2002). *Los asentamientos irregulares, entre prevenir y curar*. Montevideo: Paper presented at the Primeras jornadas uruguayas de asentamientos informales.

Özler, S. I. (2003). *Squatters stand up: Political institutions and demand making in the developing world*. (Ph.D.), University of California, Los Angeles.

Panizza, F., & Pérez Piera, A. (1988). *Estado Y Sociedad*. Montevideo: FESUR.

Portes, A., & Walton, J. (1976). *Urban Latin America*. Austin: University of Texas Press.

Rama, G. (1971). *El Club Político*. Montevideo: ARCA.

Roberts, B. (1973). *Organizing strangers: Poor families in Guatemala City*. Austin: University of Texas Press.

Roberts, B., & Portes, A. (2006). Coping with the free market city. Collective action in Six Latin American cities at the end of the twentieth century. *Latin American Research Review, 41*(2), 57–83.

Schneider, C. L. (1995). *Shantytown protest in Pinochet's Chile*. Philadelphia: Temple University Press.

Semanario-Voces. (2011). Julio Villamide "No creció el número de asentamientos sino la cantidad de personas que vive en ellos". *Semanario Voces*. Retrieved from http://www.voces.com.uy/entrevistas-1/juliovillamide%25E2%2580%259Cnocrecioelnumerodeasentamientossinolacantidaddepersonasquevivenenellos%25E2%2580%259D.

Stokes, S. (1991). Politics and Latin America's Urban poor: Reflections from a Lima Shantytown. *Latin American Research Review, 26*(2), 75–101.

Stokes, S. (1996). *Clients and radicals*. [S.l.]: [s.n.].

Tarrow, S. (1989). *Democracy and disorder*. Oxford: Clarendon Press.

Tilly, C. (1978). *From mobilization to revolution*. Reading: Addison-Wesley.

Veneziano Esperón, A. (2005). *Reflexiones sobre una reforma orientada al ciudadano. La descentralización participativa de Montevideo*. Madrid: Instituto Nacional de Administración Pública.

Viana, I., Zuccolini, S., & Casanova, R. (2006). *Mercado de suelo urbano formal-informal*. Montevideo Lincoln Institute of Land Policy-Instituto del Suelo Urbano.

Villamide, J. (s.d.). Crecimiento Imparable. *Revista Propiedades, 183*, 3–5.

Walton, J. (1998). Urban conflict and social movements in poor countries: Theory and evidence of collective action. *International Journal of Urban and Regional Research, 22*(3), 460–481.

CHAPTER 6

Politics on the Ground

The white walls of the modest yet solidly built house in the middle of a squatter neighborhood in Montevideo, where I interviewed Manuel Gómez, were lined with all sorts of trophies he delighted in showing me one by one. In the same way as we all tend to fill our living rooms with pictures of our loved ones, our favorite places, and maybe a collection of ornaments or paintings that allow a glimpse at our tastes and lifestyle, this squatter community leader had his own very peculiar gallery. The centerpiece seemed to be a picture of Manuel with his arms around Tabaré Vazquez, former Montevideo mayor and later Uruguayan president for the leftist coalition *Frente Amplio;* it was surrounded by a host of newspaper clippings of articles about the neighborhood and a picture of Mario Carminatti, once candidate for city mayor from the traditional center-right *Colorado* Party. There was another picture of Manuel, this time with Jorge Zabalza, a former city councilor, who lives in a squatter settlement, politically located to the left of the left, once a member of the *Tupamaros* guerrilla movement, and who has helped and promoted the creation of many settlements in the city. Perhaps the most surprising trophy of all, was a letter in a golden frame that Manuel climbed up a chair to take down and show me. Signed by the then President Julio María Sanguinetti, from the Colorado Party, it congratulated Manuel for the "thriving human group that moves this neighborhood ahead." I was surprised by the celebrity of the sender of course, but I was also puzzled by the paradox of Manuel—about whom I had repeatedly heard rumors of fraudulent transactions—being congratulated for building a neighborhood considered irregular for its location on a rural area where the Montevideo Municipal Government forbids urbanization.[1]

M.J. Álvarez-Rivadulla, *Squatters and the Politics of Marginality in Uruguay*, Latin American Political Economy, DOI 10.1007/978-3-319-54534-9_6

More than the meaning of each particular letter, article, or picture described in these field notes, what was even more curious was their combination in the same place. It was not mere chance. Just as Manuel saved each of these objects, I saved this vignette because I remember it as one of those moments in ethnographic fieldwork when suddenly everything falls into place, micro windows through which you can see the bigger picture, seconds that reveal what months of research had hidden not because they are anecdotal but because they synthesize what you have already seen but only as confused and fragmented. A broker's role is to connect, and rather than being fixed, it is relational and mobile. In this case, Manuel played this role most of the time, connecting squatters with the political system and, ultimately, with the state, but party state officials and party members sometimes acted as brokers as well, connecting Manuel to the others or the state.

In an exaggerated manner, this room illustrates one of the mechanisms by which some squatter communities in Montevideo seized political opportunities created at national and municipal levels: brokerage through the strategic use of multiple political networks. As mentioned earlier, opportunities were particularly abundant between 1989 and 2004, years of great competition for the votes of the urban poor in the city periphery and during which the national government was held by one of the two traditional parties and the municipal government belonged to Frente Amplio, the coalition of leftist parties that also won the presidency in 2004 and has been in power ever since. This mechanism consisted in opportunistic face-to-face relationships of squatter leaders with politicians from various factions and parties, as intermediaries to get much-needed state goods, such as water, building materials, electricity, roads, and ultimately, land tenure. Colombian scholars have dubbed this multiple particularistic political networking, *market clientelism,* as opposed to one that is loyal to one political party (Dávila León de Guevara and Delgado 2001; García 2003; Gutiérrez Sanín 1998).

Planned land invasions like this one were deeply embedded in political networks, as developed in the previous chapter. Here, I zoom in on one story that shows how relevant those networks were and how skillful brokers (mainly neighborhood leaders and party members) built and used them and in so doing connected squatters to the state. Through politicians, some squatters reached goods that other squatters without the (right) connections did not.

The study on the ground political networks of the poor in Uruguay has not received the same attention as other cases in the region (Auyero 1999, 2000a, b; Stokes 2005), although, as mentioned in Chap. 2, they are constitutive of Uruguayan politics (Buquet and Piñeiro 2016; Luna 2004; Panizza and Pérez Piera 1988; Rama 1971). Yet, they are relevant not only because they have been overlooked but also because they engage in unsolved debates on the literature on clientelism. Thus, this case shows the richness of a broad definition of face-to-face politics rather than the narrow definition of vote buying or monitorable exchanges, if the goal is to understand on the ground politics. It shows the endurance of face-to-face politics even in modern democracies with shrinking states and increasing accountability. It highlights the material as well as the symbolic exchanges that circulate through political networks. It shows that, under certain conditions such as electoral competition on the one hand and deprivation on the other, politicians and brokers may invest in political networks even if the pay, vote, or favor, respectively, is uncertain. The case also highlights the continuous nature of clientelistic exchanges beyond electoral times. Finally, the case shows that clientelism may coexist with different degrees of agency and mobilization and that both increase when electoral competition is high because this tilts the power balance toward brokers and clients.

Clientelism, a Contested Concept

Political clientelism refers to the particularistic exchange of favors for political support, generally understood as taking place in an unequal relationship between politicians and clients. Although previously believed to identify politics in underdeveloped societies, it has appeared in different contexts, including wealthy democracies. Agreements about the concept finish there. Clientelism means different things to different people, including academics. The kinds of goods are contested. Some consider that clientelism is the exchange of individual goods, while others consider it the exchange of collective goods also. Emphasis on material versus other types of goods, including symbolic goods, also varies. The concept of political support is also contested since, for some, it refers only and specifically to votes while others think of it as including other forms of support such as going to rallies.

Most of these debates can be summarized as an opposition between minimalist and maximalist definitions of clientelism. The minimalist definition considers clientelism a very specific exchange in which a politician or a party offers material benefits in exchange for votes. Recipients are generally individuals or small groups of citizens provided their vote can be monitored (Brusco et al. 2004; Kitschelt and Wilkinson 2007; Medina and Stokes 2007; Stokes 2005). This definition is becoming common wisdom in the political science literature and has the virtue of very clearly defining what it leaves in and what it takes out, although observing the conditionality of the exchange and the monitoring mechanisms is always a challenge. Yet, this definition leaves out many of the political networks observed on the ground, including the ones observed among Montevideo's squatters.

The broader definition, in turn, includes not only the exchange of political support for favors, contingent or not, but also subtler exchanges, i.e., when (often low quality) policy aimed at vulnerable populations is later rewarded electorally and is therefore conceived as a favor rather than a right. Gay calls the former *thick* clientelism and the second, *thin, institutional,* or *implied* clientelism (Gay 1997, 2001). The broader more encompassing definition has the virtue of being adjustable to different contexts and it betters illustrates what I found among squatters and politicians in Montevideo of the late twentieth century. The political networks I observed among squatters and politicians in Montevideo of the late twentieth century fit more precisely to the second broader definition. Thus, I deliberately interchangeably use face-to-face politics, on the ground political networks, particularistic political exchanges, and clientelism. I hereby sacrifice parsimony for depth and validity.

Methods

This chapter is based on the ethnographic fieldwork conducted in Uruguay during 2006 and 2007, as well as on a follow-up during the last national elections in November 2009. In this article, I zoom in on the story of one particular squatter neighborhood, *New Rock,* and its leader. But the analysis is always comparative, with the other settlements that I investigated through the multi-method study that included 25 mini-ethnographies and statistical analysis of the cycle of land invasions in Montevideo from 1947—the date of the first land invasion I could track—to the present. As mentioned in the Introduction and developed in detail in the methodological appendix (Appendix A), the aim of the broader study was to understand the *conditions under which* squatter settlements were more likely to emerge and, from a perspective of mechanisms, to understand *how* squatters had interacted with these conditions to produce (different types of) squatter settlements. I also focus on a mechanism that emerged as crucial in this study: brokerage through multiple political networks.

Fieldwork in *New Rock* included a multiplicity of data. To begin with, I conducted oral histories with some neighborhood referents and tried to reach their founders and leaders as well as ordinary early residents, I walked through the neighborhood taking field notes, filling a neighborhood observation template, and taking pictures. I had previously identified one of the leaders, Manuel, through other interviews. His name turned up in some of the interviews with politicians and officials as did the neighborhood he founded, labeled by some as a fraudulent sale, and by others as an example of planning and organization. I decided to look for him.

To find Manuel, I randomly called people in the phone book with his name and asked if they lived in New Rock until I eventually found him and arranged an interview. The day of the interview, Miriam, another founder, was also there and so I had the chance to ask both of them about the history of the neighborhood. It was Manuel who introduced me to a family of early residents I also interviewed on that long afternoon.

Those oral histories guided me in my search for new interviewees and in crosschecking the stories or considering the same information from another point of view. I interviewed former city councilors from different political parties, social workers, and local authorities at the Local Community Center (CCZ), one of the main directors of the Ministry of Housing, two other local brokers that knew the main New Rock leader, a Cooperative Housing Movement leader, and asked all of them about New Rock and its main leader, Manuel. I also looked at newspaper articles, and managed to gain access to the minutes of the City Council's Special Commission on Squatter Settlements for the day on which they received a group of neighbors from New Rock.

I have used this plentiful information obtained from these sources in several ways (e.g., the date of settlement for the statistical modeling). But for this chapter, I have focused on the strategies used to build the neighborhood, and in particular to contact the state. By carefully reconstructing the genealogy of the settlement and the main leader's political network, I tried to illustrate the most common patterns or mechanisms involved in reaching the state.

Becoming a Neighborhood, Becoming a Broker: The Genealogy of a Flexible Political Network

From the very beginning, New Rock and its main leader, Manuel, our opening character, were embedded in political networks. They became a squatter settlement and a neighborhood leader, respectively, through political networks.[2] Manuel had always lived in the area next to the settlement called *Rock,* where a few clustered poor houses were the only sign of urbanness in the middle of an enormous green area of small family farms, in the northeast of Montevideo. They did not have good electricity, running water, or any other services. They were in the middle of nowhere. According to Manuel, he had "always thought that the way to progress was to bring people in."

The opportunity came, Manuel and another neighborhood representative, Miriam, remember when, in November 1995, "we occupied this plot because FUCVAM [the cooperative housing movement, related to the Socialist Party faction of Frente Amplio] had a group of people evicted from a cooperative and did not know where to put them." They were interested in the plot next to where Manuel and Miriam lived, a plot that had been empty for 30 years, and nobody knew who its owners were. Manuel, who in his own words had always been "just another neighbor," started to turn into the leader of what would later be New Rock.[3]

Unlike the slow reaction that some settlements on public land had experienced, since the land invasion was on private land, the police came immediately and took everybody to the police station. As Manuel recalls it, "The owners appeared immediately (…) but we agreed that they would sell and we would buy." The invaders did not have any money to pay for the land, but Manuel had an idea. He opened a bank account, divided the plot into about 250 small plots, and started receiving people who would pay 2500 Uruguayan pesos each, equivalent to around 200–250 dollars at the time. People did not need to pay the whole sum upfront. Most people paid in small installments, depositing directly into the bank account and giving the receipt to the neighborhood association.

As was true for many other owners of private land in what is considered by the municipality a rural area, this was probably a good deal for the owners of the unproductive land on which New Rock is currently located. Since protected rural areas cannot be subdivided, owners could have only sold the whole plot, for much less than the amount they received from New Rock neighborhood association. How much money was exactly involved in the transaction between the New Rock neighborhood association and the owners remains obscure. Different sources have different numbers, and some accuse Manuel and the others of having kept some money for themselves. Manuel and Miriam deny any profit from the transaction.[4]

The early days of the neighborhood were busy. Much knowledge from the cooperative housing movement was transmitted to the planning of this neighborhood, through the alliance of Manuel with the FUCVAM leaders. Yet, when New Rock was founded, Manuel still belonged to the Colorado Party, which held national office at the time. He had been a Colorado follower since he was young, although he had switched factions within the party because once "they came and got me a job at the municipality." After invading and squatting, he started using his political contacts in the Colorado Party to obtain things for the neighborhood. For instance, he got money to fund a children's soccer team through the then president of the public electricity company, and found help to make the roads with another party friend, the Minister of Public Works. During those years, Manuel founded a workers' cooperative for himself and some other men in the neighborhood who were hired by the Colorado administration to bring water to his and other squatter settlements.

Yet, his loyalty slowly started leaning toward those who helped him create the neighborhood. And he voted for the Socialists in the 1999 election. However, he eventually left the Socialists because of fundamental discrepancies. He considered them too sectarian for his needs:

> What happened? If you said to the Socialists that someone from the Colorado party was coming to bring water [to the neighborhood], they said no, no, no. If you told them someone from the Blanco Party was coming to solve the electricity problem, they said no, no, no. That's how it started. We can be your friends but we need to do the public works. If we don't do them, people are going to start revolutionizing and we need to get the things. If we don't...

Other Frente Amplio factions also showed an early interest in the neighborhood. Manuel remembers the president of the City Council at the time, Jorge Zabalza, defending them at the City Council. (He was one of the characters in the pictures from the opening vignette, who at the time of this interview still belonged to the most radical faction of the leftist coalition, the MPP, and who I had also mentioned in the previous chapter given that he was related to different planned invasions). While speaking about this, Zabalza told me that at the time of the land invasion, the left was divided regarding the settlement. Some thought they should not help because it was built in a forbidden area, there was money involved, and Manuel was building his political career within the Colorado Party through it. "And what *we* thought was that there were more than 400 families solving their housing needs." For him and others in the radical left, squatter settlements were a sort of sui generis land reform that they should support and help organize. Although grateful to Zabalza, Manuel never voted or promoted his faction in the neighborhood. They never offered him anything tangible for the neighborhood.

As already mentioned, in 2004, 2 years before my fieldwork, the national government switched from being held by the Colorado Party to being run by the Frente Amplio. Right before that election, Manuel switched factions, which he proudly showed with a huge sign of the faction's candidates hanging at the entrance to his house. He was actually on that faction's municipal ballot "as filler in the 30th place" he clarifies. According to Manuel, "all types of politicians came here" and he mentions several from the whole political spectrum.

That faction did well in the primary, national, and municipal elections, so once the party was in office, they gave them the vice-presidency and the leadership of the Ministry of Public Works (Although coparticipation among the two traditional parties ended with the Broad Front victory, it continued within the Broad Front among its different factions). At the time when I conducted fieldwork, Manuel's working cooperative had a contract with the Ministry of Public Works. They were building bus stops along some main roads around Montevideo's periphery and nearby areas. Manuel recalls the story of this contract as part of a negotiation to promote his new faction in the neighborhood. In his words, "we work politically with a sector, with the vice-president's. So I went and told him 'if you want me to work for you politically, there are two things we have to think about: first the neighborhood and second, jobs. I can give you credit, but I am not going to work for free'."

Manuel was not the only one switching from the Colorado Party to the Frente Amplio in the neighborhood. Those belonging to his inner circle followed suit.[5] In a long interview with Luis and Betty, a middle-aged couple who have been in the neighborhood almost since its foundation, and who used to be Colorado voters, they said that they also voted for that Frente Amplio faction in the last election, following Manuel. They are both skeptical about politics. As Luis puts it "I don't identify with any party because politicians are all the same." They have had a life of hardship and they do not feel that politicians have helped them much. Yet the one who has helped them—even more than their own families—is Manuel. He was the one who took their disabled child to the hospital, the day he was knocked down by a car, in a truck belonging to the water company for which he was doing some work—again, through his political contacts. Manuel also lent them money to pay for Luis' mother's funeral, since her death found them broke. Once, at Easter, when they could not buy any chocolates for their kids, Manuel came and brought some. He also gave Luis a job in the workers' cooperative he founded. They feel indebted to him. As Betty puts it, "he is always there when you are not ok (…). We matter as people to someone. He cares if something happens to us. That's enough. So in appreciation we … if he asks me for help in a soup kitchen, even if he cannot pay me, I'm there." And when he asked them to vote for his new Frente Amplio faction, they did.

Today, New Rock houses about 3500 people, not counting *New Rock II*, a second nearby neighborhood, also created by Manuel. As shown in the pictures in Fig. 6.1, it is pretty consolidated. Despite still awaiting complete legalization, paved streets, and other improvements, the neighborhood has achieved a lot in a period of about 20 years. Its residents were able to stay on the plot and build in a rural area. They have a bus line that connects them to the city, and a neighborhood kindergarten born of an alliance between the neighborhood association and the municipal government. To achieve all this, Manuel and others in the neighborhood used different strategies; for example, having representatives in the local council. Manuel and other neighbors have been elected as local councilors at the *Centro Comunal Zonal*, one of the 18 local governments into which the city is divided since the Frente Amplio promoted city decentralization (Canel 2010; Chávez and Goldfrank 2004; Goldfrank 2002; Veneziano Esperón 2005).[6] But the most frequently used and effective strategy has undoubtedly been to pull the right strings in Manuel's political networks.

Fig. 6.1 New Rock squatter settlement. Montevideo, 2007. Clockwise from upper left: **a** New Rock's corner with a bakery on the left. Streets are not paved and houses are unfinished but the neighborhood blocks have been carefully planned **b** Neighborhood kindergarten, the result of an association between the Municipal Government and the neighborhood association. **c** Two of the best houses in the neighborhood. All houses are made of solid materials (a necessary condition to stay in the neighborhood) but there is great variation in the quality and completion of the constructions. **d** Very typical image of a squatter settlement street: houses in construction with a pile of bricks or other construction materials outside. For many squatters houses are always slow, ongoing projects which they go back to every time they can save some money or when there is a family need, such as the marriage of a child who will live there

Political Networks in the Mud

The story of this neighborhood speaks to some of the main debates in the literature on nonprogrammatic politics and clientelism in particular.

Enduring Importance of Particularistic Exchanges with Politicians Rather than Disappearance in Modern Democracies

Undoubtedly, this squatter settlement, like other planned settlements in Montevideo, has been deeply embedded in political networks in which, on the one hand, politicians are trying to help by seeking political support and, on the other, squatters are in great need of that help in order to satisfy some of their basic needs. Those settlements with political networks with politicians holding office at some state agency were more successful than the rest, and those with several contacts, across factions and parties, were generally even more successful.

The story of New Rock shows that face-to-face contacts and particularistic exchanges continue to be important for modern Uruguayan politics as the literature has now pointed out repeatedly for other examples (Kitschelt and Wilkinson 2007; Piattoni 2001). Particularistic face-to-face contacts and exchanges were not just tied to traditional politics and destined to disappear with the modernization of political parties and the modern use of the media to spread political messages and attract voters; rather, people still like politicians who come to them and get stuck in. Politicians, in turn, need to obtain more votes and in so doing, face-to-face interactions and exchanges seem to still be effective. Political brokerage is crucial in these relationships and squatter leaders often play that role, connecting the neighborhood with politicians and ultimately the state.

As mentioned earlier, it took some effort and time for Frente Amplio to learn to communicate with leaders from the popular classes, which, like Manuel, were from the more traditional Colorado and Blanco parties. But in a context of electoral competition for the urban poor's votes, some Frente Amplio factions were eventually able to. As one of the leftist politicians involved in the foundation of New Rock told me:

- I used to work with these people. They are very peculiar comrades… they have many codes that I think were never really understood by the left. It takes a lot to understand these codes. But these leaders have served the people in an unconditional manner, but at the same time they have acted as bandits.

  Interviewer—I've heard Manuel switched parties…
- Yes, they were all from the right. This has to do with another debate we had in the left. I always thought being a leftist militant was

> sectarian. And even more so in my generation. You had to smoke a particular brand of cigarettes, wear boots, jeans and have long hair and listen to folk music.... The Beatles were bourgeois. (...)

> [Bringing these leaders to the left] was an arduous job. They were all from the right, but from the right right, anticommunists. And now, they are all leftist militants. This is a great achievement. And it's a product not just of giving them a book to read but of really going and getting stuck in with the people. We were in the land seizure, we worked, we saw, we learned.

The literature on clientelism in Uruguay has highlighted its historical importance (Luna 2004; Panizza and Pérez Piera 1988; Rama 1971) and its current recession, mainly due to state retrenchment and reform (Buquet and Piñeiro 2016; Filgueira et al. 2003; Luna 2006). Recent comparative research has also highlighted the low levels of vote buying in the country (Nickerson 2010). However, my research shows that on the ground political networks are still active among poor voters, particularly, those who live in squatter settlements. The kind of collective goods squatters need such as connections to water or electricity are still available in opposition to the old goods that used to be exchanged through clientelistic networks such as jobs and pensions.

This discussion of the persistence of particularistic networks in politics becomes even more relevant with recent discussions of forbearance (Holland 2017). The state may redistribute by just letting squatters squat. It does not necessarily take traditional goods or services for political networks to survive. Tolerance sometimes becomes a good that politicians may exchange in the hope of receiving political support in exchange or, at least, in the hope of not being electorally punished for repression. In the case of Uruguay, it was clear during the 1990s, that nobody wanted to pay the political cost of eviction. As mentioned earlier, forbearance increases with electoral competition, so even if our states are smaller and more accountable now, forbearance gives politicians some degrees of maneuver.

Now that that Frente Amplio has held national and municipal power since 2004 in Montevideo, it becomes relevant to ask what is likely to happen with these networks. The party has always criticized traditional parties' clientelistic practices. Yet, as we have seen, some members and some factions learned to play the game. Many questions arise. Will on the ground political networks end now that there is less competition for the urban poor in Montevideo? Or will they become active again after this period of economic bonanza? Will Frente Amplio develop a hegemonic machine similar to the Peronist one (Auyero 2000b; Levitsky 2003) in order to stay in power? Or will the strong fight between factions in the leftist coalition reproduce the old fight among parties? The future is uncertain but promises an interesting case to keep following particularistic political networks.

The Symbolic Aspects of Clientelism Rather than Its Exclusive Focus on Instrumental Exchanges

Far from being a merely instrumental relationship, face-to-face on the ground politics has a strong symbolic content. Manuel has achieved many more or less tangible goods for the neighborhood though his political networks, from an implicit permit to build a neighborhood in a rural area to obtaining roads, water, electricity, and other services for the neighborhood. He has also used his networks to get jobs for himself and for some of his neighbors. However, it is not only goods that circulate through these ties. As the literature has repeatedly pointed out, clientelistic exchanges rest on a balance of affective and instrumental ties (Auyero 2000a; Scott 1977a, b).

The physical presence of the politician in the neighborhood enhances and raises the status of the leader who brings him or her there. It also serves the image of the politician, who people see as one of them, at least for a little while. Manuel is very grateful, for example, to one politician from the Colorado Party who worked at the state water company. He remembers him as someone who helped many squatter settlements by bringing them water, and, essentially, as a very modest man, who would come and "eat *chorizos* (sausages) with us." During my fieldwork, I repeatedly found this idea of the good politician being one that comes to the neighborhood, is unpretentious, speaks people's language, walks around the neighborhood, and "steps in shit," listens, shares food, or drinks *mate* with the neighbors. In a nutshell, a good politician is one who shows understanding and closeness, as he or she knows it is important. As a current city councilor of the same political faction as Manuel once told me, "he feels important when he stands side by side with someone who is important."

This is why politicians continue to spend a great part of their campaign visiting small towns and, in this case, squatter settlements. To give another example, before the 2009 presidential elections, New

Rock received Victor Rossi, the then Minister of Public Works and one of Manuel's patrons, and María Julia Muñoz, the then Health Minister, also from Manuel's faction. "We invited them to a stew, and we got her to cook!" Manuel says proudly, showing how important it is to reduce the inequalities in the relationship, at least for an illusory moment. But they were not the only ones who visited before the election. Other visitors included Mujica (former president of Frente Amplio), and Magurno (a traditional Colorado politician, from its populist faction, known by squatters for sometimes bringing blankets and food). And, as shown in the opening vignette, Manuel feels great pride in those visits.

It becomes important to understand these symbolic aspects of clientelism and political networks more generally. Political networks are a source of recognition for all those involved, clients, brokers, and politicians. Beyond the instrumental exchanges, these symbolic exchanges appear to be behind the enduring relevance of face-to-face politics.

Uncertainty Rather than Monitoring and Conditionality

The minimalist definition of clientelism as an exchange of favors contingent of clients' votes supposes a degree of certainty I could not find in my fieldwork. Most of the exchanges I was able to observe were uncertain rather than contingent on squatters' votes. This uncertainty was associated to monitoring problems. While squatters built relationships with different politicians at the same time, some politicians complained about their help not being compensated. At the same time, brokers experienced high tension in choosing who to work with since they did not need promises but actual goods or services in order to safeguard their legitimacy as leaders in their communities. In Manuel's words:

> You have to be very careful in choosing who you are going to work with in order to get things. Otherwise they [politicians] disappear and then.... [you are left alone]. Currently, you can't work for nothing. [You have to ask] what do you have? What can you get me? You can be a good person but if you don't get something for the neighborhood, you are useless. You are a neighborhood leader depending on what you achieve for your neighborhood (...) Otherwise you don't exist.

In his study of patronage politics in nineteenth-century Brazil, Graham (1990) describes what Manuel experiences in this quote as anxiety. For him, patrons, clients, and brokers experienced great anxiety because their social status was at risk around the fulfillment of the patronage exchange.

Many of the settlers in the planned settlements I visited, mentioned that they had received help from more than one party and then voted for whomever they wanted. In fact, most of them practiced a strategy I call *a political performance* in which they pretend to have no interest in political affairs. One of the early founders of a settlement explained to me that even though invaders were from the left, once they squatted "there were no political parties." Early on, the neighborhood association did not let people put political signs in their houses.

"We are apolitical here" was a common phrase among leaders of squatter settlements, especially the more organized ones. Given the many stories of contacts with politicians to get this or that, this latter phrase sounded a bit paradoxical. In fact, one could substitute apolitical for hyper-political and it would make perfect sense. But what squatters really mean when they say they are apolitical is not that they *are* politically neutral since most of them have their clear preferences, but that they *behave* or *perform* as if they were apolitical. Part of that performance is "opening doors to everybody" as they claim they do. If they publically show preference for a party, they would probably not get many of the things they want that are not under the control of that single party. They might even get less from that party as well.[7]

Seen from the other side of the network, a city councilor with a lot of experience in working with squatter settlements told me:

> It is like a market. Politicians offer... We offer (I'm not going to play the raped girl here) services and people pay with votes. Just like in a market. (...) Among these squatter leaders there is great variation. There are some who let anybody enter and then promote the one who helps, no matter which party he belongs to. They make his help public (...). But there are also those who let anybody who wants to help in, they let him help, they get stuff, but then they either promote him or not depending on his political affiliation. This is more common among leftist squatters who let others [from traditional parties] get the things, but then they put a lot of effort into it going unnoticed.

To what extent these statements are true remains an enigma, precisely because it is difficult to monitor how squatters vote. Although clientelistic ties rely on trust, most of the literature on clientelism emphasizes some monitoring capacity on the part of the politicians giving away goods. Stokes (2005), speaking of clientelistic ties in current Peronist Argentina, points at informal monitoring devices where the ballot is secret. There, "machines use their deep insertion into voters' social networks to try to circumvent secret ballot and infer individual votes" (p. 315). Moreover, no matter how difficult it gets to infer individual voting behavior, counting votes in the district where the machine is operating enables an evaluation of the aggregate performance of the machine. This latter condition is not present for most squatters in Montevideo, since they have moved recently without changing their electoral registration, and therefore tend to vote close to their old residence, not close to their new squatter neighborhood.

Local leaders may however invent other instances to prove their strength to politicians, which provides a means to monitoring. Manuel talked about election to local councils as a way to measure his power. If he got elected, as he did three times, he could show that he had many votes. He also mentioned the Frente Amplio internal elections of 2006 as an instance in which he could show strength. These were elections for party authorities, organized by the party, in which people could vote in any of the party's authorized places. There was one authorized precinct in New Rock, and Manuel was indeed able to show votes for his faction.

> Nin Novoa [vice-president at the time of the interview] and Victor Rossi [Minister of Public Works] came and asked us for help in the party elections with the 738 [their list]. They wanted to know whether we really had people. So I bet Nin Novoa that here in the neighborhood, the 738 was going to have more votes that the other lists altogether. (...) He said –you are crazy, Manuel, I bet you two lambs.

Although Manuel won that bet by showing that his faction within Frente Amplio was stronger in the neighborhood, there is no way to know this for the different parties. This is why I repeatedly found myself puzzled during fieldwork when trying to find out about monitoring. Yet the paradox is that despite that uncertainty, politicians continued going on visits and doing favors. High competition for squatter votes stimulated them to do so.

Continuity Rather than Sporadic Electoral Exchanges

Although inflamed around electoral times, political networks of squatters were regularly active, and to understand them, we need to look at political networks beyond electoral moments, precisely to better understand electoral moments. Planned invasions were more likely on electoral years (see Chap. 5 and Appendix B). Electoral campaigns increased politicians' visits to squatter settlements. Moreover, elections were perceived by brokers as good opportunities to ask for goods, not only because politicians were more likely to respond but also so that people in the neighborhood could "remember." Manuel puts this eloquently:

- We have to repair the roads. But I don't want to do that until the next elections.
- Interviewer—Why?
- Because you do the streets now and they forget. By the time the elections come round, people forget. And for politicians to keep doing what you need, you need to show them strength. If you don't have strength, they don't do anything for you.

Yet, contacts with politicians are by no means constrained to electoral times. Squatters also resort to incumbents once they are in power. They have many more needs than the ones they can solve around election times. An example of this is the meeting Manuel organized with the then president Tabaré Vazquez. According to him, they had sent Vazquez a letter before the 2004 election to talk about his policies on squatter settlements, but he never answered. Once he was elected, they sent another letter scolding him for not having replied. He gave them an appointment immediately. Manuel went to the meeting with some people he knew from squatter settlements in his area. In his words,

> What we said to the president was that we disagreed with the Emergency Plan (basic income program).[8] Instead, we want to solve our unemployment problems. One of the arguments was that the people who work for state agencies as builders, maintenance staff, cleaners, and so on are people from squatter settlements. But the ones who get the contracts are big companies that pay low salaries. So it's better that they teach people from squatter settlements, who are the ones that need the most, how to organize themselves, create their own small company, their own cooperative, NGO, whatever.

This was the origin of the already mentioned working cooperative Manuel founded and in which I found him working with contracts with the Ministry of Public Works. Besides, speaking of inter-temporal, continuous, exchanges, this quote also describes another characteristic of squatters' political networks: agency.

Agency Rather than Submission

Far from being passive recipients of help used by politicians, brokers, and clients of organized invasions had relative agency and strategizing capacity, associated to a context of high electoral competition from squatters' votes and in a context of no monopoly of public goods or hegemonic machines. Of course, most types of political relations, even the most unequal ones, have some level of agency. Deciding to support someone because it is convenient implies agency. Clientelistic exchanges, even under great inequality, can be combined with some forms of resistance to submission. But when the inequality in the relationship decreases, the bargaining power of brokers and clients increases considerably.

Switching parties and factions himself was not Manuel's only strategy. In the neighborhood organization, they formed teams. One worked with the Blanco Party, another with the Colorado Party, and a third, led by Manuel, with Frente Amplio. As Manuel put it, "I worked with everybody and I didn't work with anybody, you understand?" Or more clearly:

> We had to flirt [franelear] a lot with politicians. If you don't flirt, you don't get anything. You have to use them as they use you. Politicians today don't give you anything if they are not getting something from you. If here the Ministry of Public Works and the President gave us jobs it is because of something. If they connected the electricity or water, it is because of something.

Extreme loyalty to just one party was especially inadequate during the years in which New Rock emerged. Not only were the municipal and national authorities between 1990 and 2004 from different political parties, so were the relevant ministries, following the Blancos and Colorados' tradition of coparticipation. For example, during the 1995–1999 Colorado national government, the Housing Ministry was in the hands of the Blanco Party.

Political exchanges between politicians and the poor do not necessarily imply passiveness and submission. In a pluralist democratic context, clientelistic exchanges can be a part of the strategic repertoire of the urban poor to advance their own interests. This has been reported in other cases such as in Burgwal's (1995) study of the conscious use of clientelism as a strategy by Quito's squatters despite being critical of it. Very similar is Gay's (1994) report of a Brazilian favela with a much-empowered leader very similar to Manuel, who was able to play the clientelistic game to his advantage. This also appears to be the case in other parts of today's Brazil (Borges 2007; Nichter 2010) and in Colombia, where some authors talk about "market clientelism" to highlight the capacity of clients and brokers to choose from various patrons and not to be tied to pyramid networks (Dávila León de Guevara 1999; Dávila León de Guevara and Delgado 2001; García 2003; Gutiérrez Sanín 1998), as we will see shortly. Although this capacity for agency almost always exists in any clientelistic relationship, the greater the competition for clients, the greater the agency they have. Agency is greater under market clientelism than it is under the loyal or monopolistic clientelism. In the following sections, I describe these two types of clientelism, both present among Montevideo's squatters.

Market Clientelism

By market clientelism, I refer to those fragile clientelistic networks, based on competition among patrons, which give more power to clients and brokers and are based more on short-term exchanges than they are on long-lasting loyalties. Clients and brokers are able to switch patrons or combine them in unprecedented manners. I draw this concept from scholars of Colombian politics (Dávila León de Guevara and Delgado 2001; García 2003; Gutiérrez Sanín 1998). They developed the concept of market clientelism to understand the changes that the 1991 constitutional reform brought by introducing decentralization. According to these scholars, decentralization has increased political options and political competitors. This, in turn, has developed into what they dub market clientelism, which is characterized by unstable networks that are less asymmetric than in the past because the client acquires greater weight in the relationship. Early scholars of clientelism already thought of the changes electoral competition may cause to clientelistic relationships. In his study of Southeast Asia, Scott (1977a) argues that electoral competition had improved clients' bargaining power.

Like other forms of clientelism, market clientelism is a form of citizen–politician linkage that, unlike programmatic linkages, is based on direct tangible goods aimed at individuals and small groups of citizens in exchange for (the promise of) electoral support. The peculiarity of market clientelism is that it defies the common ideas of a passive client because it shows a very strategic one, who is willing to change bands and "flirt" with many politicians at the same time in order to obtain concrete goods.

Manuel's self-representation, his practices, and the stories that others in his network and outside told me about him, strongly contrast with other experiences of clientelistic relationships that are highly unequal and in which the lower class leader assumes "an attitude of submission or even servility vis-à-vis the powerful" (Stokes 1991). Way beyond passiveness or submission, and also beyond hidden resistance in Scott's (1990) terms, Manuel's strategy is explicit and active. Using Merklen's (2003, 2005) metaphor to illustrate the behavior of squatters in Argentina, Manuel's logic and practices resemble those of a *hunter* more than those of a *farmer*. He is always attentive, ready to grab any opportunity.

Besides flirting, to use his word, he has actually switched parties and factions several times, and, as he explained, he left one particular Frente Amplio faction because it demanded too much loyalty or exclusivity. Others' descriptions do not situate him in a submissive attitude either. "A popular urbanist," "a rogue (*pícaro*) from a Cervantes' novel," "a person who only defends his pocket," "an intelligent man that always goes towards where there is [political] strength," are some of the phrases both fans and detractors have used to describe him. Although poor and in a position apparently subordinate to any politician, Manuel has power and has used it strategically to his and his neighborhood's benefit. Those squatters who, like Manuel, learned how to use these networks in a market-like way were the most successful in reaching the state, particularly during this context of high electoral competition for the popular vote and of a divided government (different political parties in different state agencies).

Loyal Clientelism

No doubt market clientelism was the most successful strategy for squatters' organizations and leaders that wanted to get the state's attention. Yet, in the varied universe of squatter settlements I found, although less frequently, other less strategic uses of political networks, based on the long-term loyalties and strong affective ties.

The Distributor, a local Colorado Party broker who earned his nickname because he has organized many squatter settlements in one of the most deprived areas of the city and distributed land in them to many people, is an example of a more traditional type of broker than Manuel. He has always been very much involved in political networks but he has never left his party. As he put it looking at me with fixed, wet eyes:

> If the Colorado Party has a vote, that's my vote. I have had offers by the Blancos, the *frenteamplistas* ( ) They offered a blank check to switch… but how can I do that? With myself.…I can't do that as easily as others change colors. What would I say to my children?

The squatter settlements organized by The Distributor were, however, visibly less developed and upgraded than New Rock. He has a single patron, someone who was twice a representative and once a candidate for mayor but who has not been in office since 2000. The Distributor, therefore, does not have access to much for his constituency. Once in a while, the patron comes and distributes mattresses and blankets and invites people to a barbecue. However, although The Distributor once got a job through the party, today he is unemployed. "I am one of the living dead—he says—(…) I live off my wife." He gets sporadic personalized help from his patron. Once in a while, he gives him some money, but it doesn't feel dignified, and he also got medical attention through him. But the relationship appears to survive for reasons other than the goods exchanged. Loyalty and belonging seem crucial.

The contrast between Manuel and The Distributor illustrates different means by which to obtain state resources through political contacts with different degrees of effectiveness. In the 24 different cases of land invasions I visited,[9] three patterns were clear. First, a leader or neighborhood association with political ties helped the neighborhood acquire services. Those neighborhoods whose initial leaders had political ties with any party, and that used any brokerage modality indiscriminately, have better services today and a better urban life quality in general. Second, accretion invasions did not have this type of leader. Politically well-connected leaders are often present in planned invasions and sometimes in subdivisions and sales (see Table 6.1). Finally, among the connected leaders or neighborhood associations, those that had ties with different political parties were more successful in obtaining a greater variety of state resources (something that gives them the best urban quality).

The effectiveness of Manuel's market clientelism is a product of the increasing electoral competition between parties, and even between factions, for the urban poor, as well as the divided government brought about by coparticipation (see Chap. 2), and the left winning the municipal government but not, as yet, the national government. In the past, being loyal to one party could be effective. In fact, the squatter settlement

Table 6.1 Presence of political ties at the moment of settlement by land invasion type (study sample)

Invasion type	*Presence of leader or neighborhood association at the beginning of the invasion with political ties*	*Total number of invasions in the sample*
Accretion	0	6
Planned	14 1 unknown	15
Subdivision and sale	1	3
Total	15	24

that has achieved the greatest recognition from the state in the history of the informal city in Uruguay has been *Casabó*, whose leaders were very loyal to the Colorado Party for many years. They are the only ones whose case, after being discussed by the Parliament, is backed by a law that recognizes their property of the land and promises to upgrade the neighborhood. Yet in the 1990s and at least until 2004 when the left took office and put an end to coparticipation of different parties in state agencies, flirting with many parties became more effective.

Clientelism Fostering Rather than Inhibiting Mobilization

This case also contributes to the debate on clientelism and mobilization. Clientelistic networks are often portrayed as an explanation or consequence of poor people's demobilization or submission. Squatters or generally deprived populations are often portrayed as either rebellious or clientelistic as if these were the two opposites of a continuum (Stokes 1996). Different studies have shown this dichotomy to be false (Auyero 1999, 2000a, b; Burgwal 1995; Gay 1994). The case of New Rock also proves it false, even for such a centralized network.

First, for many residents becoming involved in a planned invasion meant becoming mobilized for the first time. Luis and Betty, members of Manuel's network's inner circle, are a good example of this. Before coming to live in New Rock they had never participated in any organization. In Luis' words, "the only thing we used to do was vote." When they started building their current house, the neighborhood was just starting and there were a lot of people in need. Betty started participating in a soup kitchen. She remembers that the Colorados donated them pots, glasses, clothing, etc. "We used to give milk, rice with milk, bread and jam that INDA (the National Institute for Nutrition) gave us for the children here. In the winter, it was cold, it rained and they were barefoot." Interestingly, Betty did this with Manuel's wife and daughter. Betty and Luis became members of the neighborhood association, and, as members, it was the first time they talked to politicians face-to-face, the first time they went to the City Council, and so on. In general, however, they worked in the neighborhood—dividing the plots, building streets, filling some irregular parts of the plot, organizing celebrations, building their own house, and helping others with theirs—letting Manuel and a few others do the public relations work.

Yet, another interesting example of the connection between clientelism and mobilization is that a group of neighbors from New Rock mobilized *against* Manuel. Having paid for their plots by depositing the money in the bank account that Manuel opened to pay the landowner, and not having received a property title and only elusive answers from Manuel, they went to the City Council and said, "we want you to help us defend our rights."[10] This group of neighbors resorted to the channels of the municipal government, which has been, at least formally, an enemy of land invasions in rural areas and of those suspicious of fraudulent transactions. Moreover, they explicitly denounced the centralized clientelistic network, as these meeting minutes illustrate:

> There is no interest in neighbors' organization because they work with the old *caudillo* to which neighbors are hostages. There are a lot of accusations to make but since we don't have solid arguments to found them, we can't mention them…because that can lead to a lawsuit (…). What we want is for New Rock to be more democratically organized. We want to have the support of the City Council, of the Municipal Government and the Local Councils -people who are neutral here- and promote the creation of a good neighborhood association that is truly representative.[11]

Hence, far from being opposites, clientelism and mobilization may have a recursive relationship with many types of outcomes (Auyero et al. 2009). Rather than a theoretical opposition, the relationship between these two concepts invites us to ask empirical questions such as how and under what conditions does clientelism enhance or inhibit mobilization?

Discussion and Concluding Remarks

The story of New Rock is not representative of the more than 400 squatter settlements in Montevideo. Yet many of the things I found here and there in my visits to 25 of those neighborhoods, in my interviews with bureaucrats and politicians, and in my statistical analysis of the land invasion cycle more generally, I found—all in one place—in New Rock. Many separate features appeared condensed and exaggerated in this social universe, as in a Weberian ideal type. I have focused on the neighborhood leader's crucial brokerage role in connecting squatters with the state and highlighted what I dub *market use of political networks* as a tool to obtain things for himself and his neighborhood. Through the use of multiple political ties at the same time, switching patrons, performing or behaving as if they were apolitical and in the meantime opening doors to different parties, some squatters were able to transform the political opportunity of electoral competition for their promise of loyalty and votes into new land invasions and new services for their neighborhoods.

As mentioned in the introductory chapter, some scholars of contentious politics are switching from the study of big causes to the study of mechanisms across different types of contentious events and processes, from revolutions to (why not?) land squatting (McAdam et al. 2001; Tilly and Tarrow 2007). Brokerage is one of those mechanisms, and Manuel's case shows its relevance for successful squatting. Manuel showed us one type of brokerage, one that has a central location in the network, one that controls his inner circle but that at the same time can generate strong opposition networks, and fundamentally, one that is able to adapt to change and switch or combine the sites it connects to. It was through brokerage that the political opportunity of electoral competition became materialized in organized land invasions and later in neighborhoods. Understanding how these mechanisms work is crucial to comprehending how structural conditions transform themselves into mobilization.

Notes

1. Neighborhoods and people's names are fictitious to comply with confidentiality. Only the names of public figures are real.
2. The process of becoming brokers, patrons, and clients has received little attention from the literature, which often focuses on already working networks (Auyero 1997).

3. This expression is more a product of retrospective interviewing than it is real. He was probably never just another neighbor. He had some political networks; he had some leadership features that the FUCVAM people noticed in order to choose him to organize the neighborhood.
4. It was not only other interviewees (such as a neighborhood leader of another area of the city) that suggested that Manuel had kept some of the money, some of the *New Rock* neighbors, accused him at the City Council, according to the minutes of the City Council's Special Commission on Squatter Settlements.
5. And according to Manuel and to the signs in people's houses by the time of the last election in 2009, the majority of the neighborhood voted for the Frente Amplio. Yet this cannot be attributed to Manuel's political network, whose patrons got very little votes in general. Neighbors voted like the majority of Uruguayans, supporting the faction of the former President José Mujica.
6. This has recently changed. Now the city is divided into eight municipalities. I do not have updated information on Manuel's current participation.
7. Nichter (2009) describes a similar dilemma suffered by Brazilian Northeastern voters who wonder and calculate the benefits of declaring their voting choices or not.
8. One of the *Frente Amplio's* main campaign plans, and one of the first measures the administration implemented once in office, was a new social welfare program for poor families, in response to the big economic crisis that had hit the country in 2002–2003. The plan, popularly known as *Plan de Emergencia* (Emergency Plan), was a conditional cash transfer program and had two main objectives: immediate assistance (e.g., basic income of about 50 dollars per month, health care) and support to get out of poverty (e.g., educational programs, labor programs).
9. I studied 25 different invasion cases, but one of them was a case of eviction, so I could not visit it but just reconstruct its history from the perspective of a local leader of the broader neighborhood and the local authorities that avoided the occupation of a public plot.
10. *Minutes of the City Council's Special Commission on Squatter Settlements*, October 3, 2003.
11. Ibid.

References

Auyero, J. (1997). ¿ Favores por votos. Estudios sobre clientelismo político contemporáneo. Buenos Aires: Losada.

Auyero, J. (1999). From the client's point(s) of view. How do poor people perceive and evaluate political clientelism. *Theory and Society, 28*, 297–334.

Auyero, J. (2000a). The logic of clientelism in Argentina: An ethnographic account. *Latin American Research Review, 35*(3), 55–81.

Auyero, J. (2000b). *Poor people's politics. Peronist survival networks & the legacy of Evita*. Durham, NC: Duke University Press.

Auyero, J., Lapegna, P., & Page Poma, F. (2009). Patronage politics and contentious collective action: A recursive relationship. *Latin American Politics and Society, 51*(3), 1–31.

Borges, A. (2007). Rethinking State Politics: The Withering of State Dominant Machines in Brazil. *Brazilian Political Science Review 1*, 108–56.

Brusco, V., Nazareno, M., & Stokes, S. C. (2004). Vote buying in Argentina. *Latin American Research Review, 39*(2), 66–88.

Buquet, D., & Piñeiro, R. (2016). Uruguay's shift from clientelism. *Journal of Democracy, 27*(1), 139–151.

Burgwal, G. (1995). *Struggle of the poor: Neighborhood organization and clientelist practice in a Quito squatter settlement*. Amsterdam: CEDLA.

Canel, E. (2010). *Barrio democracy in Latin America. Participatory decentralization and community activism in Montevideo*. University Park: The Pennsylvania State University Press.

Chávez, D., & Goldfrank, B. (Eds.). (2004). *La izquierda en la ciudad. Participación en los gobiernos locales de América Latina*. Amsterdam: Transnational Institute.

Dávila León de Guevara, A. (1999). Clientelismo, intermediación y representación política en Colombia: ¿Qué ha pasado en los noventa? Estudios Políticos, *Universidad de Antioquia 15*, 61–78.

Dávila León de Guevara, A., & Delgado, N. (2001). La metamorfosis del sistema político colombiano: ¿Clientelismo de mercado o nueva forma de intermediación? In F. Gutiérrez Sanín (Ed.), *Degradación o cambio. Evolución del sistema político colombiano*. Bogotá: Norma.

Filgueira, F., Garcé, A., Ramos, C., & Yaffé, J. (2003). Los dos ciclos del Estado uruguayo en el siglo XX. In I. d. C. Política (Ed.), *El Uruguay del siglo XX. La Política*. Montevideo: Banda Oriental.

García, M. (2003). *Ciudadanía Avergonzada?: democracia local y construcción de ciudadanía en Bogotá*. Bogotá: CESO-Universidad de los Andes & IEPRI-Universidad Nacional.

Gay, R. (1994). *Popular organization and democracy in Rio de Janeiro. A tale of two favelas*. Philadelphia: Temple University Press.

Gay, R. (1997). Entre el clientelismo y el universalismo. Reflexiones sobre la política popular en el Brasil urbano. In J. Auyero (Ed.), *¿Favores por votos? Estudios sobre clientelismo político contemporáneo*. Buenos Aires: Losada.

Gay, R. (2001). The Even More Difficult Transition from Clientelism to Citizenship: Lessons from Brazil. *Working Paper 01-09g*. Princeton: Center for Migrationand Development, Princeton University.

Goldfrank, B. (2002). The fragile flower of local democracy: A case study of decentralization/participation in Montevideo. *Politics and Society, 30*(1), 51–83.

Graham, R. (1990). Patronage and Politics in Nineteenth-century Brazil. Stanford: Stanford University Press.

Gutiérrez Sanín, F. (1998). *La ciudad representada: Política y conflicto en Bogotá.* Bogotá: TM Editores-IEPRI.

Holland, A. C. (2017). *Forbearance as redistribution. The politics of informal welfare in Latin America.* Cambridge: Cambridge University Press.

Kitschelt, H., & Wilkinson, S. I. (2007). Citizen-politician linkages: An introduction. In H. Kitschelt & S. I. Wilkinson (Eds.), *Patrons, clients and policies. Patterns of democratic accountability and political competition.* Cambridge: Cambridge University Press.

Levitsky, S. (2003). *Transforming labor-based parties in Latin America.* Cambridge: Cambridge University Press.

Luna, J. P. (2004). *La Política desde el llano. Conversaciones con militantes barriales.* Montevideo: Ediciones de la Banda Oriental.

Luna, J. P. (2006). *Programmatic and non-programmatic voter linkages in two institutionalized party systems: Chile and Uruguay in comparative perspective.* (Ph.D.). Chapel Hill: University of North Carolina.

McAdam, D., Tarrow, S., & Tilly, C. (2001). *Dynamics of contention.* Cambridge: Cambridge University Press.

Medina, L. F., & Stokes, S. (2007). Monopoly and monitoring: An approach to political clientelism. In H. Kitschelt & S. I. Wilkinson (Eds.), *Patrons, clients, and policies.* Cambridge: Cambridge University Press.

Merklen, D. (2003). Vivir en los márgenes: la lógica del cazador. In M. Svampa (Ed.), *Desde Abajo. La transformación de las identidades sociales.* Buenos Aires: Biblos.

Merklen, D. (2005). *Pobres Ciudadanos. Las clases populares en la era democrática (Argentina 1983–2003).* Buenos Aires: Editorial Gorla.

Nichter, S. (2010). Declared Choice: Citizen Strategies and Dual Commitment Problems in Clientelism. Paper prepared for presentation at the 68th Annual National Congress of the Midwest Political Science Association, Chicago, April 23.

Nickerson, D. W. (2010, April 15). *Detecting vote buying in Latin America using list experiments.* Paper presented at the presentation for the center for the study of democratic politics Seminar.

Panizza, F., & Pérez Piera, A. (1988). *Estado Y Sociedad.* Montevideo: FESUR.

Piattoni, S. (2001). *Clientelism, interests, and democratic representation: The European experience in historical and comparative perspective.* Cambridge, NY: Cambridge University Press.

Rama, G. (1971). *El Club Político.* Montevideo: ARCA.

Scott, J. (1977a). Patron-client politics and political change in Southeast Asia. In S. W. Schmidt, L. Guasti, C. H. Lande, & J. C. Scott (Eds.), *Friends, followers, and factions. A reader in political clientelism*. Berkeley: University of California Press.

Scott, J. (1977b). Patronage or exploitation? In E. Gellner & J. Waterbury (Eds.), *Patrons and clients in Mediterranean societies*. London: Duckworth.

Scott, J. (1990). *Domination and the arts of resistance: Hidden transcripts*. New Heaven, CT: Yale University Press.

Stokes, S. (1991). Politics and Latin America's urban poor: Reflections from a Lima Shantytown. *Latin American Research Review, 26*(2), 75–101.

Stokes, S. (1996). *Clients and radicals*. [S.l.]: [s.n.].

Stokes, S. (2005). Perverse accountability: A formal model of machine politics with evidence from Argentina. *American Political Science Review, 99*(3), 315–325.

Tilly, C., & Tarrow, S. (2007). *Contentious politics*. Boulder and London: Paradigm.

Veneziano Esperón, A. (2005). *Reflexiones sobre una reforma orientada al ciudadano. La descentralización participativa de Montevideo*. Madrid: Instituto Nacional de Administración Pública.

CHAPTER 7

Conclusion

The new century found Uruguay enmeshed in its worst socioeconomic crisis. The recession period starting in 1999 and epitomized by the banking crisis of 2002 added a new layer to the long-term trends of impoverishment and precarization. If the period of growth rife with inequality that characterized the 1990s had hurt the poor, this new recessive period was even more harmful. Poverty and unemployment rose to unprecedented levels and household incomes dropped considerably (Amarante and Arim 2004).[1] Hunger and despair flooded the city of Montevideo. However, no wave of land invasions accompanied or followed this crisis. Although some settlements did receive new families during the worst years of the crisis (2002–2004) becoming denser and even more precarious, land invading was not a massive strategy used by those affected by the crisis, at least not in the city.[2] This greatly contrasts with the two previous decades when, at the conjunction of democratization and neoliberalism, Montevideo was the setting of a silent yet lasting revolution: an enormous growth of the informal city and two waves of squatters' mobilization as this book has documented.

Although it is true that it takes grievances to squat, the case of Montevideo in the crisis of the 2000s illustrates that it takes more than just grievances to squat. Mixing the parsimonious and inferential power of statistics and the depth of ethnographic research, this book has emphasized the role of political opportunities in interaction with grievances, in squatting mobilization as well as brokerage as the mechanism that connects the disenfranchised with those opportunities.

M.J. Álvarez-Rivadulla, *Squatters and the Politics of Marginality in Uruguay*, Latin American Political Economy, DOI 10.1007/978-3-319-54534-9_7

Actual and potential squatters are constantly trying to survive. In the midst of hardship they use individual, family, and collective strategies to keep their heads above water. From invading an individual plot, to stealing electricity or dedicating themselves to street vending, squatters all over the world often violate rules starting by the most crucial for capitalist societies: property law. Bayat (1997) poetically refers to this as "the quiet encroachment of the ordinary." Some see everyday forms of resistance (Scott 1985) or insurgent citizenship (Holston 1999, 2009) in these everyday practices of survival. Yet, there are contexts in which collective strategies become more prevalent, moments in which contextual factors make economically rooted grievances become different forms of mobilization among squatters.

The case of Montevideo becomes significant in the study of squatters' mobilization in at least two ways. First, it offers a near "pure" case of the effects of deindustrialization and political opening for the less educated in urban environments. In the new open economy, one of the main inequality generating mechanisms is the increasing differential returns by education, especially in economies like the Uruguayan one, so highly dependent on the service sector. The squatters of Montevideo are not principally rural–urban migrants as in most Third World cities. They used to be formal urban dwellers expelled from the formal city not being able to afford to live there anymore. The concept of expulsion, developed by Sassen (2014) to refer to new processes of dislocation or dispossession not completely captured by more traditional notions of poverty and inequality, seems particularly relevant to understand the urban dwellers that had to move to a squatter settlement in the 1990s. Second, the study is significant because of its historical scope and the variation it offers both in the political economy of the city and in the urban poor's grievances and strategies to solve their housing needs. Many studies of social movements analyze only a snapshot, a moment, or a brief period of time. In contrast, here I study the whole history of land squatting in one city, from its beginnings in mid-twentieth century to the present. This sheds light on many variations throughout political periods. Changes occur in the passing of democracy to dictatorship and back again; in models of development, going from import substitution to neoliberalism, from periods of growth to periods of recession; and variation in the types and intensity of squatters' mobilization.

The case shows two different moments in which squatters mobilized collectively in Montevideo in the recent past. Both coincide with moments of political opening and grievances, yet they differ in interesting ways. The first mobilization happened among the poorest squatters, scavengers, and other informal workers living in very precarious shacks, and under the threat of eviction. This threat transformed their everyday practices of mainly individual resistance into collective action. Threats of losing a benefit have mobilizing power in general (Pierson 1995), and for squatters in particular (Bayat 1997). This threat coincided with the relative political opening of a dictatorship that had been harsh with any type of mobilization and harsh toward squatters and the urban poor in general. However, we do not completely understand what happened without paying attention to the brokerage role of local catholic parishes and NGOs. They helped squatters avoid evictions, find resources, and, more exceptionally, scale up, connect to other settlements in the same situation forming an unprecedented umbrella organization. The second mobilization had a slightly different social basis. Around 1990, previous urban dwellers who could not afford the formal city any more, with some previous organizational experience from unions, cooperatives, and leftist militancy, started a wave of planned invasion in the periphery of Montevideo. Their needs were activated under a new moment of political opportunity under democratic times characterized by electoral competition for the popular vote. Again, brokers became crucial, yet this time, under democracy, they were not local priests or NGOs but rather local leaders with political capital who connected squatters to the state.

Brokers are vital as activating mechanisms for different types of contentious politics (McAdam et al. 2001), yet they become absolutely crucial for those with few resources to mobilize. They connected those most disenfranchised with the resources that would otherwise be out of reach. As Eckstein (2001) pointed out, "protest movements among the economically and politically weak are especially likely to occur when a community of people with social and cultural bonds experience sudden material deprivation, when they lack attractive alternatives to exit and seek individual solutions to their plight, and *when they have the support of better-situated individuals and groups*" (p. 347). Yet, what remains underspecified in this explanation is that this support from better-situated individuals and groups does not happen in an abstract context but rather through networks in which brokerage roles are crucial. In reconstructing these micro-networks, this book has emphasized the agency among squatters and the moments in which that agency has greater chances of becoming collective action.

A Bitter-Sweet Ending

"Things got worse before they could get any better," says McCann (2013: 159) describing the sad unraveling of the favela mobilization of 1970s' Rio. This mobilization, which had helped bring democracy and pushed for municipal reforms to better integrate favelas into the city, soon found its limits. Rio was bankrupt by natural disasters and hyper-inflation and, to make matters worse, drug trafficking permeated favelas and their organizations. The story of Montevideo is similar, yet less tragic and with more nuances, perhaps because the time span of the analysis is longer than in this case for Rio. The similarities are interesting and put the Montevideo case in a comparative perspective. This sad ending seems to be the curse of many of squatters' mobilizations. The social capital that mobilization activates is, in most cases, neither enough nor sustainable over time to compensate the lack of economic and cultural capital squatters are subject to in Third World cities (Álvarez-Rivadulla 2007 [2000]).

Outcomes of social movements often receive less attention than their emergence, particularly those indirect or unintended outcomes (Giugni 1998). Squatters' mobilization in Uruguay has been partly successful and partly unsuccessful particularly if we look at its unintended outcomes in terms of residential segregation and social fragmentation. On the one hand, both the squatters of MOVIDE—the movement of a group of very poor squatter neighborhoods toward the end of dictatorship in Uruguay—and those that more recently starred the wave of planned invasions have gained their right to the city, their right to land and urban services. Most of them would not move out from where they are. They value their place in the world although they definitely want to improve it. Some even entered the upgrading and land-titling program through which they will eventually obtain property rights. This program, promoted and funded (in part) by the Inter-American Development Bank (IADB) like in other Third World cities, has finally been implemented in the city, regularizing and improving the living conditions of several settlements. Its interventions have reduced the number of people living in squatter settlements (PMB-PIAI 2013),[3] and a favorable international political economy has helped the general improvement of the urban poor in Montevideo, including recent squatters. While the First World struggles to recover from the global financial crisis and its effects, Latin America has been growing since the mid-2000s. Uruguay has been growing steadily (4.8% yearly from 2006 to 2015), although the rhythm of growth has started to decelerate mirroring the situation in the region (World_Bank 2016). Moreover, in contrast to the 1990s, this growth came with redistribution. Formal employment has been on the rise; poverty and inequality rates have dropped considerably; and the leftist government implemented a progressive tax reform and a myriad of other social policies, including conditional cash transfer programs received mainly by the poorest residing in squatter settlements.

Despite this, squatters' dream of belonging to the city seems as unattainable as ever. The city and its society have changed. Lasting fractures are evident in rising delinquency and fear. Some invasions—those that were successful in reaching the state and, at the same time, were able to control norms and population within their borders—were able to become part of the city as regular neighborhoods. But for many, it was an impossible task. "Organizing strangers" (Roberts 1973) is very difficult, particularly in contexts of unbearable need, and new problems (such as the emergence of drug consumption and trafficking). Moreover, residential and educational segregation have increased, in part, because of the expansion of a poor periphery (Kaztman et al. 2004; Kaztman and Retamoso 2007). The upper middle classes are exiting public education and fearful and stigmatizing of those living in squatter settlements (Álvarez-Rivadulla 2016). Squatters currently live in more segregated conditions than in the past, especially those who came from formal areas in the city. Moreover, they are exposed to the pernicious effects of concentrated disadvantage (Wilson 1996), which, once in action, is difficult to reverse in some of its mechanisms (Kaztman 2001). The following final ethnographic account illustrates these processes.

Ethnography in the Margins

Paradoxically, improvements in the country's general situation, in the concrete income of squatters, and in their infrastructure have not been enough to counteract different layers of exclusion accumulated over time. In 2014, when I visited *Nuevo Cauceglia* and *Villa Libre*, two adjoining planned invasions I started to visit in 1998 (2 and 3 years after they occupied, respectively), I was surprised by the changes in their infrastructure. The area is much more connected to the city, and although no bus goes there directly, residents can now get closer by taking a bus to the newly built Cerro bus terminal. Shirley, a former neighborhood leader, went to pick me up on her motorbike for what was only a 5-min ride. There is a brand new extended day school very close, in the *La Boyada* neighborhood, a nearby already regularized settlement. Shirley delivered this news with great pride because they have been fighting for this school ever since she was president of the neighborhood association 17 years ago. A generation went without it, and the consequences are visible.

Some of the kids I met when I first went there to help build a soup kitchen for the children, robbed the soup kitchen years later. Another one has killed two brothers that Shirley assures I also knew from that time. Often shots are heard at night. "*Pasta base* marked a change in the neighborhood," she says, referring to a derivative of cocaine, similar to crack, whose consumption skyrocketed—especially among the poorest youngsters in the city—around 2002 coinciding with the economic crisis. There is now a drug selling point in the neighborhood (*boca*), "but they do not steal here." Shirley's eldest started to study Law at the Public University but dropped out before finishing the first year and currently lives with a boyfriend in their own shack in the settlement. The two of them work together in street markets, selling nail polish, make up products, and clothes, and they move the stock around on her motorbike and a cart. They also own another motorbike and a car that often does not work very well. The car garage doubles up as an Evangelical Church on Tuesdays. Shirley's house has improved a great deal over the years; it has gone from being a small shack to a two-floor house with three bedrooms and improvements she proudly shows me every time I visit. However, the neighborhood as a whole has not improved very much; its streets are still unpaved and some new and very precarious shacks have sprouted around the settlement, which greatly upsets Shirley. She did not want her neighborhood to look like a cantegril. Their main struggle was for the neighborhood to become a legal and regular neighborhood. They are currently entering the regularization process but they are not likely to have the neighborhood they dreamt of when they invaded. They only wanted working-class people and yet now, even their own working-class identity is under threat.

Shirley's story illustrates the effects of residential segregation and accumulated layers of exclusion. In the country's best economic moment in many years, the best work she can do with her low level of education is to be a street vendor, which now allows her to buy a flat TV set and eat every day, but is still a very precarious job. The neighborhood is much more violent than in the past and, although it finally seems to be becoming a regular neighborhood, there are questions about the potential of infrastructure to change structural conditions, the dynamics of drugs and violence, and place stigma. This sheds doubt on the potential of squatters' mobilizations to go beyond survival and improvements in infrastructure, to being solidly integrated into the city (Harvey 2008; Holston 2009) if conditions of segregation and inequality continue.

Far from being a local exception, this glass ceiling to squatters' mobilization is more of a global trend. Murphy (2015), for example, signals the limits of the "housing question" for the Chilean case, in which improvements in infrastructure are undeniable. Yet, he opens the issue regarding improvements in citizenship, and highlights problems where the exclusion situation of the now owners of social housing—former *pobladores*—remains the same in terms of education or employment, and sometimes becomes more significant because of residential segregation and social fragmentation in such an unequal society. Moreover, "violence in the margins," to paraphrase Auyero and Berti's (2013) books about Argentina, is growing among youngsters in poor neighborhoods of many cities of the Global South. Without ever experiencing a sense of belonging to the formal city, a new generation of Montevideans and millions of other "Third World urbanites" are growing up, living their entire lives, and having children in squatter settlements. How this affects their worldviews, practices and their "capacity to aspire" (Appadurai 2004) remains an open and worrisome question.

Notes

1. Poverty reached 40.9% of Uruguayan households, almost doubling the percentages for the 1990s decade (Arim and Vigorito 2007).
2. According to anecdotal evidence, squatter settlements did grow in the metropolitan area around the crisis years (along the northern Costa de Oro, for example). Also, it becomes important to mention that other forms of mobilization did occur in existent squatter settlements such as the organization of soup kitchens, like in other popular neighborhoods (Falero 2004).
3. This program started in 1996, but its implementation in the city government was slow until the national and the municipal government finally had the same (leftist) orientation.

References

Álvarez-Rivadulla, M. J. (2007 [2000]). Asentamientos irregulares montevideanos: la desafiliación resistida. *Cadernos metrópole PUC/SP & IPPUR/UFRJ, 18*, 207–249.

Álvarez-Rivadulla, M. J. (2016). *Middle classes in Bogotá and Montevideo: "People should know their place"*. Paper presented at the LASA, New York. https://www.academia.edu/28723761/Middle_classes_in_Bogot%C3%A1_and_Montevideo_people_should_know_their_place_.

Amarante, V., & Arim, R. (2004). El mercado laboral: cambios estructurales y el impacto de la crisis, 1986–2002. In OIT (Ed.), *Uruguay. Empleo y Protección Social. De la crisis al crecimiento*. Santiago: Oficina Subregional de la OIT para el Cono Sur de América Latina.

Appadurai, A. (2004). The capacity to aspire: Culture and the terms of recognition. In V. Rao & M. Walton (Eds.), *Culture and public action* (pp. 59–84). Stanford, CA: Stanford University Press.

Arim, R., & Vigorito, A. (2007). *Un análisis multidimensional de la pobreza en Uruguay, 1991–2005*. Documentos de Trabajo Instituto de Economía. Montevideo. Retrieved from http://www.iecon.ccee.edu.uy/publicaciones/DT10-06.pdf.

Auyero, J., & Berti, M. F. (2013). *La violencia en los márgenes: Una maestra y un sociólogo en el conurbano bonaerense* (Vol. 2040). Buenos Aires: Katz Editores.

Bayat, A. (1997). *Street politics. Poor people's movements in Iran*. New York: Columbia University Press.

Eckstein, S. (2001). Power and popular protest in Latin America. In S. Eckstein (Ed.), *Power and popular protest. Latin American social movements.* (2nd ed.). Berkeley: University of California Press.

Falero, A. (2004). Sociedad civil y construcción de nueva subjetividad social en Uruguay: condicionamientos, conflictos, desafíos. In J. Seoane (Ed.), *Movimientos sociales y conflicto en América Latina*. Buenos Aires: CLACSO.

Giugni, M. G. (1998). Was it worth the effort? The outcomes and consequences of social movements. *Annual Review of Sociology, 24*, 371–393.

Harvey, D. (2008). The right to the city. *New left review*, (53), 23–40.

Holston, J. (1999). Spaces of insurgent citizenship. In J. Holston (Ed.), *Cities and citizenship*. Durham, NC: Duke University Press.

Holston, J. (2009). Insurgent citizenship in an era of global urban peripheries. *City & Society, 21*(2), 245–267.

Kaztman, R. (2001). Seducidos y abandonados: el aislamiento social de los pobres urbanos. *Revista de la CEPAL, 75*, 171–189.

Kaztman, R., & Retamoso, A. (2007). Efectos de la segregación urbana sobre la educación en Montevideo. *Revista de la Cepal, 91*(133).

Kaztman, R., Corbo, G., Filgueira, F., Furtado, M., Gelber, D., Retamoso, A., & Rodriguez, F. (2004). *La ciudad fragmentada: mercado, territorio y marginalidad en Montevideo*. Paper presented at the Latin American Urbanization in the Late 20th Century: A comparative study.

McAdam, D., Tarrow, S., & Tilly, C. (2001). *Dynamics of contention*. Cambridge: Cambridge University Press.

McCann, B. (2013). *Hard times in the marvelous city: From dictatorship to democracy in the favelas of Rio de Janeiro*. Durham, NC: Duke University Press.

Murphy, E. (2015). *For a proper home: Housing rights in the margins of Urban Chile, 1960–2010*. Pittsburgh, PA: University of Pittsburgh Press.

Pierson, P. (1995). *Dismantling the welfare state? Reagan, Thatcher and the politics of retrenchment*. Cambridge: Cambridge University Press.

PMB-PIAI. (2013). *Informe Técnico: Relevamiento de Asentamientos Irregulares. Primeros Resultados de Población y Viviendas a partir del Censo 2011*. Montevideo.

Roberts, B. (1973). *Organizing strangers: Poor families in Guatemala City*. Austin: University of Texas Press.

Sassen, S. (2014). *Expulsions*. Cambridge: Harvard University Press.

Scott, J. (1985). *Weapons of the weak*. New Heaven: Yale University Press.

Wilson, W. J. (1996). *When work disappears: The world of the new urban poor*. New York: Alfred A. Knopf.

World_Bank. (2016). Uruguay. Overview. Retrieved from http://www.worldbank.org/en/country/uruguay/overview.

Appendix A
Mixed Methodology to Study Elusive Collective Action

Social movements and, more generally, contentious politics are complicated sociological objects. They have, either despite this or because of it, provoked sociological imaginations to think creatively about how to grasp these amorphous, mobile, unstable, and difficult-to-limit type of social phenomena. Studying social movements as processes rather than snapshots leads to an additional difficulty. Scholars have developed several methods for collecting and analyzing historical data, newspaper data being one of the most common. There are examples of collective action, however, that do not always make it to the press or to any other record, or at least not systematically. These *elusive* forms of collective action require additional efforts from researchers who want to provide accurate accounts of their development over time.

Broadly speaking, I wanted to understand *when* and *under which conditions* squatter settlements were more likely to emerge. Yet, I did not have any systematic sources to extract event data such as land invasion dates to build the time series usually used to illustrate such issues. Ethnographic fieldwork had to help. In this case, qualitative and quantitative methods are deeply intertwined. Part of the quantitative analysis came directly from ethnography. Yet ethnography was also analyzed qualitatively to understand *how* squatters had interacted with these conditions to produce (different types of) squatter settlements.[1]

I conducted the bulk of my fieldwork during an entire year from August 2006 until July 2007. Since then, I have been updating information with the press, government documents, interviews, secondary

M.J. Álvarez-Rivadulla, *Squatters and the Politics of Marginality in Uruguay*, Latin American Political Economy, DOI 10.1007/978-3-319-54534-9

bibliography, and several visits to a group of three settlements I have been following since 1998. Also, in 2015, and with the help of an MA History student, María José Bolaña, I collected press data and secondary information on the creation and development of a movement of squatter settlements towards the end of dictatorship (1979–1989).

Protest Event Analysis

In order to describe squatter settlements in Montevideo and obtain information on when and under what conditions different types of land squatting had been more likely, I built a catalog of land invasions with their location, type of invasion (i.e., accretion, planned, or land subdivision and sale), date of settlement and land property. Results from this catalog are exposed in Chap. 3. In addition, I transformed this catalog into a time series of squatting events per year, including some predictors based on the theories I wanted to put into dialog: grievances and political opportunities. Chapter 5 and Appendix B are based on this effort.

When I started this project, I was able to obtain a list of settlements from the Ministry of Housing and another one from the Municipality of Montevideo, for some of which, they had the dates of settlement. When they listed the same settlements, they usually had very similar dates minus or plus 1–3 years. With this information, I assembled a time series of 136 settlements, which I could have used as my final data set, but I was afraid that it was not representative of the whole universe of the more than 400 settlements in the city. My fear was not so much based on the sample size but on its biases. I feared that the settlements in those lists were among the more organized, given that they had some sort of contact with the state and got registered in their files. I also feared they were not representative of the different types of occupied land types. Specifically, I feared that occupations of private land would be underrepresented, given that the state did not keep a record of them, and that those squatters on municipal or state land would tend to be overrepresented. This was why I became engaged in the difficult enterprise of building an event data set, without newspapers, without much archival information, and basically based on retrospective inquiry.

For about a year I worked, among other things, on building this time series mixing the *métier* of a sociologist with that of historian and ethnographer. By the time I started, the Bureau of Statistics and the program for slum upgrading and regularization had just released a map with

412 polygons of squatter settlements in the city, defined as groups of 10 or more houses whose inhabitants were owners of the house but illegal occupants of the land (INE-PIAI 2006).[2] The polygons had a geographical reference to which I wanted to link dates, types of land invasion and land ownership, as well as any other information I could collect. It took many interviews, and different triangulation efforts to build this data set. As I mentioned earlier, government agencies are now interested in the informal city. They see it as a problem they need to locate, count, and in relation to which they need to act. But it is not their main task to systematize information on its history.

I started my inquiry by taking a list of squatter settlements and a map to the local governments. Montevideo was divided into 18 local governments after the 1990s city decentralization program. Those administrative and political units are the ones that best understand the reality of their area. However, each area took much more than one interview. Information was fragmented and social workers, architects, local politicians, and old time local residents often had parts of the puzzle. Only in one local government did I find a folder with files for each of the more than 60 settlements of the area with some characteristics, including settlement date. In the others, I had to rely on retrospective information from key informants. This often required previous interviews to find the right informants, with more and reliable knowledge. Luckily, people were willing to take the time to talk to me. No matter how much I looked, those areas with stronger local participation, and stronger relationships between the local government and civil society had more precise information. This constitutes a source of bias I tried to solve by interviewing more people in some areas and by using other sources.

I also used information from the neighborhood visits and the oral histories I describe below to crosscheck dates and find dates the local governments did not have. Early residents had the most reliable information regarding the date on which the settlement started as the beginning had been part of their experience. They often connected that date to some other personal event, such as the birth of a child. Often, those early residents also knew about the dates of settlement of nearby informal neighborhoods because they had seen them start and grow.

As a third source, I used previously unprocessed archival material that I found rather unexpectedly. In 1998 and 2001, the Bureau of Statistics made a list of the country's squatter settlements and asked key informants a number of questions. I obtained access to the hard copies of the forms, which were resting on an office shelf, and I generated an electronic data set with some of the questions. I used that information as the last source for those cases for which I did not have any other information, or had contradictory or imprecise information from the previous sources.

Besides helping me fill in some missing data on dates, this new source provided me with 15 "dead" events. It had information about places that were squatter settlements in 1998 but that had been relocated or regularized by 2001. These data were interesting for different reasons. First, they led me to a very interesting case, which I later conducted oral histories for. It was a case of a planned land seizure whose leaders used their political contacts very efficiently and reached services and regularization in record time despite being located in a protected rural area where the municipality forbids construction. Since they were regularized, they are not legally squatter settlements any more. In addition, the geographical location of the "dead" events taught me something important about the politics of relocation. The three squatter settlements that were once in the central neighborhoods of the city (old city and surroundings) had been relocated. That is why there are none in those areas today. The squatters that had managed to find an open space in expensive areas of the city had been relocated.

Combining these three main sources, I was able to assemble a data set with the exact or approximate date of origin of 382 out of 427 land occupations.[3] Approximations, such as "the 90s" or "between 1985 and 1986" are from two main sources. One is related to the nature of the settlement, which in many cases is an accretion process. My criteria was always to find out the year in which the first settlers occupied, regardless of the fact that more came in the following years, but sometimes I could not find an exact year for this. This is precisely the other source of ambiguity: the lack of accurate records and the imprecision of memory.

Triangulation was useful to determine some of the dates (e.g., when one source refers to 1990–1995, and the other helps with a more accurate 1994, I took the more precise figure to be the initial land invasion date). For the general descriptive analysis of the cycle in Chap. 3, I made use of every single piece of information on dates, the more or the less precise, trying to locate invasions at least in a period of time. Still, for the event history analysis in Chap. 5 and Appendix B, I only used those cases for which I had an exact year of settlement. I therefore ended up with 257 events for 58 years (i.e., 1947–2004) for the Poisson regressions shown in Appendix B and with 258 events for 65 years (i.e., 1947–2011) for Chap. 2.

The analysis of number and types of land invasions over time was very illustrative. However, the study of retrospective dates is problematic. The ethnographic analysis showed that even the best planned invasions kept receiving newcomers years after they started. However, there is something to be said about using the date on which the "early birds" or pioneers settled. Early residents are the ones who break the rules initially; they are the ones who violate property rights, the ones that show that it is possible to settle there, the ones that test the chance of repression and eventually face the police or the owner, and the ones that widen the repertoire of possibilities for other urban poor that may start to see the plot as a possible new home. The moment in which some people seize a plot of land is often the most contentious in the history of the settlement. This is why studying squatting over time becomes so important.

Mini-Ethnographies

In order to understand *how* squatting occurred, I selected a group of neighborhoods and tried to reconstruct their history. The basis for selection was the official list and map of squatter settlements that the agency in charge of squatter settlements in Uruguay and the Bureau of Statistics had just finished building when I started my fieldwork. However, I also included two cases that were not on that list. One was not listed because it had already been regularized and therefore it was not legally a squatter settlement anymore but a formal neighborhood in which dwellers were owners of their land. The case was however interesting to me, because of the moment in which the land invasion occurred and the squatters' success in getting the state to pay attention to them by providing urban services and ultimately land titles. The other was not on the official list, because it was a failed invasion, deterred by neighbors and local authorities the day it happened. It was interesting precisely for being a non-event.

The criterion for selecting neighborhoods was guided by my original questions about the cycle of land invasions and the influence of politics. I wanted settlements that originated at different points in time in order to cover different political periods. I therefore sampled settlements formed before the dictatorship, during the dictatorship, during the transition to democracy, and during each electoral period thereafter.

I ended up visiting 25 different squatter settlements, trying to also look at a variety of types of settlement to represent both the more and the less planned land seizures and variation in the geographical location in the city.

Although I collected other types of information, the focus of my fieldwork was on the earliest days of settlements, how the early settlers got to the piece of land, how they started building, how they solved everyday needs and obtained (or failed to obtain) public services such as water and light, how they solved collective action problems (if they did), who helped them, and whether they faced any eviction attempt. To obtain that information, I conducted 41 oral histories with early residents, using a questionnaire template (at the end of this section), very flexibly, but always making sure I got detailed information about initial times. While interested in the role of politics, I never asked about it directly and only pursued the issue after a name or event appeared in the interviewee's narrative. To avoid vagueness, after trying out the interview a few times, I included a question that turned out to be crucial. I asked: *If you had to choose the three people or institutions that were most helpful to this neighborhood, which would they be?* This question often gave me relevant tips and names that I could later pursue, and pushed some interviewees that had only said the common phrases "we are apolitical here" or "we did everything ourselves" to think and tell me about political and institutional helpers.

Finally, I interviewed leaders and non-leaders to crosscheck information.[4] Besides helping to fill gaps in the information, non-leaders gave me less grandiose and less articulate stories than leaders. They also sometimes helped me understand the final link in the political network chain, as it became explicit in the analysis of a clientelistic network in Chap. 6. The shaded box below includes a characterization of respondents. When leaders and non-leaders from the same settlement or some other informant gave me information contradicting what another had said, I often tried to explore those contradictions further. Sometimes, it was a matter of one remembering incorrectly. But in other cases, there were just different perceptions of the same reality, based on the differential positions of the interviewee. In those cases, there was nothing to solve or clarify but just two equally interesting though different perceptions of the same reality based on experiences. The most common example was the story of a leader who tells his story of sacrifice for his neighborhood without much recognition, and a non-leader that sees him as a corrupt person that only participates to fulfill personal interests.

One important bias in this study is the absence of those who arrived at the settlement later on. Given that the goal was not to reconstruct the variation in memories within each settlement according to respondents' position and especially according to arrival time, I did not include newcomers as informants. This could be interesting to carry out in the future.

The rationale for choosing oral histories as a technique was based on Blee and Taylor's (2002) recommendations: "oral history interviews aim to elicit a robust or 'thick' description of a historical period or situation from the perspective of those who lived through that time." Oral histories are particularly valuable research tools for studying social movements that, like squatting, do not leave great documentary evidence. They are also valuable for unveiling aspects of movements that tend to be underestimated in written accounts, such as the role of women (Blee and Taylor 2002). In addition, they offer the possibility of studying the memory of protest, which I would like to do as a future project. However, retrospective oral accounts, just like all sources, can be misleading if not used with caution. For example, they tend to under-represent conflict, relations of domination, and differences between earlier and later beliefs, processes, and goals (Blee and Currier 2005). Considering these possible biases, I conducted oral histories with differently situated persons and combined them with other sources.

As often happens in ethnographic fieldwork, whenever one of the residents mentioned an external actor in the interview, I tried to find information regarding this actor and often also interview him or her. Some people appeared in more than one interview and, as mentioned below, that was often an indicator of an important node. Thus, I talked to former and current local authorities and city councilors, lawyers, social workers and other professionals, the ex-major of Montevideo and current Minister of Housing and his advisors, and so on, totaling 44 formal interviews.

From the three types of invasions I worked with (accretion, planned and land subdivisions and sales), the latter was the most difficult to track. I included three invasions that started in this way, but I could not always talk to all the actors, like I tried to do for the other types. In one case, for example, the settlement started as a fraudulent sale and settlers never really knew where their money went. I could not find those fake sellers either. Yet the story of Manuel in Chap. 6 compensates for this a little bit, since it provides an in-depth illustration of how subdivision and sales start and develop. Accretion invasions, in comparison to planned invasions, were also more difficult to study because due to the lack of collective planning at the beginning, there was no collective history to tell. Interviews were much shorter, no matter how much I probed my interviewees.

Every time I visited a new neighborhood, I used an observation template to systematically observe spatial features such as the existence of streets, public services and collective buildings or spaces such as soup kitchens. I also collected documents such as neighborhood reports conducted by professionals or NGOs and a few press articles. In some neighborhoods, leaders had neighborhood documents such as pictures, meeting minutes, and local press articles, which I also collected.

For the analysis, I tried to reconstruct neighborhood histories by putting together all the sources and exploring contradictory information. I analyzed the way in which the histories vary through time and space. However, I did not use the neighborhood histories just to compare them using the traditional comparative method based on Mill's most similar or most different cases. I paid attention to similarities and differences in order to be able to identify relevant types of invasions. But I also analyzed connections among stories. References to other settlements, leaders, or to the same politicians appearing in more than one neighborhood, were often indicators of something worth pursuing further. This is perhaps best illustrated in the analysis in Chap. 6.

During the analysis and the writing, which often went hand-in-hand, I used the stories to understand and illustrate the cycle of land invasions (and to build it as I will explain below). I paid particular attention to squatters' strategies for invading plots and building neighborhoods, often including connecting with the state either directly or through a political contact. I also paid attention to the squatters' and politicians' perceptions of each other.

The reconstruction of these neighborhood histories helped me better understand what it took and what it meant to seize land at different moments in time and with different degrees of organization. Political networks and particularly the action of local political and/or economic brokers appeared to be crucial in the organization of settlements. Those that did not have brokers tend to be poorer. As I will develop in Chap. 4, time and space mattered and the settlements that emerged in the 1990s and that were located in the western part of Montevideo were often more organized.

About my interviews with squatters:
I interviewed 41 squatters (16 women, 25 men), all early residents of the settlements I visited, some leaders and some ordinary residents.

Age: On average, middle aged (mid 40s ranging from 33 to late 70s). Even though I explicitly looked for the earlier residents, I ended up talking to a middle-aged group, in general. This is not surprising given that squatting has mainly been a housing strategy of recently formed families. While the average age of household heads and their partners in the formal city was 53 in 2006 (ENHA 2006), their counterparts living in squatter settlements are on average 11 years younger. Yet squatters tended to look older. Their harsh lives, poor health care, and poverty were evident in their lack of teeth, early wrinkles and tired looks. During fieldwork, I was mostly impressed by the early aging or quick lives of women. I met Jenny about 10 years before this fieldwork trip when I started visiting *Freedom Village*. A life of scarcity and fighting to make ends meet with several children and now early grandchildren, who also live with her, made her look much older than the mid 40s she was.

Jobs: My informants tended to survive on low paid informal jobs just like the population of squatter settlements in general. According to the ENHA (2006), 60% of workers from squatter settlements had informal jobs (i.e., without contracts or benefits) whereas that percentage is 31% for the formal city. Some were scavengers, in general as a cushion job held in certain periods when they did not find anything else; some had small businesses in their houses; some were temporary workers in construction; two women were maids. A small group was receiving state benefits: two were receiving the governments' basic income; two were living on their pensions and one was receiving unemployment benefits. Only two of my interviewees resembled the ideal of the working class (i.e., relatively skilled, manual, protected jobs): a soap factory worker and a carpenter working for a building company.

Four others, however, also belonged to the manual working class, but their jobs were much more temporary, and dependent on short-term contracts with the state. Two of them were scavengers who at the time were part of a NGO state funded project that worked with scavengers from the poorest area of the city.

Two others were building bus stops as part of a short-term contract with the state. Their jobs reflect a new trend in some Latin American states that after the huge retrenchment policies of the 1990s had started new welfare programs to attenuate the social consequences of liberalization. Some of these programs include short-term employment and training projects for those that would otherwise be unable to leave unemployment.

Also, among my interviewees I found a few non-manual working class or even bourgeois employees: a lawyer, the secretary of a congressional representative, and a public employee. They were among the most educated of their neighborhoods. In addition, I found two retired low rank military men and the wife of one that was in Congo at the time, as part of a UN mission. Finally, 5 of the women worked in their houses as housewives.

Urban trajectory: Before becoming squatters, the great majority of my interviewees lived in formal neighborhoods, either renting or with family, in nearby neighborhoods or at least in the same general area of the city as their squatter settlement. Only four came directly from outside Montevideo, and even in those cases, they were not rural migrants but came from other urban areas. They all had urban experience.

How they found out: Most respondents learned that a new invasion was being planned or that one had just occurred through word of mouth and personal networks. Only one woman, who bought her plot of land in what turned out to be a fraudulent sale, learned through a newspaper.

Politics: Most respondents identified with *Frente Amplio*, the leftist coalition that was in office when I was conducting the fieldwork, just like the majority of Uruguay's population at the time. I made sure to interview people from different political leanings, and I got at least six *Blanco* Party voters and five *Colorado* Party voters.

Leaders versus non-leaders: People leading land invasions did not belong to different social universes from the rest of the population. However, at least among my interviewees, leaders tended to have two features that made them stand out from the rest: they had some political or organizational capital and they knew how to talk. They tended to have some organizational experience in unions, cooperative housing movements, neighborhood associations or political parties before the invasion. In fact, they somehow translated that experience and the capital that came with it to the organization of the squatter settlement. They knew how to do things, whom to talk to and how to talk, how to organize neighborhood associations and assemblies, how to petition and so on.

I found non-leaders that trusted leaders and were willing to help them and others that were distrustful because they considered them to be pursuing personal gains or not communicating all their information.

Neighborhood leaders work hard. But squatter settlements have mobile populations and leaders are not an exception. Those that after the invasion stayed in the neighborhood are likely to stay in charge forever. They become a reference for others who, whenever there is a problem, can easily find them in their houses. For many, the neighborhood is their big oeuvre in life and that is part of the motivation behind the hours, money and effort spent in what they perceive as helping others. Leaders perform different types of tasks such as finding out about a plot to invade, facing the police or the owner, organizing squatters, measuring, dividing and distributing plots, selecting new settlers, writing letters, petitioning, waiting for hours at a public office to get a water connection for everybody, getting birth certificates for kids whose parents do not know how to do it or do not have the money to pay a bus ticket to the city, calling an ambulance when somebody is sick, evicting people that try to build in what were considered public spaces, talking to politicians when they come to visit the neighborhood, among many other things.

Many define their work as "social work in politics" or "the social," which they at least explicitly consider to be different from regular politics, less strategic and more for the people, more because they care about the poor. Leaders complain because the work is hard and others do not participate. They also complain because the neighbors, politicians, and state officials they work with do not give them enough recognition for their hard work. An anecdote from my fieldwork illustrates this latter point very well:

When I arrived at the office of a Frente Amplio city councilor to interview him that day, he let me in but he was talking to someone else, an angry woman. This happened the week before the internal elections of the party and both the woman and the local councilor belonged to the same party faction. The woman was complaining because she said that the party had not given her enough support and that "those things hurt." She had been in charge of the door-to-door political work convincing people to vote for their faction. According to her, they had not given her enough flyers to distribute in her neighborhood, which I later learned was a squatter settlement in which the city councilor had some constituents. Besides, they had only given her one banner that, she emphasized, was old and worn out. She felt that she could not convince others to vote for their faction if the party did not back her up. At one moment, the councilor had to go outside and she told me, "I cannot work like this. The other day, I brought 50 people to the meeting. It cannot be that they don't give me anything."

Her story, the story of feeling unsupported or in some cases underused by what they perceive as ungrateful others illustrates what some leaders feel: a frustrated search for recognition. Part of the rewards of being a leader is being able to show that you are well connected.

The story of a leader and the relevance of language and political capital: I was struck by a very charming and politicized woman, who expressed herself using elaborate language not only in our two long interviews but also when talking in public. She surprised me from the beginning. To break the ice, I asked her if I should interview her as a local politician or neighborhood leader. She told me "first of all, I'm a woman, and I am Uruguayan" and she broke into a huge laugh. Her elaborate phrases did not fit with some orthographic mistakes I could see in the handwritten quotes she has stuck on the walls throughout her welcoming but extremely poor house. They did not match her formal education either. She had suffered a life of deep economic and social exclusion. She told me she had to quit high school when her parents divorced and she was institutionalized with other homeless girls. She later became a prostitute, got married to a guy that eventually sold their house and left her and her children homeless again. Organizing with others to create what is now a consolidated neighborhood was a way out for her, the opportunity to have a place of her own for her family. It was a space in which she has participated from the beginning. She also participates outside her neighborhood, in the local council. Digging into her past, I realized this political capital went back in time. Her family was from the Communist Party. She remembers going to meetings when she was a child. She remembers her aunt taking her to strikes in the factory she used to work at. She remembers working clandestinely for the Communist Party during the military period. When the Communist Party took away her membership upon learning she was a prostitute, she showed her resilience once again by continuing to participate in a different Frente Amplio faction. She acknowledges how much that "political education"—her words—helped her in her participation in the neighborhood, and through her helped the neighborhood to get recognition and services. Once, she and some other neighbors went to the city council to ask for sponsorship and some material help for a local meeting in which they were going to talk about the main problems of their area of the city. Her speech was long and provocative:

I always say I am very proud to belong to a squatter settlement and I add that nobody gave us anything. (...) I am telling you this so you get to know the reality, because I haven't seen many of you walking through my neighborhood or through the area in which we live (...) I would like to explain to you what it means to live in a shack. It means that when it's 6 or 7 pm [in the winter] you have to go to bed dressed because the cold is atrocious. And you are lucky if the roof doesn't leak and your floor is not just mud. If the school is more than two blocks away, you often have to take your kids barefoot or with sneakers and then wash their feet in some puddle to be able to put their shoes on.[5]

Knowing how to talk came up several times during my fieldwork as a necessary condition for becoming a leader, both among non-leaders explaining why so-and-so was the leader or among leaders themselves telling me why others delegated things to them. Communication skills become very important when you are so dependent on others, as squatters are on state institutions to survive. They are crucial also for brokerage purposes, when you have to speak two or even three languages: that of the state, that of politicians, and that of fellow squatters. Conducting retrospective fieldwork, it is difficult to know whether leaders gained communication skills with the land occupation and neighborhood organization or whether they already had them. Judging from the oral histories, a mixture of both is probably closer to the truth. Some, as already mentioned, had experience in participating in organizations in which they also had to talk in public before invading a plot of land. But for some, participation in the neighborhood organization was a politicizing experience in which they learned many things, including how to communicate effectively, in order to reach out, to build ties, and bring resources to the neighborhood.

Archival Research

Although the previously described ethnographic fieldwork included the collection of all the documents I could find, there was a specific archival work I conducted to understand the creation and development of MOVIDE (analyzed in Chap. 5). With the help of a historian, María José Bolaña, we researched press archives to understand the dates and the characteristics of this mobilization.

We analyzed press from 1982 when, according to oral histories, the nine evicted settlements start to meet, until 1989, when mention of the movement disappears from the press. From 1982 to 1985, we used the Archive of the Center of Interdisciplinary Uruguayan Studies (CEIU) at the School of Humanities, Universidad de la República. From information from 1986 to 1989, we resorted to the Legislative Palace Library. We sampled 4 different newspapers, two weekly and two daily. For most years, we reviewed two months. We chose October and November because Homeless Day, established in 1986, is in early October, and we assumed there was going to be more information on the housing problem around that time. However, for some particular years, such as 1983 and 1984, when the dictatorship ended leading to great mobilizations and democratic negotiations, we analyzed the whole years. We chose sources from different perspectives in the political spectrum: *Opinar*, a Colorado weekly that functioned during the dictatorship and until 1985; and another weekly, *Aquí*, associated to the Christian Democratic Party established in 1983 (our search in this weekly went up to 1989). The newspapers were the two most traditional ones, one tied to the Colorado Party, *El Día*, and the other one to the Blanco Party, *El País*. In general, the two weeklies had much more information regarding the housing problem, evictions, and specifically MOVIDE than the daily publication. Our key words for searching were: MOVIDE, Organización San Vicente, Calera Vieja/La Cachimba del Piojo, cantegriles, desalojos, CONAPRO.

Besides the press research, we searched for documents available in the archive of one of the communities involved in the movement: Organización San Vicente, and we used two secondary sources that were crucial to reconstruct the organizational processes in San Vicente (Basanta et al., s.d.; Clara 2012) and in La Calera (Ricci Cabrera 1993). Finally, we used the audio archives of a radio program conducted in 1988 in the San Vicente area, with the testimonies of priest Cacho and cantegril dwellers. The journalist, Graciela Salsamendi, whom we interviewed at her home, decided to donate all the cassettes to be digitalized at the Archive of the Center of Interdisciplinary Uruguayan Studies (CEIU), School of Humanities, Universidad de la República.

Conclusion: Qualitative or Quantitative?

When conducting multi-method work, it is a huge temptation to write some parts as a quantitative researcher and others as a qualitative researcher, and in so doing make things easy for ourselves. Because of disciplinary traditions, methods determine not only a research choice but the way results are reported, the journals in which they can be published, the rhetoric to be applied, the authors cited, the audiences appealed to, and so on. Nevertheless, I have tried to avoid contributing to the seemingly essential division between quantity and quality. Many of the things we count and use as variables in regression analyses are often based on "qualitative" judgments.

In this work, no chapter is exclusively qualitative or quantitative. As expressed here, the building of the event catalog of invasion events required ethnographic information. The interpretation of the cycle and its explanation relied heavily on the contextual information I could find. At the same time, the initial statistical patterns I started to find helped me shape the lenses through which I was conducting the oral histories, reading documents, and so on.

Oral History Questionnaire

I am María José Álvarez, and I am a Ph.D. student at the Department of Sociology at the University of Pittsburgh in the US. I am conducting a study of squatter settlements in Montevideo, and I am interested in the story of your neighborhood. The interview will take approximately 90–120 min. Dr. John Markoff, Professor of Sociology at the University of Pittsburgh, is supervising my progress on this project.

Record on Template. Do not Tape	• Date: • Location of Interview: • Neighborhood: • Role of interviewee in the neighborhood (type of activities performed and since when): • Demographic information: (age, gender, race, class identification, occupation, education, household composition, and residential trajectory—previous neighborhood, childhood neighborhood, date the person moved to the squatter settlement and plans to move out if any):
Neighborhood data: Open question about neighborhood origin first. It's important to let the interviewees speak freely to later analyze their narrative construction. After that, ask specific questions if the information does not come up as specifically as needed. Focus on how they solved problems (do not ask directly about clientelism).	1. How did this neighborhood start? What do you know about its history? Make sure the following issues are covered. If not, probe or ask directly. • When did it happen? • Name (who named the settlement and why?) • Who were the first settlers? • Number of initial settlers. • Did settlers know each other from before (e.g., coworkers, neighbors, members of the same political group, etc.)? • What were the previous neighborhoods of initial settlers? • Why did people decide to move to a squatter settlement? • Who were the initial leaders and how did you choose them? • Who owned the land? • Very specific description of the first day or days of settlement (was there a planned invasion? If planned, how planned? By whom? Where did they/you meet to plan? How did they/you choose the land? How did they/you choose the date? Did you have government authorization? • Role of external actors: Did they/you receive any help from non-settlers (e.g., lawyers, politicians, other settlements, NGO, government official, judge, land owner, etc.)? Particularly important is obtaining information on the role of political groups (formal/informal, before/after the occupation, party, type of help and timing).

(continued)

- Did they/you receive any threat of eviction (e.g., police, politician, government, court, land owner, etc.? When and in what way? What were the consequences? (Reaction of neighborhood, follow-up by police, politician, etc.).
- How many and what types of groups did you have at the beginning?
- How often did they meet?
- Who participated in these organizations? (Number and characteristics).
- Did women and men participate in similar or different ways? (Older and younger? Employed versus unemployed? People from the city versus people coming from elsewhere?)
- Did you have any relationship with other settlements or with social movements such as the labor movement or the cooperative housing movement?
- (Specifically about space) Who planned the neighborhood layout and why? And what has happened with the original plan?
- Did you ever feel you were breaking the law or defying the authorities?
- When the settlement was first established did it identify itself with any political party?

After the origins, ask about the evolution.

2. What happened after the initial days? How did you solve the neighborhood problems?

Focus on one or two issues (housing, water, light, food) and explore in detail how they obtained those goods. Probe for specific answers (including names and dates) in order to reconstruct the process and the social networks involved. Remember that you want to know whether there are family, neighborhood, political or other networks that play a significant role and what is the role of the interviewee in these networks. You want to understand if clientelism plays a role, and if so, how. Make sure you get data on:

- Who initiated and was in charge of the actions (a politician, a neighborhood group, a leader, the government)
- What type of strategy was used (e.g., writing a letter, a person contacting somebody, a group contacting somebody, etc.)?

3. If you had to choose the three people or institutions that were most helpful to this neighborhood, which would you mention?

(continued)

Current Mobilization	4. How is the neighborhood currently organized? Make sure the following issues are covered. If not, probe or ask directly. • How many and what types of groups are functioning in the neighborhood right now? • When were they created and why? • How often do they meet? • Who participates in these organizations? (Number of people and characteristics). • Do women and men participate in similar or different ways? (Older and younger? Employed versus unemployed? People from the city versus people coming from elsewhere?) • Do you participate in inter-neighborhood associations? Have you ever gotten together with any other neighborhood organization? For what? Which neighborhoods (location, name). Do you have any relationship with other social movements such as the labor movement or the cooperative housing movement? • Who are the leaders and who chose them? • What are your goals as a neighborhood? • What are your main problems? • What have been the main successes? • Are there any political clubs in the neighborhood? Who participates and what do they do? • Does the neighborhood association identify with any political party? Why? • Does the neighborhood participate in the local government? How? • Compare the neighborhood of today with its initial state? What has changed? What is the same? • Are there any rules regarding who visits/lives/or works here? What are they? • How would you characterize this settlement politically? Is there a primary political party? Is there a political club in the neighborhood or close by? Which party would you say got the most neighborhood votes in the last election? • What's the most famous politician in this neighborhood? • How would you characterize the relationship of the neighborhood with the administration? (Local and national)?

(continued)

Individual data. Personal motivation to move, personal history of activism and personal problem solving networks.	5. Now I'd like to ask you some questions about yourself in relation to your neighborhood. Why did you move here? And why at that particular moment? 6. (For leaders) How did you become a neighborhood leader? (For non-leaders) were you ever in a leadership position in the neighborhood? Why or why not?). Have you ever participated in other organizations outside the neighborhood? 7. What were your steps (if any) in neighborhood or political militancy? Have you ever participated in organizations outside the neighborhood (parties, unions, neighborhood association, etc.)? 8. I have already asked you about the neighborhood, but how have you solved your personal problems such as housing, labor, and so on? 9. Which party do you identify with (if it did not come up during the interview)? Why? Which party did you vote for in the last elections of 2004? Why?
Additional questions will be asked to clarify or expand on answers given by subjects.	

Appendix B
Interactive Models for an Interactive Theory: Event Analysis for Land Invasions

Throughout the book, I have described the cycle of land invasions based on contextual historical evidence. In this appendix, I show a more quantitative part of my research, based on protest event analysis. Although crucial to my argument, I have decided to include it in the appendix to avoid breaking the narrative of the book. I test an interactive theory of political opportunities and hardships to understand squatting events. I take the moment of land invasion as a squatting event. *The main hypothesis behind the analysis (and the book in general) is that moments of political opportunities mediated and intensified the effect of hardship on the likelihood of new land invasions.*

Definition of Contentious Event

Social movements and other forms of collective action are composed of different kinds of events. The study of just some of those mobilization events is therefore a gross simplification; however it still enables sophisticated and parsimonious explanatory analysis. There is no single definition of what a contentious or a protest event is. Sampson et al. (2005), for example, consider "collective action events," two or more individuals engaging in some sort of non-profit, political, public act that is not part of routine political activity (initiated by the state or political parties) or part of regularly scheduled gatherings such as self-help group meetings. For Koopmans and Statham (1999), any instance of claims-making

M.J. Álvarez-Rivadulla, *Squatters and the Politics of Marginality in Uruguay*, Latin American Political Economy, DOI 10.1007/978-3-319-54534-9

by migrants and ethnic minorities appearing in German or British daily newspapers was considered an event. Here, I consider an event to be the invasion of a plot of land by a group of people who intend to build their houses on it. It is a contentious moment because it involves going against one of the most sacred principles of capitalist societies: property rights.

Data

As explained at length in Appendix A, I used various sources to build the data set of the dates of land invasions. I was able to assemble a data set of 257 out of a total of 427 land occupations, covering 58 years, from 1947 to 2004. This information was used to build my dependent variable, *number of land invasions per year*. The data set was completed with a series of variables that I thought would be good predictors, based on the interactive theory of hardships and political opportunities already explained, and a number of controls.

As an indicator of hardship, I have used average yearly *real wages* of workers. Thanks to the work of economic historians, a time series of real wages, or wages adjusted for inflation to make them comparable across time, is available for Uruguay from 1870 to 2002 (Historia Económica 2008). Historically, real wages are a better measure of quality of life, especially for the lower classes, than the more artifactual GDP per capita (Aghion and Williamson 1999). Other series of relevant indicators of hardship such as poverty rates, number of evictions or housing prices is only available as from the late 1980s and therefore not appropriate for longer-term historic analysis. However, real wages correlate strongly with other possible measures of grievances such as the yearly number of renters' evictions ($r = -0.87$). Figure B.1 shows the bivariate relationship between real wages and the number of yearly land occupations.

The widespread number of land invasions at low values of real wages and the low occurrence of invasions at higher values of real wages suggest that real wages might be a necessary but not sufficient condition for the occurrence of land invasions, which usually suggests an interactive relationship between one or more pairs of variables. The scatterplot also shows an outlier year, with low average real wages and the highest yearly number of land invasions (40). This point corresponds to 1990, and it is the year for which a peak was detected in Fig. 5.2 in Chap. 5. As stated earlier, my interest here is to explain variation throughout the period, and not only to understand the peak. However, it is important to control

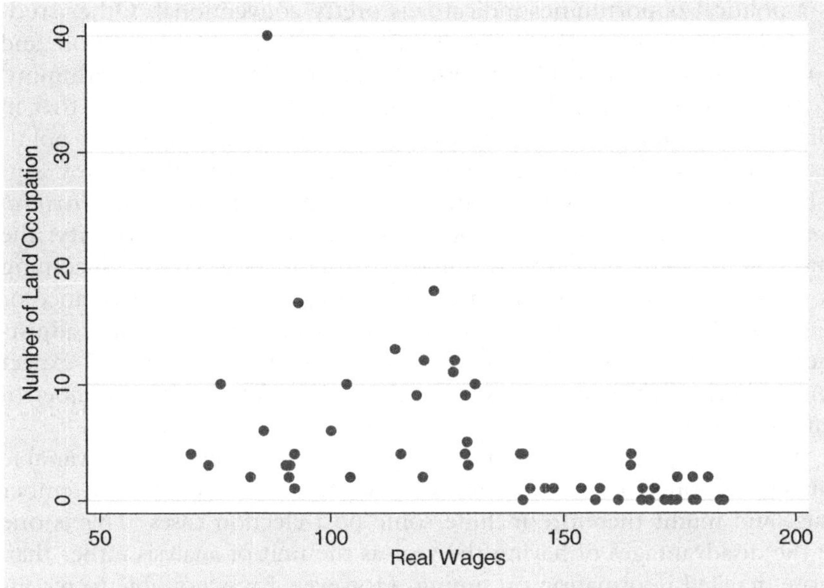

Fig. B.1 Scatterplot of real wages and number of land invasions by year, Montevideo 1947–2002[6]

for this in order to avoid having a data point influencing the results inordinately. It is also important to run the models without that data point to check whether results hold without the outlier.

Rather than including a dummy variable to account for a single outlier, which would be an a-theoretical ad hoc solution given that land invasions increased after 1989, I preferred to include a dummy variable to account for the whole period after 1989, coded 1 if the year was 1990 or later, and 0 otherwise. Therefore, if there is something special about that period, we should see a positive effect of the *1990-and-beyond dummy* on the number of land invasions, controlling for the other factors. This dummy also accounts for the Frente Amplio city government, which started in 1990, and for a contingent political opportunity. Yet my goal was to also account for more systematic ones. As indicators of political opportunities, I have therefore used two dummy variables: *electoral year* and *post-electoral year*, both coded 1 if the year was electoral or post-electoral respectively, and 0 otherwise. The use of election times as a political opportunities indicator is pretty conventional. Other studies have suggested a relationship between electoral competition and squatters' mobilization (Özler 2003; Schneider 1995). The first dummy, *electoral year* is supposed to capture the campaign effect. Given that in Uruguay, elections are held in November, parties and individual politicians have that entire year to campaign, meaning that this dummy captures what happens before elections. The second dummy, *post electoral year,* captures a different type of political opening or opportunity: the one that happens once the winning party is in power (e.g., incoming government paying favors, perhaps the perception of more tolerance or more overlooking by the authorities due to the confusion and adjustment of the first months in power, or some other mechanisms). I expect one or both of these dummies to be positively related to the number of land invasions.

It becomes important to note here that the election year variable introduces some noise into the analysis because it includes December data, and might therefore include some post-election cases. This is one of the disadvantages of having the year as the unit of analysis rather than more detailed information on timing. However, I was not able to reconstruct invasions' exact date of settlement.

I have also included a 1 year *lagged number of invasions* in the models for two connected reasons. On the one hand, this is a customary practice in time series analyses because data points are not independent as regression models assume: what happens in a certain year is probably influenced by what happened the year before. If, at an extreme, the dependent variable were entirely predicted from last year's values, one would have no evidence that the exogenous variables were causing anything to happen the current year. The other reason is more theoretical. This lag captures a diffusion process. Once a group of people invades land, they open the possibility for others to do so too. Thus, I expect this lag to be positively related to the number of land invasions.

Finally, to test the type of interactive or conditional effect of grievances and political opportunities suggested earlier, I have included two *interactive terms* in the model. They are interactions (multiplications) of real wages with the electoral year dummy and with the post electoral year dummy. The signs and significance of the coefficients of these interactive effects do not mean much in themselves (Brambor et al. 2005; Braumoeler 2004). As explained below, their interpretation requires a more nuanced analysis.[7]

Methods

I estimated the yearly number of land invasions using a Poisson regression, which is appropriate for use with count data, where the use of the linear regression model usually results in inefficient, inconsistent and biased estimates (Barron 1992; King 1988; Long and Freese 2006; Minkoff 1995, 1997).[8] Since the unit of analysis is the year, there are 55 observations (1947–2002). I ran all the models using STATA.

After estimating the models, I predicted the count of yearly land invasions using the *predictnl* command in STATA used for post estimation of nonlinear predictions. The estimation of parameters in non-linear regression models such as Poisson can be used to predict and plot probabilities. Probabilities of the dependent variable are more intuitively meaningful to interpret than the coefficients, especially when we have interactive terms.

Results

Table B.1 shows the Poisson regression results, both for the simpler model and for the model with interaction terms. In both models, most variables are significant and with their signs in the expected direction. However, with the presence of interaction effects, we cannot interpret coefficients as if we were in a world of simpler linear additive regressions. (Remember that in models with interaction effects the main effects' coefficients represent the effect of one the variables when the other is zero. In this case, for example, the coefficient of the electoral year represents the effect of an electoral year when real wages equal zero, which is an inexistent situation). The exception is the lag variable, which surprisingly turns out to be not significant. Apparently, the number of invasions at t−1 does not affect the number of invasions the following year, but it does not rule out all possibilities of diffusion. There is no evidence of diffusion of squatting experiences from year-to-year, but perhaps our yearly measures do not account for shorter-term diffusion processes occurring say, month-to-month. The coefficient for the *1990-and-beyond dummy* is significant and positive which means that after controlling for hardships and other political opportunities, invasions were more likely to happen after 1989; that is, after Frente Amplio won the city government. It is important to note that the outlier of 1990 with 40 land invasions is not drawing the data to this result. I have run the analysis without that year and results hold.

Table B.1 Poisson regression estimates of the influence of selected predictors on the number of land occupations per year, Montevideo 1947–2002

N invasions total		
Real wages	−0.022***	−0.011**
	(0.003)	(0.004)
Election year dummy	0.508**	1.970**
	(0.174)	(0.728)
Year after election year dummy	0.546***	2.976***
	(0.150)	(0.677)
Real Wages*Election Year		−0.013*
		(0.006)
Real Wages*Year after election year		−0.022***
		(0.006)
1990 and beyond dummy	1.488***	1.409***
	(0.176)	(0.178)
Lag (*N* total invasions t −1)	0.003	0.007
	(0.009)	(0.010)
Constant	3.298***	2.056***
	(0.321)	(0.492)
N	55	55
LR Chi2	281.000	294.78
P > Chi2	0.000	0.000
Pseudo R-squared	0.546	0.573

Standard errors in parentheses
***$p < 0.001$, **$p < 0.01$, *$p < 0.05$

Both models give significant results for theoretically relevant predictors. Both political opportunities (election year and the year after) and hardship (low salaries) have increased the number of land invasions per year during the 1947–2002 period. There are several criteria for choosing one model over the other. Parsimony is one common criterion, predicting power is another. Combining the two, the option would be the simpler model because it is more parsimonious without losing goodness of fit (log ratios are not very different between the two models). However, in this case, I choose to analyze the interactive model because it is the one that derives from my theoretical model. Both grievances and opportunities are required for mobilization and mobilization, in turn, depends on their interaction. Following this logic, the model without interaction terms is underspecified.[9]

Thus, given the fact that we have included interaction terms, the interpretation of our theoretically more relevant predictors is not intuitive. The coefficient for, say *real wages* does not represent the average effect of yearly real wages on the number of land invasions. It only indicates the effect of *real wages* when both the *post electoral dummy* and the *electoral dummy* are 0; that is, in between election years. As Kam and Franzese (2007) remind us, each variable involved in the interaction terms of interactive models has multiple effects, depending on the values of the other interactive variables, and not a single, constant effect.

Figure B.2 offers a more intuitive understanding of the effect of real wages on the number of land invasions. It shows the predicted count of land invasions for different types of years (electoral, post-electoral and other) for the different levels of real wages. The first thing that is clear from the figure is that there are more land invasions when real wages are low and that there are almost none when real wages are high. Clearly, hardship does have an effect on the probability of land invasions happening. Yet that effect is conditional on the year. Post electoral years tend to have a greater number of land invasions, followed by electoral years.

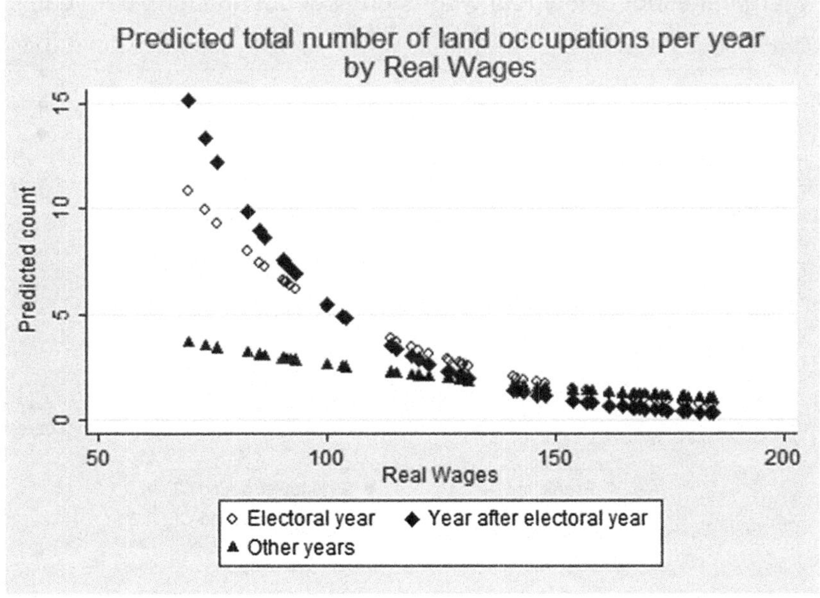

Fig. B.2 Predicted total number of land occupations per year by real wages

Years in between elections, however, do not witness many land invasions even if average salaries for people are low.[10]

Figure B.3 illustrates the magnitude of the differential effects of real wages on the number of land invasions, depending on the type of year, with the corresponding confidence intervals.[11] The effect of real wages on the expected count of land invasions is negative. When real salaries are low, the number of land invasions increases. But that effect depends on the type of year. The greatest effect occurs in post-electoral years, followed by electoral years. In other years—years between elections—the negative effect is still negative but almost insignificant. The upper limit of the 95% confidence interval is almost 0.

These results, supporting the hypothesis of a conditional effect of real wages on the number of land invasions per year, refer to the whole population of land invasions. As stated earlier, however, land invasions are far from homogeneous in Montevideo. While some are planned before the invasion, others start by accretion, and others still start by somebody subdividing the land and selling it to people often fraudulently

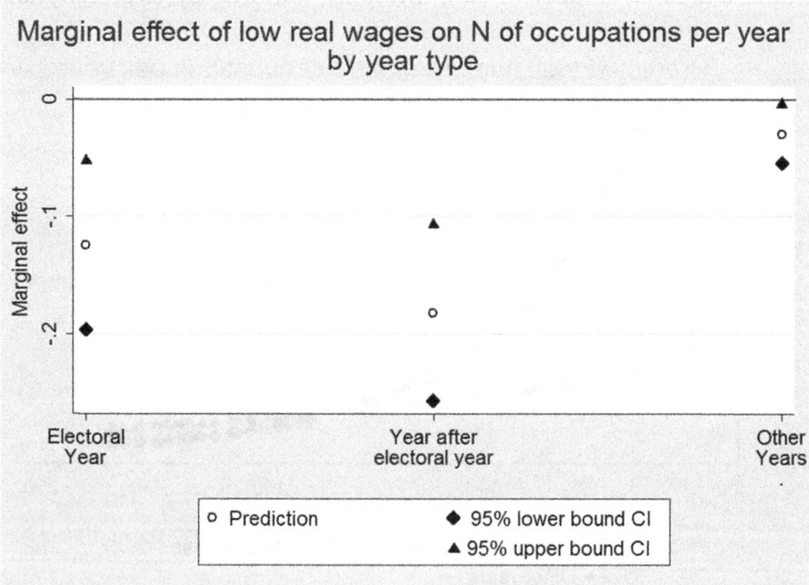

Fig. B.3 Marginal effect of low real wages on total number of occupations per year by year type

(see Chap. 2). In the following section I explore the possibility that these three types of settlement formation are different kinds of collective actions, triggered by different factors.

Comparative Results

Table B.2 shows the results of running the same interactive model as in Table B.1, but this time also for the three different types of land invasions separately.

Table B.2 Poisson regression estimates of the influence of selected predictors on the number of land occupations per year for three types of occupations, Montevideo 1947–2002

	Total	*Organized*	*Accretion*	*Land subdivision and Sale*
Real wages	−0.011**	0.003	−0.011*	0.007
	(0.004)	(0.012)	(0.006)	(0.031)
Election year dummy	1.970**	6.329**	0.719	9.326
	(0.728)	(2.191)	(1.104)	(5.699)
Year after election year dummy	2.976***	5.178**	3.472**	3.446
	(0.677)	(1.790)	(1.043)	(3.990)
Real Wages*Election Year	−0.013*	−0.046*	−0.003	−0.074
	(0.006)	(0.018)	(0.009)	(0.047)
Real Wages*Year after election year	−0.022***	−0.039*	−0.027**	−0.020
	(0.006)	(0.016)	(0.010)	(0.033)
1990 and beyond dummy	1.409***	2.346***	0.800*	3.875**
	(0.178)	(0.458)	(0.315)	(1.167)
Lag (*N* total invasions t−1)	0.007	0.029	−0.001	−0.018
	(0.010)	(0.018)	(0.019)	(0.047)
Constant	2.056***	−2.221	1.451*	−4.667
	(0.492)	(1.637)	(0.700)	(4.273)
N	55	55	55	55
LR Chi2	294.78	132.03	67.75	45.21
P > Chi2	0.000	0.000	0.000	0.000
Pseudo R-squared	0.573	0.6023	0.309	0.482

Standard errors in parentheses
$^{***}p < 0.001$, $^{**}p < 0.01$, $^{*}p < 0.05$

The *1990 and beyond dummy* and the *lagged number of land invasions* behave similarly across the four models. For all types of land invasions, the expected count was greater after 1989. Yet looking at the magnitude of the coefficients, and comparing the models for each type with the model for the total, we can see some interesting differences. The entrepreneur invasions seem to be the ones more likely to occur after 1989, followed by the organized invasions. In turn, none of the three types seems to be triggered by temporal diffusion processes since the lagged number of invasions is not significant for any of the models. Again, it becomes important to note that this only rules out diffusion year-to-year, but not week-to-week or month-to-month.

To interpret the conditional effect of real wages on the expected count of land invasions per year for each of the three types of invasions, I have calculated predicted counts and marginal effects for the three models (following the same logic explained in footnotes [10] and [11]). Figures B.4, B.5, B.6, B.7, B.8 and B.9 show these calculations graphically.

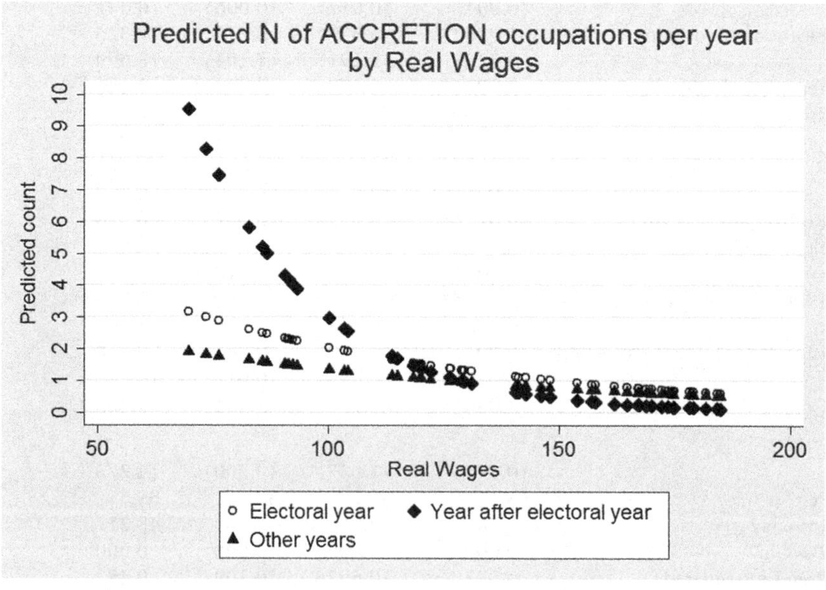

Fig. B.4 Predicted number of ACCRETION occupations per year by real wages and year type

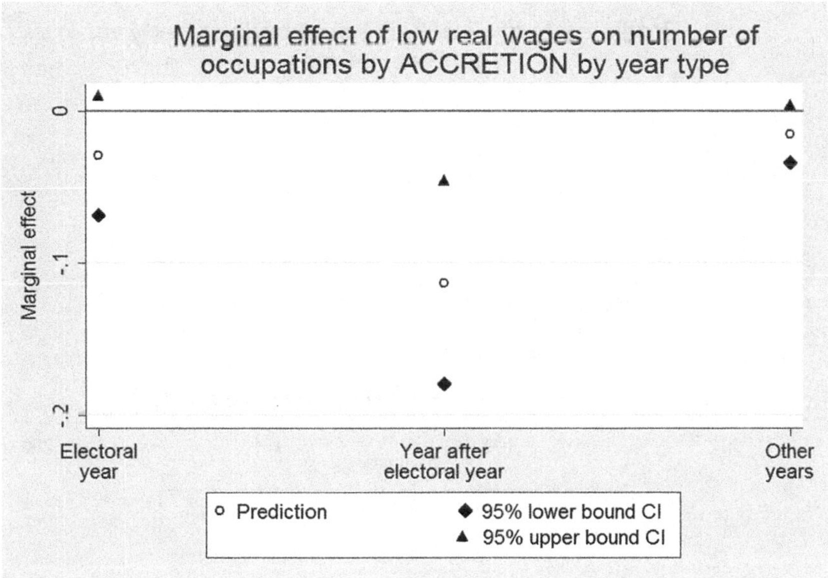

Fig. B.5 Marginal effect of low real wages on number of ACCRETION occupations by year type

The comparative analysis of the models for the three different types of land invasions shows variation that remained hidden in the overall analysis. Accretion invasions are the closest to the general pattern (e.g., it makes sense because accretion invasions are the majority, so they influence the overall results). The expected number of invasions is greater as the yearly real wages decrease (Fig. B.4). Yet the effect of real wages is much greater in post electoral years. In fact, if we look at Fig. B.5, we see that low real wages are only significant for post electoral years. This is quite different from planned invasions, which are more likely to occur when the salaries are low but also when elections are looming in election years (Figs. B.6, B.7). Post electoral years also positively affect the expected count of planned land invasions but to a lesser extent (e.g., the effect of low real wages in post electoral years is close to being insignificant).

Although entrepreneur invasions seem to behave similarly to planned invasions in the estimated counts (Fig. B.8), when we look at the marginal effect of low real wages on the expected count of land invasions

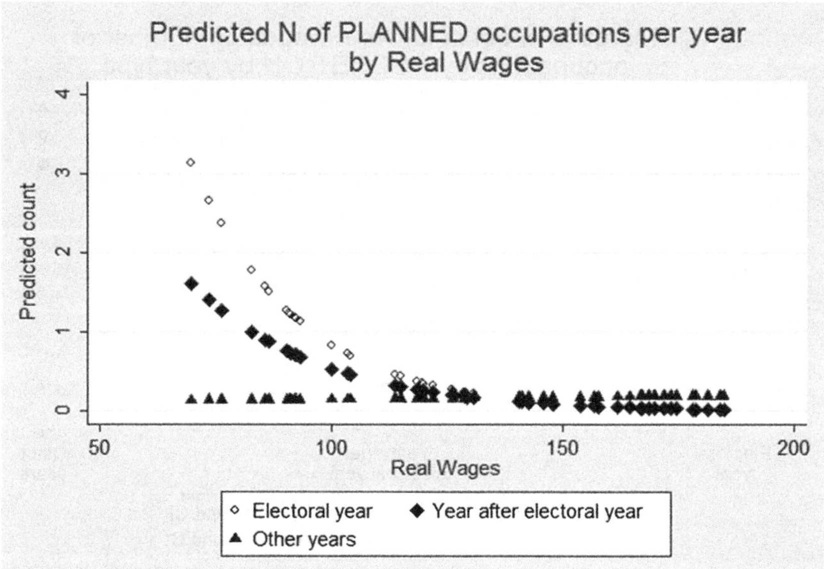

Fig. B.6 Predicted number of PLANNED occupations per year by real wages and year type

(Fig. B.9), we can see that it is not significant for any of the year types. Thus, entrepreneur invasions seem to be yet a different type, unrelated to grievances and political opportunities, at least as measured here.

Brief Discussion

As expressed earlier, the results of this analysis underlie the whole argument of the book. Yet, specifically, this quantitative analysis shows that, as expected, as real wages diminished, land invasions grew. Land invasions are generally a strategy employed by the urban poor who are obviously the most significantly affected by overall indicators of hardship such as low real wages, but this is just part of the story. It takes more than just hardship to make people squat. The effect of low real wages is enhanced if there was an election the year before. Electoral years also increase the effect of real wages on the number of land invasions.

As it seems, land invasions cannot be explained only by looking at individual or family attributes. Another level or mechanism is needed. Based

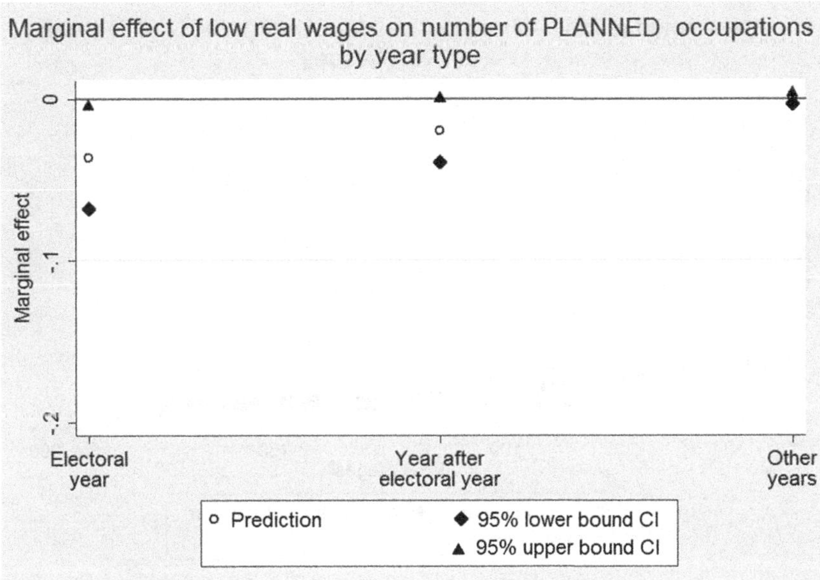

Fig. B.7 Marginal effect of low real wages on number of PLANNED occupations by year type

on my broader fieldwork, I hypothesize that isolated individuals or families may feel ready to squat when their salaries are low or when they have a series of other hardships, but often the intervention of brokers, leaders or entrepreneurs is needed before those families take action. This is especially true for planned invasions, and it takes us to another discussion point.

More interestingly, the interactive effect of grievances and politics varies for different types of land invasions. This is especially clear for accretion and planned invasions. Accretion invasions tend to take place in post electoral years while planned invasions tend to happen in election years. This finding can be understood in the broader context of the fieldwork I conducted in the city of Montevideo, visiting squatter settlements across the city and interviewing more than 80 residents (leaders and non-leaders), politicians, state employees, and other key informants.

To give just one sharp indicator, while interviews with residents of accretion invasions lasted less than half an hour, interviews with residents of organized invasions never lasted less than two hours, and

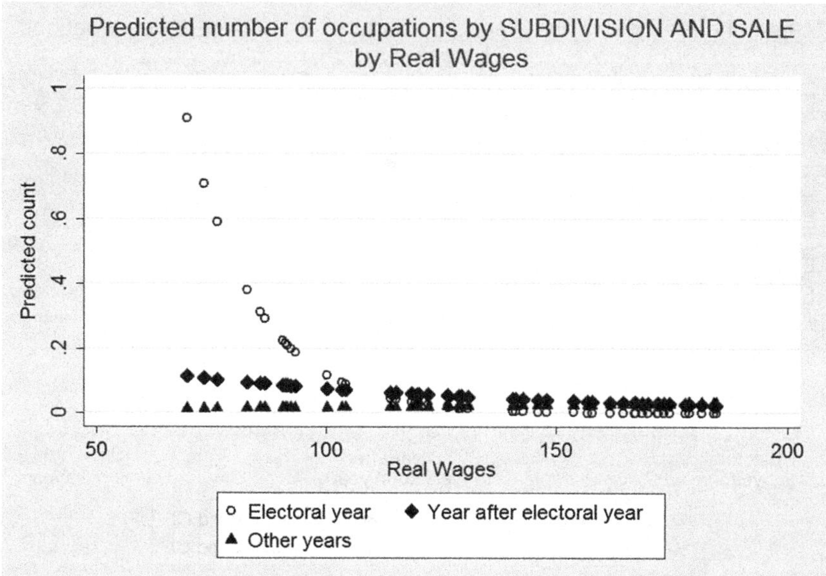

Fig. B.8 Predicted number of LAND SUBDIVIDSION AND SALE occupations per year by real wages and year type

sometimes even several visits. In accretion, invasions there is not much of a collective story to tell, which was what the interview schedule was about. Of course, there are lots of stories, and lots of examples of solidarity among neighbors. But when asked about how they got to the occupied land, and what they did when they first arrived when had to build their houses and deal with the lack of services, most of these stories were individual and not stories of neighborhood organizations. With residents of planned invasions, after listening to epic stories about the old days (e.g., organizing beforehand, finding a safe plot to squat, resisting the police, building houses together, sharing a soup kitchen, discussing everything in assemblies with direct democracy, and so on), I was the one who sometimes had to cut the interview short because information was becoming redundant after the third hour or so and because I had to run to the other extreme of the city to my next interview. Planned invasions, especially at the beginning, were more proactive. Interestingly, they frame their squatting in terms of rights, in this case, demanding a

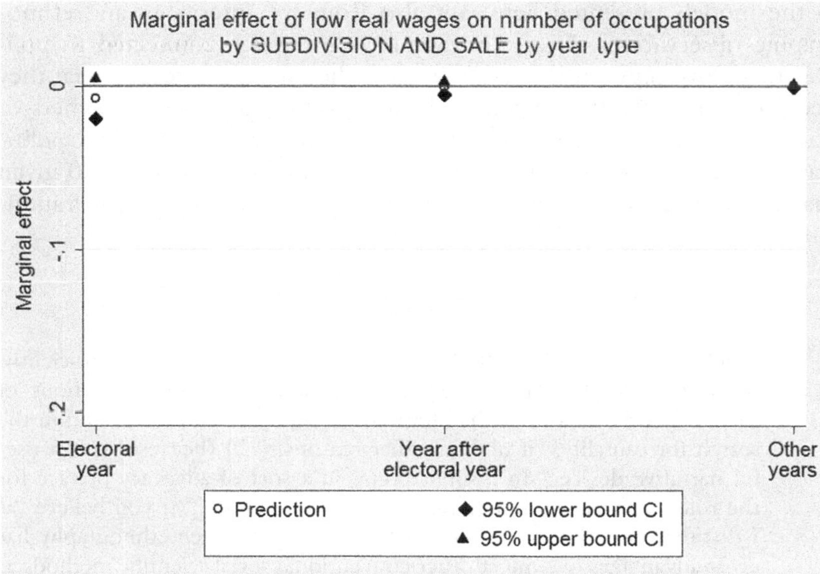

Fig. B.9 Marginal effect of low real wages on number of LAND SUBDIVISION AND SALE occupations by year type

place in the city. This might be the reason for which they tended to squat in electoral years, during the campaign, just like more organized social movements and pressure groups.

There may be several reasons why accretion invasions tended to occur in post-election years. Using the framework of all my data, I hypothesize two mechanisms as important. On the one hand, once in office, politicians and new state officials may have repaid their constituents for their votes by letting them squat. In addition, most of the politicians and state officials that squatters are connected to are those in office, the ones that have resources to give away. On the other hand, individual families or small groups might have decided to invade a plot straight after elections in the safety of the confusion of a change of authority.

Finally, entrepreneurial invasions are a new type, which does not seem to be use hardship or elections as political opportunities. Since they start with subdivisions and the sale of plots by the owner or by a fraudulent broker, they might follow more of a market logic that is not captured in the models presented here. Yet also from my interviews and ethnographic observations, I can say they are very much connected to politics. Elections might not determine when they start, but to get what they need (e.g., streets, information, tolerance, water, and so on), owners or fraudulent brokers need to be in contact with state officials and politicians. It is a puzzle that they seem to have proliferated since 1990 given that the Frente Amplio government has dealt with such, often fraudulent, sales harshly.

Notes

1. Following Katz (2001, 2002), I believe that "when refined sufficiently, descriptions of how people act merge seamlessly into explanations of their behavior," and that therefore ethnography should not abandon the search for causality, "if not for other reasons, (...) [because] it is a useful narrative device." In a similar vein, in a sort of advocacy preface for the role of political ethnography, Tilly (2006) wrote: "If you believe (as I do) that how things happen is *why* they happen, then ethnography has great advantages over most other conventional social scientific methods as a way of getting at cause–effect relations."
2. More recently, the slum upgrading program, working with the 2011 census and satellite pictures speaks of only 332 settlements. It is likely that many of the ones that I had without dates were not settlements but deteriorated urban areas, or that they were two polygons next to each other constituting just one squatter settlement. Also, the number decreased because the program has regularized several neighborhoods, which are now no longer considered squatter settlements (PMB-PIAI 2013).
3. The total is more than 412. These include the ones currently existing in the city, because I included a few "dead events," meaning settlements that changed into cooperative housing or that were relocated by the government to a different area.
4. The idea of interviewing both leaders and non-leaders comes from Collier's (1976) historical study of squatter mobilization in Peru. He interviewed initial leaders and non-leaders as a crosscheck.
5. Transcription from the Special Commission of Squatter Settlements of Montevideo City Council, Minutes No 7537, May 13, 2005.
6. Real wages are measured using an index base 100 (which corresponds to the year 1913).
7. In general, predictors are not correlated among each other. The only problematic correlation is that of the lagged dependent variable and the 1990 and beyond dummy ($r = 0.72$). Yet, when I run the models

without the lagged variable, the effect of the 1990 and beyond dummy remains, which indicates that multicollinearity is not taking away the effect of any variable vis-à- vis another one.

8. The choice of Poisson over negative binomial comes after running negative binomial models, and comparing them. The negative binomial model is a generalization of the Poisson model that corrects for overdispersion. When data is overdispersed, the Poisson model gives spuriously small standard errors. In none of the cases was the additional "alpha" parameter (the one that accounts for overdispersion) in the negative binomial models significant.
9. An autocorrelogram (using the acplot routine in STATA) does not show serious autocorrelation problems in the time series model. In any case, as explained in the text, I include the lagged dependent variable as a control.
10. To predict the number of land invasions for different types of years I used the *predictnl* command in STATA, with three different equations. I let real wages vary freely and held all other variables constant using a central measure (median for dummy90andbeyond and median also for the lag dependent variable). Given the Poisson equation $\mu_i = \exp\ (x_i\beta)$, I used the following equation to predict the count of land invasions in electoral years:

    predictnl p_invtot_electoralyears =
    exp(β_0 [cons] +
    β_1 [real wages]* real wages +
    β_2 [electoral year]*1 +
    β_3 [post electoral year] * 0 +
    β_4 [interaction realwages_electoral year] * real wages * 1 +
    β_5 [interaction real wages_postelectoral year]* real wages * 0 +
    β_6 [dummy90andbeyond]* median value of dummy90andbeyond +
    β_7 [lagged n invasions]* median value of lagged n invasions)

    In this equation, the value for the dummy electoral year is set to 1 (both in the main effect (β_2) and in the interaction term (β_4)), whereas the value for the dummy postelectoral year is set to 0. The equations for postelectoral years and for other years, were similar but with the values changed in the dummies and the interaction terms.
11. As stated earlier, the effect of real wages on the number of land invasions is not just the coefficient for real wages (β_1). To calculate that effect we need to take the first derivative of y (number of land invasions) with respect to x (real wages), as suggested by Kam and Franzese (2007) and Friedrich (1982). When we have two-way interactions as is the case here (real wages interacts with the two types of year dummies), and the

outcome is categorical or count data, the marginal effect of x_i on y (p in the equation) is:

$$\frac{\delta p}{\delta x_i} = \frac{\delta p}{\delta F(XB)}(\beta_i + \beta_{ij}x_j + \beta_{ik}x_k)$$

In the Poisson model, this translates into:

$$exp(x_i\beta) * \beta_i + \beta_{ij}x_j + \beta_{ik}x_k$$

Thus, to calculate the effect of real wages on the expected count of land invasions, I used the following equation, using the *predictnl* command in STATA:

predictnl derivate of *n* land invasions for low real wages =
exp(β_0 [cons] +
β_1 [real wages]* low real wages +
β_2 [electoral year]* electoral year +
β_3 [post electoral year] * postelectoral year +
β_4 [interaction realwages_electoral year] * low real wages* electoral year +
β_5 [interaction real wages_postelectoral year]* low real wages * postelectoral year +
β_6 [dummy90andbeyond]* median value of dummy90andbeyond +
β_7 [lagged n invasions]* median value of lagged n invasions) *
(β_1 [real wages] +
β_4 [interaction realwages_electoral year] * electoral year +
β_5 [interaction real wages_postelectoral year]* postelectoral year)

I also calculated confidence intervals for the effect. Since the ultimate goal was to show this graphically and there is one marginal effect for each value of real wages, I had to hold that variable fixed at a certain value. Because substantively I was interested in hardships, I held real wages constant at a low value (minus 1 standard deviation). I let the types of years dummies vary, and held the dummy90andbeyond and the lag n of invasions constant at their medians.

Bibliography

Aghion, P., & Williamson, J. G. (1999). *Growth, inequality, and globalization: Theory, history and policy*. Cambridge: Cambridge University Press.

Barron, D. (1992). The analysis of count data: Overdispersion and autocorrelation. *Sociological Methodology, 22*, 179–220.

Basanta, M., Larrosa, M., Ripa, R., & Olveyra, G. (s.d.). *Mis vecinos de San Vicente (Padre Cacho). Una comunidad barrial con memoria*. Montevideo: San Vicente Organization.

Blee, K., & Currier, A. (2005). Character building: The dynamics of emerging social movement groups. *Mobilization: An International Quarterly, 10*(1), 129–144.

Blee, K., & Taylor, V. (2002). Semi-structured interviewing in social movement research. In B. Klandermans & S. Staggenborgh (Eds.), *Methods of social movement research*. Minneapolis: University of Minnesota Press.

Clara, M. (2012). *Padre Cacho. Cuando el otro quema adentro*. Montevideo: Trilce.

Collier, D. (1976). *Squatters and oligarchs. Authoritarian rule and policy change in Perú*. Baltimore: The John Hopkins University Press.

Friedrich, R. J. (1982). In defense of multiplicative terms in multiple regression equations. *American Journal of Political Science, 26*(4), 797–833.

Historia Económica, B. d. d. d. (2008). Serie de tiempo de salario real, Uruguay 1870–2003. Retrieved 2008, from Facultad de Ciencias Sociales, UdelaR.

INE-PIAI (Producer). (2006, February 2009). Relevamiento de Asentamientos 2006. Retrieved from http://www.ine.gub.uy/piai3/inepiai.htm.

Kam, C. D., & Franzese, R. J., Jr. (2007). *Modeling and interpreting interactive hypotheses in regression analysis*. Ann Arbor: The University of Michigan Press.

M.J. Álvarez-Rivadulla, *Squatters and the Politics of Marginality in Uruguay*, Latin American Political Economy, DOI 10.1007/978-3-319-54534-9

Katz, J. (2001). From how to why. On luminous description and causal inference in ethnography (Part 1). *Ethnography, 2*(4), 443–473.

Katz, J. (2002). From how to why. On luminous description and causal inference in ethnography (Part 2). *Ethnography, 3*(1), 63–90.

King, G. (1988). Statistical models for political science event counts: Bias in conventional procedures and evidence for the exponential poisson regression model. *American Journal of Political Science, 32*(3), 838–863.

Koopmans, R., & Statham, P. (1999). Challenging the liberal nation-state? Postnationalism, multiculturalism, and the collective claims making of migrants and ethnic minorities in Britain and Germany. *The American Journal of Sociology, 105*(3), 652.

Long, J. S., & Freese, J. (2006). *Regression models for categorical variables using Stata*. College Station: Stata Press.

Minkoff, D. C. (1995). Interorganizational influences in the founding of African American organizations, 1955–1985. *Sociological Forum, 10*(1), 51–79.

Minkoff, D. C. (1997). The sequencing of social movements. *American Sociological Review, 62*, 779–799.

Özler, S. I. (2003). *Squatters stand up: Political institutions and demand making in the developing world*. Ph.D. Thesis, University of California, Los Angeles.

PMB-PIAI. (2013). *Informe Técnico: Relevamiento de Asentamientos Irregulares. Primeros Resultados de Población y Viviendas a partir del Censo 2011*. Montevideo.

Ricci Cabrera, M. (1993). *Historia de la calera. Una cooperativa distinta*. Montevideo: Obsur.

Sampson, R. J., McAdam, D., McIndoe, H., & Weffer-Elizondo, S. (2005). Civil society reconsidered: The durable nature and community structure of collective civic action. *American Journal of Sociology, 111*(3), 673–714.

Schneider, C. L. (1995). *Shantytown protest in Pinochet's Chile*. Philadelphia: Temple University Press.

Tilly, C. (2006). Afterword: Political ethnography as art and science. *Qualitative Sociology, 29*, 409–412.

INDEX

Note: Page numbers followed by *f* and *t* refer to figures, and tables respectively

M.J. Álvarez-Rivadulla, *Squatters and the Politics of Marginality in Uruguay*, Latin American Political Economy, DOI 10.1007/978-3-319-54534-9

The manufacturer's authorised representative in the EU is Springer Nature Customer Service Centre GmbH, Europaplatz 3, 69115 Heidelberg, Germany. If you have any concerns regarding our products, please contact ProductSafety@springernature.com

Printed and bound by CPI Group (UK) Ltd, Croydon, CR0 4YY

07/01/2026

02030927-0001